MUSICAL HEROES

Robert Ponsonby was Organ Scholar of Trinity College, Oxford, from 1948 to 1950, and President of the University Opera Club. Engaged by Glyndebourne in 1951, he organized the Festival of Sussex, a country-wide celebration, under the umbrella of the Festival of Britain. At the same time, he worked as assistant to the Director of the Edinburgh Festival, Ian Hunter, whom he succeeded in 1956. Resigning after the 1960 festival, he eventually gained a job with the Independent Television Authority. He returned to music in 1964, being appointed to administer the Scottish National Orchestra. His eight years in Glasgow were professionally happy and apparently successful, for he was head-hunted by the BBC, who in 1972 appointed him Controller, Music, in succession to William Glock. This post he held until 1985. He directed the Canterbury Festival in 1987 and 1988; and since 1985 he has filled advisory roles with the Purcell School, the Young Concert Artists Trust, the Council for Music in Hospitals and Wingate Scholarships. Currently, he is on the committee of the Michael Tippett Musical Foundation. He holds the Janáček Medal from the Czech Government, is an Hon RAM and was made a CBE in 1983. (For a fuller biography, see 'About the Author'.)

MUSICAL HEROES

A Personal View of Music and the Musical World Over Sixty Years

Robert Ponsonby

dlm

First published in 2009
by Giles de la Mare Publishers Limited
53 Dartmouth Park Hill, London NW5 1JD

Typeset by Tom Knott
Printed by Cromwell Press Group
Trowbridge, Wiltshire

A CIP record of this book is available
from the British Library

ISBN 9781900357296 paperback original

To

Mickie and Beth

&

Gwen and Tom

with love

ACKNOWLEDGEMENTS

The essays in this book were all written after I left the BBC in 1985, but they refer back in my own recollection as far as the 1940s – and in the case of the obituaries often much further. (Robert Mayer was born in 1879, Adrian Boult in 1889.)

The obituaries were published in *The Times*, *The Independent* and *The Guardian*. Other pieces appeared in *The Listener* and the BBC *Music Magazine*. The tribute to Sena Jurinac appeared in *Opera* magazine, though in a cut version: the full original text is printed here. 'A Mysterious Business' – about conductors and conducting – was published by *The Oldie*. The interview with Pierre Boulez was reproduced in *Tempo* magazine. Sixteen of the essays have not previously been published. Nor, of course, have the summarizing pieces – Prospects and Retrospect.

I am most grateful to the publishers of *The Times*, *The Independent* and *The Guardian*; to the BBC and specifically, to BBC Publications; to John Allison, editor of *Opera*, to Calum MacDonald, editor of *Tempo*, and to Richard Ingrams, editor of *The Oldie* – for their permission to reprint.

I am also most grateful to my half-brother, Nigel Jaques, who originally suggested that Giles de la Mare, my publisher, might be interested in my writings – and to Giles himself. I am a techno-wimp and he has been the very soul of patience and persuasiveness. Julia Bailey, an old friend, and Wendy Sanford have between them successfully converted my manuscripts and typescripts into a CD-ROM – whatever that may be.

Specially grateful thanks, too, to the friends who have encouraged me, in particular the dedicatees; and to Janet Baker for her generous introduction.

CONTENTS

ACKNOWLEDGEMENTS vi

INTRODUCTION
by Dame Janet Baker xi

PROSPECTS
at January 1951 1

CONDUCTORS 5
- Adrian Boult 5
- Thomas Beecham 8
- John Pritchard 12
- Paul Sacher 15
- Carlo Maria Giulini 17
- Rafael Kubelík 21
- Alexander Gibson 24
- Rudolf Kempe 27
- Jascha Horenstein 29
- Norman Del Mar 31
- Djura Jakšić 34
- Charles Groves 37
- Günter Wand 40
- Hans-Hubert Schönzeler 43

COMPOSERS 46
- Hans Gál 46
- William Walton 48
- Michael Tippett 52
- Robin Orr 56
- Iain Hamilton 58
- Luciano Berio 62
- John Buller 66
- György Ligeti 68

PERFORMERS 73
- Sena Jurinac 73
- John Kentish 76
- Clara Haskil 77

Yehudi Menuhin 79
Evelyn Rothwell 84
Mstislav Rostropovich 87
Jacqueline du Pré 88
John Ogdon 90
Sidonie Goossens 93
Philip Jones 96

ADMINISTRATORS 100
Moran Caplat 100
Ian Hunter 102
John Drummond 106
Chris Samuelson 111
William Glock 112
Ernest Warburton 117
Norman Platt 119

FRIENDS 122
Andrew Pavlovsky 122
Anthony Besch 124
Thomas Armstrong 126
Robert Mayer 130
Ursula Vaughan Williams 132

MISCELLANY 135
Moving South: Walton, Henze and Boulez 135
Hungary Diary: Music for a Lime-green Cat 138
Langham Diary 141
Prom-bashing 144
Planning the 1986 Proms 147
A Mysterious Business 150
Pierre Boulez in Conversation 152

RETROSPECT
at January 2009 171

WHO'S WHO 180

ABBREVIATIONS 186

PHOTO CREDITS 187

ABOUT THE AUTHOR 188

INDEX 191

ILLUSTRATIONS

Between pages 116 and 117

1 Dinner at the Mitre Hotel, Oxford, 1912, with Adrian Boult and Noel Ponsonby
2A Adrian Boult in old age at the Royal Albert Hall, *c.*1977
2B Sena Jurinac coaching Amanda Roocroft in 1988
3 Sena Jurinac, *c.*1950
4A Thomas Beecham at Edinburgh, 1956
4B Isaac Stern and Myra Hess at Edinburgh, 1960
5 Clara Haskil at the keyboard, Lausanne, 1957
6A Clara Haskil, Besançon Festival, 1956
6B Sam Bor, Jacqueline du Pré and Daniel Barenboim playing chamber music, 1967
7 Günter Wand rehearsing the BBC Symphony Orchestra, *c.*1983
8 Pierre Boulez rehearsing the BBC Symphony Orchestra, *c.*1975

page 154 Boulez's hands
page 189 Thetis Blacker's caricature of the author and herself as Narbal and Anna in *The Trojans*, Oxford, 1950

INTRODUCTION

One of the truly great privileges is to spend one's working life among charismatic, interesting and gifted people. It has clearly been the experience of Robert Ponsonby during his many years of artistic administration and he writes about it with obvious delight. The world of the arts is a fascinating one but those involved in it don't have an easy ride through life and the stress often shows itself in something which is commonly described as temperament. This is perfectly understandable: in the constant search for perfection, a certain degree of stress arises; to meet deadlines, or deal with the inevitable clash of egos, miracles are both required and achieved on a daily basis. There is never a dull moment and to deal with the creative, performing and administrative sides of the profession demands the utmost from everybody.

In former times it was the practice to draw a kindly veil over the idiosyncrasies of others, but now we are told that the public needs to know the truth and so a character or a life is opened up to the public gaze in ways formerly unheard of, warts and all. How refreshing, then, to read Robert Ponsonby's collection of portraits which steer such a well judged course between the light and darker sides of the human condition and give us a balanced picture of his subjects. He has a delightful turn of phrase and describes aspects of character which I found immediately recognizable and true.

It is all done with wit, perception, kindness, honesty, affection and humour, leaving this reader wanting more.

Dame Janet Baker, CH, DBE

PROSPECTS
at January 1951

This book is about a number of my heroes and heroines – musicians whose music-making, and in some cases whose friendship, has given me special pleasure. Incidentally, and subordinately, it is also about myself and a career in music which I have greatly enjoyed.

I began to go to London for concerts, opera, theatre and ballet in 1943 when it was (more or less) safe to do so. Of Myra Hess's inspired and inspiring National Gallery lunchtime concerts the first I heard – on 28th April 1943 – was a tribute to Rachmaninoff, who had just died. Dame Myra (not yet a DBE – but I cannot think of her as other than 'Dame') announced that Benno Moiseiwitsch, after a trying journey, had only just arrived; but he had agreed to 'muck about' with some of the Preludes. This Moiseiwitsch did, to brilliant effect, and became for me one of those musicians who define one's standards for life. Others, between 1946 and 1948, included Thomas Beecham in Mozart, Artur Schnabel in the *Diabelli Variations*, Wilhelm Furtwängler in Mahler, Strauss and Brahms (and later, a stupendous *Eroica* in Edinburgh); Kirsten Flagstad and Hans Hotter in Covent Garden's *Die Walküre*. Then, at Salzburg in 1950 I heard Clara Haskil in Mozart's E Flat Piano Concerto, K271, and Lisa Della Casa in Strauss's *Capriccio*. Also in Salzburg that year Julius Patzak sang the Male Chorus in Britten's *The Rape of Lucretia*, though it was not until 1952, when he was an unforgettable Florestan in London, that I fully appreciated his superlative artistry.

Meanwhile, I had joined the staff of Glyndebourne on 1st January 1951, the first day of Festival of Britain year, and had begun to learn my craft from Moran Caplat and Ian Hunter. These two had been the assistants of Rudolf Bing, who had managed Glyndebourne from its inception in 1934 and directed the Edinburgh Festival from 1947 to 1949, when he went to the Metropolitan Opera, New York.

The Glyndebourne ethos was powerful: quality was the be-all and end-all and though, in the earliest recordings, Fritz Busch used a piano for the accompaniment of recitatives and there is some dodgy pronunciation from the international casts, the spirit of Mozart shines brilliantly through. John Christie and his wife, the singer Audrey Mildmay, were the inspired creators of an amazing institution, he the eccentric visionary, she the practical artist – a dream-team without whom there would be no Edinburgh Festival. For in 1940 Glyndebourne toured a production of *The Beggar's Opera* in which Mildmay was Polly, Michael Redgrave McHeath and John Gielgud the director. One night, in Edinburgh after the show, Mildmay and Bing walked from the King's Theatre to the Caledonian Hotel. The castle was moonlit and one of them – perhaps recalling Salzburg – remarked that Edinburgh had the makings of an international festival city. The seed took root and in 1945 a Glyndebourne delegation went to Edinburgh and, not without difficulty, sold the idea to the city fathers. The Festival was launched in 1947.

One of the very earliest of the post-war festivals, it was certainly the most ambitious. Its instant success put Edinburgh on the tourist map as nothing else could have done; yet the parsimonious city fathers were wearyingly slow to provide performance facilities worthy of the international artists who were to participate. (In 1957, the technical staff of La Scala, reconnoitring the King's Theatre, where the company was to play, described it as 'un théâtre abandonné'.) Moreover, civic subsidy was barely adequate, so that – later – two directors, I in 1960, John Drummond in 1983, resigned because we could no longer live with the financial pinch or the indifference, sometimes approaching hostility, of some of the civic authorities. The visits of La Scala, the Hamburg and Stuttgart State Operas and the Royal Swedish Opera were made possible for me only by large subsidies from the originating countries and when Glyndebourne returned in 1960, after an absence of several years, the cost to the Festival (since Glyndebourne had no state grant) was much higher than the payments to the Italians, the Germans and the Swedes. But the quality of the performances was admirable. Glyndebourne, at its very best, brought Joan Sutherland in *I Puritani* and Geraint Evans in *Falstaff*, both conducted by the masterly Vittorio Gui, and John Pritchard, another master, gave us Poulenc's *La Voix Humaine* and Busoni's *Arlecchino*, a fascinating double-bill.

The first ten years of my working life, when I was employed primarily by the Edinburgh Festival, whose director I became in 1956, were, it now seems to me, an apprenticeship. There was a lot to learn; great artists to sustain and – sometimes – to placate; foreign agencies to deal with; uncomprehending bureaucrats to cajole into collaboration; and, of course, the press to feed with news and 'stories'. Thus, Thomas

Beecham[1] gave me (comic) trouble in 1956, Maria Callas[2] had to be defended in 1957 and Otto Klemperer[3] – in a small tragi-comedy about his accommodation – called for appeasement in 1958. In 1959, the Czech Philharmonic disgracefully threatened to break their contract (on political grounds) and I had to stand firm (on contractual grounds), so that in the end they did not appear. In 1960, the Leningrad Philharmonic did appear, though only after tiresome negotiations with grey Soviet suits.

But Beecham and Callas (though not absolutely in best voice) and Klemperer all delivered tremendous performances, as did the Leningrad Philharmonic under the great Evgeny Mravinsky. And during those years there were other glories: Britten conducting Britten and accompanying Peter Pears, Menuhin in concertos and chamber music, Isaac Stern with Myra Hess, the young Fischer-Dieskau and Irmgard Seefried in Hugo Wolf, Victoria de los Angeles in *La Vida Breve* and in recitals with the indispensable Gerald Moore.

I began to perceive that, as an administrator, I had a single overriding professional obligation: somehow to secure for the artists conditions which would enable them to perform at their utmost standard; a congenial programme; a fine theatre or concert-hall with responsive acoustics; adequate (if possible, ample) rehearsal-time; a large and attentive audience; comfortable, convenient, above all quiet, accommodation – and a fair fee!

Of course, it wasn't often possible to provide such Utopian conditions. But I later discovered that they sometimes cropped up in unlikely circumstances.

In 1967 the Scottish National Orchestra, which I had administered since 1964, undertook a European tour which opened in Vienna's august Musikverein and ended in Rotterdam's new De Doelen – both,

1 For Beecham comedy, see page 10.

2 Callas's failure to sing the fifth and last performance of *La Sonnambula* was the consequence of a discrepancy between my contract with La Scala, which stipulated five performances, and La Scala's with her, which cited four. She had made it clear to La Scala that she would be unavailable for a fifth, but they 'hoped to persuade' her. She was of course blamed, but was blameless.

3 Klemperer had fallen for a very pretty member of the Philharmonia Orchestra and he planned to exchange his hotel suite for a room in the spartan hostel where the orchestra were lodged: in every conceivable way an unsuitable move. Some fierce words notwithstanding, he and I finally resolved his problem on the basis that he would sleep at his hotel, but was welcome – well, fairly welcome – to spend daylight time at the hostel.

in strikingly different ways, marvellous concert-halls. Our programmes, certainly congenial, were extremely well rehearsed because repeated in various combinations. Our soloists were heaven-sent: Jacqueline du Pré, who brought the Schumann, Dvořák and Elgar concertos (the last inimitable) and Janet Baker, whose Mahler *Rückert-lieder*, in Salzburg's Grosses Festspielhaus, was deeply and unforgettably moving. Alexander Gibson and the orchestra excelled themselves and throughout the tour we had very good audiences (but our Sibelius did not ignite the Germans). Though we travelled by coach, we were put up in comfortable hotels. Whether or not £100 per concert was a 'fair' fee for our soloists, I would not like to say, but it was wonderfully good value.

Similarly, after I had moved on to the BBC, the BBC Symphony Orchestra toured Japan in 1975 with Pierre Boulez and Charles Groves and produced in Yokohama a concert of uniquely memorable quality and character – Webern's *Passacaglia*, Op.1, Birtwistle's *Nenia on the Death of Orpheus* (with the splendid Jan DeGaetani) and both suites from Ravel's *Daphnis and Chloe*, to which Boulez brought scintillating colour and clarity. The hall and its acoustics were good, the audience pin-drop listeners, quite unfazed by Birtwistle, our hotel quiet and comfortable.

Still later in my career, directorship of the Proms gave me the opportunity to devise even more congenial programmes, as well as providing me with the best audience in the world (the Vienna Philharmonic, after appearing in 1984, wrote corporately to *The Times* to express their astonished appreciation of the Promenaders' concentration and warmth), admittedly controversial acoustics, though much better than detractors allow, and the ability to offer fair fees.

To have progressed from Glyndebourne, via the Edinburgh Festival and the Scottish National Orchestra, to the BBC – and hence to the Proms – was to have enjoyed a voyage not without storms (one hurricane),[1] but no shipwreck. I was very lucky.

1 The musicians' strike in 1980.

CONDUCTORS

Adrian Boult

Because Adrian Boult and my father had been contemporaries and friends, I grew up with an instinctive high regard for him. His 1944 Royal Philharmonic Society programme (referred to in what follows) which comprised Weber, Beethoven, Ravel and Strauss, was uncharacteristic, but, at Oxford, on 11th May 1948, he gave Rubbra's *Festival Overture*, Butterworth's *Banks of Green Willow*, Stanford's Clarinet Concerto (with Frederick Thurston) and Vaughan Williams's Sixth Symphony, his typically generous contribution to a festival of British music.

* * * * *

On 2nd February 1912, five young men sat down to dinner at the Mitre Hotel, Oxford. A photograph shows them in evening dress, with flowers, silver and linen on the table; they look rather self-conscious but they are likely to enjoy a meal comprising Oysters, Clear Soup, Boiled Turbot, Fillets of Beef, Roast Turkey, Plum Pudding and Cheese Custard. (The menu survives.) It is the twenty-first birthday of one of them. Of the other four, one is my father, another is Adrian Boult.

The family connection with Boult persisted after my father's death in 1928 so that in the mid-1940s I felt able to ask if I might attend his rehearsals. On one occasion he sent me a telegram to let me know that the venue of the rehearsal had been changed at the last moment. Thoughtfulness could not have gone further: I was a schoolboy and the least of his worries that day. For the concert, on 9th December 1944, was a Royal Philharmonic Society event and at the interval he was to be presented with the Society's rare and precious Gold Medal. Moreover, there was a risk of bombs and the audience was invited, in the event of an air-raid warning, 'to take shelter in the building or in the trenches in Hyde Park'. All went well, however, and Boult admirably conducted a programme which included Ravel's *Scheherazade* with the divine Maggie Teyte – the only time I heard her.

Six years later, the creator of the BBC Symphony Orchestra was retired by the BBC because he was sixty. This preposterous decision, made when its victim had a good twenty years of active work ahead, typified the BBC at its philistine worst. I hope, but I am not sure, that such a decision would never be made today. In any case, Boult was, he said, 'only unemployed for two or three days', when the London Philharmonic Orchestra sensibly engaged him. There followed a period when he was always busy but was not always engaged for concerts or recordings at the very highest level. I am myself ashamed of the fact that during my time as director of the Edinburgh Festival his only concert – on 6th September 1959 – was devoted to Vaughan Williams, because the composer had died the previous year. But working with Alexander Gibson and the Scottish National Orchestra between 1964 and 1972, I was able to make some amends by engaging him to conduct the orchestra, which he regularly did, offering his definitive Schubert Great C Major, two Brahms symphonies, much Elgar and Holst, and Wagner's *Wesendonck* songs, with Janet Baker.

When I took over the Proms in 1974, Boult was already eighty-five and, as it turned out, he would only appear in four more seasons. He liked to share concerts with younger British conductors. But that first year I asked him to share the opening concert with Pierre Boulez, his current successor with the BBC Symphony Orchestra, and he gave us a magnificent Schubert Great C Major. During the next two years he shared concerts with David Atherton, John Poole, Vernon Handley, Charles Mackerras and John Carewe, giving us Beethoven, Brahms, Elgar and Vaughan Williams symphonies, Wagner's *Siegfried Idyll* and Lennox Berkeley's *Voices of the Night*. Then, in his last year (sharing with Mark Elder, Nicholas Cleobury, James Loughran and Walter Susskind) he conducted a small anthology of his specialities: Elgar's Second, Brahms's Third, Vaughan Williams's *Job*, and – at his own particular request – music by the last and current Masters of the Queen's Music, Arthur Bliss and Malcolm Williamson. (Bliss's *Music for Strings* he had premiered at the Salzburg Festival in 1935.) I noticed after that concert, on 17th August 1977, and after many others during his last years, that an exceptionally large crowd would await him at the Artists' Entrance – well-wishing music-lovers moved to pay tribute not only to the integrity of the old man's musicianship but also to his reserve and his dignity.

After his last Prom I used to visit him and his wife, Ann, in their modest West Hampstead flat. He was by now eighty-eight but, though inclined to shuffle, he always saw me to the door and was invariably dressed in collar and tie, double-breasted suit and polished, laced shoes:

no sweater and slacks for him. Once I asked, 'Adrian, do you really *like* to have visitors?' and Ann quickly replied, 'We like to be visited by the kind of people we like to be visited by'! I was one of the lucky ones and I cherish his recollections of Nikisch, with whom as a young man he had studied in Leipzig and upon whom he had modelled his technique. 'It is impossible,' he said, 'to believe that anyone could ever (or will ever) hold orchestras in the hollow of his hand, and produce the essence of the music with the point of his stick, with such power, and with such economy and beauty of gesture.'

Boult's ninetieth birthday fell on 8th April 1979 and I was determined that, by marking the occasion with some solemnity, the BBC should expiate its bone-headed decision to retire him nearly thirty years before. I approached him privately and, though never one to want a fuss made of him, he seemed pleased by the idea. Ann Boult, as ever protective of his health and his privacy, also appeared content. So we went ahead, booking the Albert Hall and engaging three British conductors – Norman Del Mar, Vernon Handley and James Loughran – who I thought would do Boultian justice to Brahms's Fourth Symphony, the *Tallis Fantasy* and Elgar's *The Music Makers*. All was going swimmingly when intimations began to reach the BBC, at a very high level indeed, that the concert was not wanted and should indeed be cancelled. It was an awkward moment, for plans were far advanced and I guessed that Adrian, probably with Ann's endorsement, had simply got cold feet at the prospect of such an elaborate 'fuss'. After some delicate negotiations, however, it was agreed the concert would take place and, on the night, the Hall was packed. But there was one empty seat, that of the guest of honour, who at a late stage had fallen ill, but not too ill, fortunately, to record a message which we relayed to the audience and on Radio 3.

Adrian Boult's life ended in 1983, on 23rd February, the birth date of Handel and the death date of Elgar. His selfless championship of British music had been incalculably important: at his death there were at least twenty living British composers who owed to him the first performance (and often subsequent ones) of one or more of their works – and this total excluded the many who had predeceased him. But his mastery of much of the German repertoire was also remarkable: Schubert and Brahms apart, he gave a concert performance of Berg's *Wozzeck* in 1934 and – amazingly – the first performance, in Vienna in 1936, of Schoenberg's *Variations*.

So I was proud of the concert in his memory which we promoted in

December 1983. John Pritchard, his latest successor as chief conductor of the BBC Symphony Orchestra, conducted Parry's *Blest Pair of Sirens*, a small masterpiece, the *Enigma Variations* and Mahler's *Das Lied von der Erde*, in which Janet Baker was deeply moving. I felt that, at long last, the BBC had done justice to a great English musician and a kindly human being of altogether exceptional integrity.

Thomas Beecham

Thomas Beecham, like Adrian Boult, contributed to Oxford's 1948 Festival of British Music, performing, on 13th May, Bax's *The Garden of Fand*, Delius's *Paris*, Elgar's *Falstaff* and Bantock's *Fifine at the Fair*, of which the Delius was, of course, quintessential Beecham territory.

* * * * *

'God help you, sir,' said Sir Thomas on being introduced, at Eton, to the music-master who taught his stepson, Jeremy, the piano. The encounter took place at around the time that I first attended a Beecham concert, a Mozart programme with the Philharmonia Orchestra on 27th October 1946. Reginald Kell (the Jack Brymer of his day) played the Clarinet Concerto and the concert ended with the great G Minor Symphony. I was entranced by the idiomatic elegance of the performances and by Beecham's mastery of *rubato*. I became, overnight, an idolater of his artistry.

Not surprisingly, therefore, I persuaded the committee of the Oxford University Opera Club, of which I was then president, to authorize me to invite Sir Thomas to conduct an opera of his own choice under the auspices of the Club. Not surprisingly, he declined, though charmingly. Then, at the 1950 Edinburgh Festival, I heard him conduct Strauss's *Ariadne*, in the first version, which incorporates Molière's M. Jourdain (the 'bourgeois gentilhomme'). That gloriously turkey-faced actor, Miles Malleson, was the M. Jourdain who at the end of the show, complaining that he has not got his money's-worth, addresses the audience rhetorically, 'What, no bugles?' To which, unexpectedly, Sir Thomas – from the pit – was heard to reply, 'All melted down for the war effort!'

The year 1951, Festival of Britain year, saw three of Sir Thomas's finest achievements: in April, another Mozart programme, the C Minor Mass and the (C Major) *Jupiter Symphony*; in June, Delius's *A Mass of Life* (with the unknown Dietrich Fischer-Dieskau, announced on posters and programmes as FISCHER DIESKOW, *tout court*); in December,

Die Meistersinger at Covent Garden, a glowingly autumnal performance of great beauty with a cast which included the young Geraint Evans as the Nightwatchman.

All these I heard and the following summer, at the Edinburgh Festival, I met the great man. I was often deputed to meet the artists, to see them to their hotels and to settle them in. My diary records some encounters with him.

August 16
Met Sir Thomas at Waverley Station. He was in tremendous form. We discussed music critics. 'At sixty they're monsters, at seventy they're deformed and decrepit: at eighty' – in a vast *crescendo* – 'they're blistering, blathering fools! After thirty years of it no wonder they all look queer.'

'I have brought an exquisite silk waistcoat with me,' he continued. 'I want particularly to talk about it to the gentlemen of the Press. I haven't had an embroidered waistcoat for twenty-five years. I mean to make the most of it.'

August 17
After meeting Ernest Newman and his wife, I raced to the Usher Hall to put Sir Thomas onto the platform in time for the Duke of Edinburgh's arrival (and the anthem). When the moment came nothing would budge him – 'I don't want to have to wait around *up there*,' he remarked. 'I was once kept waiting twenty minutes by the Princess Royal. Stuck in a lift, you know. Having a baby at the time, I remember.' With this he sailed on and within a few minutes had embarked upon what was to prove a superlative performance of Sibelius 7.

August 19
At the evening concert (Beecham playing Mozart 34 and 38 with *Ein Heldenleben*) Josef Szigeti slipped in beside me as I sat on the Grand Tier steps. During a break he whispered, 'There is magic in what Beecham does.' Later, the RPO's leader, David McCallum, told me he had never before taken part in two such performances as Beecham had given the Mozart symphonies. The Amadeus Quartet, with whom I talked in the interval, endorsed this. Jimmy Verity, viola in the orchestra, said that any concert to equal that one would be 'heaven-sent'.

August 21
Beecham (rehearsing the opening of the *pizzicato fugato* for double basses in *L'Enfance du Christ*): 'Bogies!'

August 24
After L'*Enfance du Christ* (an afternoon performance) there was just time to attend the presentation to Beecham of an enormous jeroboam of brandy.

In May 1953, I went to Oxford to hear Sir Thomas conduct Delius's *Irmelin*. I had learned that he had had a fall in the Mitre Hotel, where he was staying, and I was lucky to find him having tea in the lounge there. Having reminded him of our meetings at Edinburgh the previous summer, I enquired solicitously about his fall:

'I fell down one flight of stairs, round the corner and down another one. I landed in the fire-bucket. That's why I kick it when I go past – *you know the expression of course*?'

Curiously, he was also 'damaged' when I went to negotiate with him over the 1956 Edinburgh Festival, my first as its director. He had had an operation on one foot and was in bed with a massive basket over his leg. I had already invited him to give the opening concerts of the Festival and he had accepted. But because the Festival was the tenth I had also asked Sir Arthur Bliss, then Master of the Queen's Music, to write a short, celebratory piece to mark the occasion, and to conduct it. Then it occurred to me that Sir Arthur deserved a better showing, indeed a half-concert – half, though, of one of Sir Thomas's. My mission was a delicate one.

Sir Thomas was in an expansive mood. 'All festivals are a kind of jollification,' he remarked, adding that Salzburg was 'a pleasing bazaar'. When I had his attention, I explained my errand: would he generously surrender half of one of his five concerts to Sir Arthur, who was writing a new work for the festival and who was – after all – Master of the Queen's Music? 'Will he appear *in uniform*?' enquired Sir Thomas.

I knew that I had got my way, but I was not to be let off too lightly: expatiating on Bliss's music, he described it as 'the apotheosis of triviality'. When the concert came, on 20th August, he was on his mettle. He arrived during the first half while Sir Arthur was conducting his Violin Concerto (with Campoli) and, instead of going quietly to the green-room, he made his way to the door onto the Usher Hall platform. This, to my consternation, he opened and, in a piercing whisper clearly audible to the back desks of the first violins, enquired, 'I*s this thing still going on*?' In the second half of the concert he gave a performance of Brahms's Second Symphony so blazingly warm and committed that all memory of Bliss's contribution was, regrettably, obliterated.

The previous evening he had conducted an effective, but somewhat idiosyncratic, performance of the *Choral Symphony*. This was not in fact the work originally agreed. I had persuaded him to conduct the *Missa Solemnis* at the opening concert of the Festival, but when the Free Church of Scotland learned that the Queen and the Duke of Edinburgh were to attend the performance of a Catholic mass, on the Lord's Day, in Scotland's capital, they made such a tremendous rumpus that the Festival Society felt obliged to back down: hence the *Choral Symphony* which, *The Times* pointed out next day, is a pagan work. After the performance I took Sir Thomas up to the Grand Tier to meet the Queen. This was a hazardous expedition because Lady Beecham was clearly not well. However, Sir Thomas tucked her under his arm and supported her up the stairs into the Royal presence where she just managed an acceptable curtsey. (I was reminded of the story of a wayward performance she had given – she was the pianist, Betty Humby – of the Delius Concerto. At the interval, Sir Thomas had observed the removal men preparing to take away the piano. He addressed them, 'I should leave that thing alone if I were you; it will probably slink off on its own.')[1]

Sir Thomas's remaining programmes included one in which Strauss's *Don Quixote* was followed by *Harold in Italy*, a glorious pairing. The others featured a number of his specialities: the Sixth Symphonies of Schubert and Sibelius, the First of Balakirev, Delius's *In a Summer Garden* and his own Suite from Grétry's *Zémire et Azor*. Encores excepted, the last work he conducted at the Edinburgh Festival (on 24th August 1956) was, aptly, Berlioz's overture *Waverley*. In 1948 he had voiced the opinion that 'the people of Scotland are damned fools to throw away £60,000 on a musical festival,' but the following year, appearing himself at the Festival, he had eaten his words. He was the ideal Festival artist – a superb performer in every sense and a gift for the press. Cecil Smith, music critic of the *Daily Express*, described his performance of Sibelius's Sixth as 'a mountain bringing forth a mouse'. Next morning, at the daily press conference, Sir Thomas stormed into the press bureau bellowing, 'Is there a Mr Smith here? I have something to say to Mr Smith.'

At a similar press conference not long before, *The Times*'s music critic, Frank Howes, had said to me, 'You can take your Toscaninis. Beecham has a more intense genius than any of these other great ones.' And if I were to be allowed to enjoy the miraculous reincarnation of just two

1 I was recently told that it was not Sir Thomas, but a member of his orchestra who made this remark.

conductors whom I had once heard, my choice would fall, unhesitatingly, on Furtwängler – and Thomas Beecham.

John Pritchard

John Pritchard's first appearance at the Edinburgh Festival was in 1952 when he stood in for Ernest Ansermet and, with the Royal Philharmonic Orchestra, gave a distinctly odd programme: Schumann's *Manfred* Overture, Rawsthorne's Second Piano Concerto and Mozart's Twenty-third (the A Major, K488), both with Clifford Curzon, and Debussy's *La Mer*. Pritchard's accompaniments were faultless.

* * * * *

John Pritchard – 'JP' to his colleagues – had a phenomenal musical talent: he was once observed, at rehearsal, conducting the orchestra with one hand while, with the other, correcting the urgently needed score of some quite different work.

Born in London in 1921, he studied with his father, an orchestral violinist, and with a variety of teachers. In his teens he visited Italy regularly to listen to opera. At twenty-two he took over the Derby String Orchestra and, four years later, when Glyndebourne fully re-established itself, he joined as a *répétiteur*. After two years he was made chorus master and by 1951 he was sharing with Fritz Busch *Figaro*, *Così* and *Don Giovanni* at Glyndebourne and *Don Giovanni* at the Edinburgh Festival.

His main orchestral opportunity came in 1952 when, with Beecham and Gui, he appeared at the Festival with the Royal Philharmonic Orchestra. Not everything he did was equally successful but here, clearly, was a young man of striking gifts. He had already been appointed to the Jacques String Orchestra and international recognition came his way with an invitation to work at the Vienna State Opera during the 1952-3 season. His debut at Covent Garden also came in 1952. He was to conduct there, on and off, for many years and to premiere Britten's *Gloriana* and Tippett's *The Midsummer Marriage*.

At the Vienna State Opera he caught the attention of the Vienna Symphony Orchestra, with whom he worked between 1953 and 1955, and of the Berlin Festival. Meanwhile, he was safely anchored at Glyndebourne. He had assumed *Idomeneo* from Busch in 1952 and the next year he conducted the second version of Richard Strauss's *Ariadne auf Naxos* in his own right. These two productions he took to the Edinburgh Festival in 1953 and 1954 respectively.

Meanwhile, Pritchard's concert career was developing fast and in 1956 the Royal Liverpool Philharmonic Orchestra had the perspicacity to appoint him their principal conductor. It is doubtful if they knew what they were taking on for, within a year, Pritchard had launched the Musica Viva series which was to establish him as a modern music man as well as a Mozartian. The concerts were introduced, examples were played, the works performed and the audience then invited to join a discussion of them. (This formula is re-invented every so often, but it was Pritchard who imported it into the UK.)

During the first season, 1957-8, the British composers were Peter Racine Fricker, Alun Hoddinott and Robert Simpson, the foreigners Berg, Boris Blacher, Luigi Dallapiccola, Karl Amadeus Hartmann, Rolf Liebermann, Milhaud, Henze, Schoenberg and Ernst Toch. Four further seasons followed, which itself suggests the concerts were successful, and these offered works by, among others, Iain Hamilton, Humphrey Searle, Peter Maxwell Davies and Elisabeth Lutyens – the natives – and Stravinsky, Carter, Bartók, Messiaen, Roger Sessions, Webern and Penderecki.

Pritchard conducted virtually everything, and certain concerts he took to London. It was an enterprise of which he remained rightly proud. Nevertheless, it was probably not the main reason for the London Philharmonic's invitation to become their musical director, a post he held between 1962 and 1966. Then, as now, London orchestras could not afford such experiments. But Pritchard's time with the LPO was characterized by interesting programmes and high standards.

In 1963 Pritchard had accepted the oddly titled post of music counsellor at Glyndebourne. To this was added, in 1968, that of principal conductor. Next year he became musical director, *tout court*. He presided at Glyndebourne for eight years during which the repertoire was enriched by the inclusion of works by Cavalli and Monteverdi, Tchaikovsky, Janáček, Strauss, Poulenc and Nicholas Maw. It was a distinguished era and the short season left Pritchard time for important activities elsewhere.

He took the LPO to the Far East in 1969 and to China – the first visit by a Western orchestra – in 1973. His American debut was at the Chicago Lyric Opera in 1969. Next year he took over from the ailing Barbirolli on a Philharmonia tour of Japan. He established a long-term relationship with the San Francisco Opera in 1970 and made his debut at the Met in 1971. His career, very astutely handled by his agent, Basil Horsfield, and by Pritchard himself, was busy and successful. And so it remained: in recent years he held the musical directorships of the Operas of Cologne, Brussels and San Francisco.

At the age of sixty-one he was knighted and returned to a leading British post, that of chief conductor of the BBC Symphony Orchestra. He was a gift to the BBC, having the huge repertoire a broadcasting orchestra needs. He gave it the cream of his experience, from Haydn and Mozart to Henze and Maxwell Davies. Out of the blue he produced a superlative Shostakovich Eleven and nobody at the First Night of the 1983 Proms will forget his Berlioz, the *Symphonie Funèbre et Triomphale*.

John Pritchard's range was astonishing and I, for one, never heard him do a single ugly thing. His Mozart was as good as you could find anywhere: Daniel Barenboim once told me his *Don Giovanni* was the best he had ever heard. His Strauss was superbly idiomatic. To early Verdi, Donizetti and Bellini he brought a special Italianate warmth and ease. You could hear both Busch and Beecham in him. Yet, for all his musicality, his popularity among musicians and his self-evident success, he was never accorded that intangible but unmistakable public acclaim that envelops the mega-star maestro. He knew this. Over lunch, when I offered him the BBC job, he said, 'You know, I won't bring you a lot of critical success.' That did not matter to me – and I do not think it mattered to him. But the music did matter (notwithstanding the days when he seemed out of sorts to the point of indolence), and he could be extraordinarily stubborn when professional principles were at stake.

Apparently quite imperturbable, his readily imitable (and much imitated) manner of speech – bland, almost epicene – concealed a tough professionalism. He survived curious accidents: a car smash near Glyndebourne, electrocution in the pit of the Paris Opéra, imminent peritonitis at a Festival Hall concert. The performance always went on.

Privately, he was witty and well informed. He had a world-wide network of acquaintance. To his close friends he was loyal and very generous. 'Good food and wine' are cited as his principal hobby in *Who's Who* and sometimes this fact was self-evident. Indeed, the struggle to lose weight to the point at which a hip-replacement joint became possible was so protracted that the good hip began to suffer. JP regarded this problem with wry, self-deprecating detachment, the same quality which caused him a rueful smile when the Promenaders unkindly shouted, 'Squelch!' as he took his seat at the harpsichord for an early Haydn symphony.

He once said that he had taken care never to give all of his affection to any one individual. Perhaps a similar absence of absolutely single-minded commitment in his professional life robbed him of the most obviously glittering prizes.

The Independent, 6th December 1989

Paul Sacher

Paul Sacher's munificence as patron was unique in the twentieth century – and his hospitality was lavish. The rather dry Swissness of his character belied both attributes.

* * * * *

Because Paul Sacher married a woman of immense wealth, it was sometimes assumed that, as a conductor, he was just a gifted dilettante. This was certainly not the case: he had been a pupil of Weingartner. Moreover, he had formed his own orchestra, the Basel Chamber Orchestra, at the age of twenty and had made his London debut in 1938, conducting a concert for the International Society for Contemporary Music. It was not until 1954, though, that he appeared at Glyndebourne, where I first met him during rehearsals for Stravinsky's *The Rake's Progress*. The neo-classical idiom of the music which, though unmistakably Stravinskian (as was every note that Stravinsky wrote), embodied equally unmistakable evocations of Mozart, seemed particularly to suit Sacher's own musical inclinations. (He was to conduct *Die Entführung* and *Die Zauberflöte* at Glyndebourne not long afterwards.)

Enchanted by *The Rake's Progress*, I also warmed to its conductor and an acquaintance persisted casually until, in 1970, I persuaded Alex Gibson that we should invite him, with Rostropovich as his soloist, to appear with the Scottish National Orchestra in Britten's Cello Symphony, then a relatively new work. The performances took place in Edinburgh and Glasgow on 23rd and 24th October. The programme we agreed with Sacher was characteristic: Mozart's 'Little' G Minor Symphony, Haydn's C Major Cello Concerto, the Britten, and a work by a distinguished compatriot of Sacher's, Honegger's *Symphonic Movement* No.2, *Rugby*. Rostropovich, whose pupil, Jacqueline du Pré, was already popular with our audiences, had not played with us before but was already on his way to being a legend. Sacher was an unknown quantity. The public responded predictably, Edinburgh with some reserve, Glasgow with open-hearted enthusiasm. Sacher, himself innately reserved, went away a happy man, for the Glasgow performance had been full of confidence and energy.

We did not meet again till 1974, when the BBC Symphony Orchestra gave a concert in Basel under Pierre Boulez, who was well known to and much admired by Sacher. After the concert we were invited to his home (whence, he told me, Adrian Boult had once chosen to walk the twelve kilometres into Basel late at night). The house, Schönenberg, was full of beautiful objects, expressionist paintings in particular and some sculptures by Sacher's wife, Maja. The supper was excellent, the occasion easy and informal. At one point Sacher said to me, 'Please come upstairs. I would like to show you one or two things.' One of the 'things' was the manuscript of Stravinsky's *The Rite of Spring*, complete with the pencilled markings of Pierre Monteux, who had conducted the notorious premiere. Another was the Sachers' Visitors Book in which, on two facing pages, were a line of music, an inscription and Bartók's signature, and, opposite, a tiny water-colour sketch and Braque's. Both thrilled me, but particularly the latter, since I had visited the painter in his Paris studio in 1956. Sacher spoke warmly of both guests, but mostly of Bartók, whose *Music for Strings, Percussion and Celeste* he had commissioned in 1937 and of which Pierre had conducted a fine performance in Vienna a few days earlier.

Sacher was in every way a generous man. In the late 1970s I asked him for a contribution to the work of the Council for Music in Hospitals, of which I was then president, and he responded with a handsome cheque, explaining that it would have been bigger had he not had recently to pay a vast sum for some Stravinsky manuscripts which were an important acquisition for the Paul Sacher Foundation. This collection, housed in a fine house in Basel's Munsterplatz, is remarkable. Stravinsky apart, it contains manuscripts, scores, sketches and books by, among many others, Webern, Martinů, Maderna, Lutosławski, Berio, Boulez, Ligeti and Birtwistle, whose *Endless Parade* he commissioned in 1986. This was one of the last of the astonishing number of works he commissioned, of some of which he conducted the first performance. Strauss (the *Metamorphosen*), Bartók, Stravinsky, Hindemith, Tippett, Britten, Henze, Carter, Lutosławski, Berio and several Swiss composers, among them Frank Martin, were all recipients of Sacher's patronage and during the 1993-4 season the London Mozart Players gave a series of seven concerts on the South Bank each of which featured a Sacher commission, Sacher himself conducting one of them at the age of eighty-seven. He seemed unchanged, undemonstrative, but clear, assured and authoritative.

Carlo Maria Giulini

Carlo Maria Giulini was more at home in Verdi's Requiem (of which he gave several performances at the Edinburgh Festival) than in the composer's *Falstaff*, whose Glyndebourne production he brought to Edinburgh in 1955. He was, I suppose, too serious a man perfectly to understand the mercurial wit which Verdi brought to one of Shakespeare's richest characterizations. But his Requiem was stupendous.

* * * * *

The name seems to signify the man: patrician, elegant, devout. The man himself was charismatic, almost saintly (Walter Legge used teasingly to call him 'St Sebastian'). When you met him you were in the presence of a personality both grand and self-deprecating. When you heard him – except perhaps towards the end of his career – there was no doubt that here was a great conductor.

Carlo Maria Giulini was born in Barletta, on the southern Adriatic coast of Italy, in 1914. At the end of the First World War, he was taken to live in the South Tyrol (formerly Austrian) and as he grew up he learned the language of Austria and absorbed its musical traditions so that when, in the 1970s, he became principal conductor of the Vienna Symphony Orchestra he did not feel a foreigner. His formal training, however, began in Rome where, initially, he studied violin, viola and composition at the Conservatorio di Santa Cecilia. Conducting, under Bernardino Molinari, came later. Indeed his professional career began as a viola-player in the Augusteo Orchestra, with whom he played under Richard Strauss, Henry Wood, Wilhelm Furtwängler, Bruno Walter, Victor de Sabata and Otto Klemperer.

It was with the same orchestra that he made his conducting debut at a concert to celebrate the liberation of Rome in 1944. The programme included one of the Brahms symphonies – probably the Fourth, which he later said was the first 'great' work he conducted. 'Brahms took possession of me with the most irresistible *prepotenza*.' Later the same year he was made music director of Italian Radio, an appointment which in retrospect looks surprising, for radio conductors need a very large repertoire. Nevertheless, it was at the Radio that he started to conduct opera, broadcasting works by Scarlatti, Malipiero and others. His reputation began to grow and he received invitations from other centres. One such came from Venice, where the Earl of Harewood heard him and was unimpressed. Malipiero, who was also present, explained, 'He was listening to the orchestra and not letting the music flow. It will be different tomorrow.' (Perhaps La Fenice's bone-dry concert acoustics had something to do with it.)

In any case Giulini was on his way. His public opera début came in *La Traviata* at Bergamo in 1950. In the same year he created the Milan Radio Orchestra, soon broadcasting Haydn's *Il Mondo della Luna* – which caught the ear of de Sabata and Arturo Toscanini at La Scala. As a result he made his début there during the 1951-2 season. He was to succeed de Sabata in 1953. Meanwhile, he visited Prague and was deeply impressed by a particular quality he found in Czech music, 'this mixture of violent rhythms and of *morbidezza*, of *tenerezza* and *tristezza*'.

At La Scala he performed *L'Incoronazione di Poppea* (in Ghedini's version: he was no purist), *Duke Bluebeard's Castle* and *Les Noces*; he worked with Callas in *Alceste* and *La Traviata*; he began to be associated with Luchino Visconti and Franco Zeffirelli. He guested successfully at Aix, the Maggio Musicale and the Holland Festival. In 1955 Glyndebourne invited him to replace Vittorio Gui, who was unwell, in *Falstaff* at the Edinburgh Festival. It was a triumphant British début for Giulini and it led, within three years, to the start of his association with the Philharmonia and, memorably, to Visconti's production of *Don Carlos* at the Royal Opera House in 1958. Lord Harewood, who with David Webster had put the production together, was later to write that it established Giulini 'as the leading conductor of Italian opera anywhere'. Webster is said to have declared that he had 'found Toscanini again'.

In the meantime Giulini's international career was burgeoning. He first conducted the Chicago Symphony, with whom he was to have a long and satisfying relationship, in 1955. He began to be in demand by all the great orchestras. In London, Walter Legge was coaxing him to broaden his orchestral repertoire: he had hitherto played no Bach and little Mozart or Beethoven. In 1958 he gave the first of many performances in Britain of the Verdi Requiem. This was with the Philharmonia. The performance was repeated at the opening concert of the 1960 Edinburgh Festival, where in the 1960s and 1970s he was a regular guest, on two occasions conducting the Requiem twice during the same Festival. Philip Hope-Wallace attended a performance of it in St Paul's Cathedral in July 1966 and recalled that 'sitting under the Dome, within a foot of Giulini's baton arm, the effect on me was stunning, overwhelmingly powerful and affecting'. Giulini also appeared frequently at the Leeds Festival, on one occasion conducting the C Minor

Mass of Mozart in memory of the Princess Royal, mother of Lord Harewood, then artistic director of the Festival.

In 1967, after giving *La Traviata* (in Visconti's production) at the Royal Opera House, he announced that he would for the time being conduct no more opera, a decision which, considering his extraordinary gifts, remains perplexing. Fifteen years were to pass before he returned to the opera house – in *Falstaff*. Meanwhile, in 1969, he was appointed chief guest conductor of the Chicago Symphony, recording his beloved Brahms Fourth Symphony for Angel after a public performance during his first season there. Later he was to record the Ninth Symphonies of Bruckner and Mahler and Dvořák's last two symphonies with the same orchestra. In 1971, with Georg Solti, he appeared with it at the Edinburgh Festival. Two years later he became Principal Conductor of the Vienna Symphony Orchestra, a post he held for three years. It is well known that he did not find Viennese musical politics congenial.

Since 1958 he had been a regular, if not frequent, guest with the Philharmonia (and New Philharmonia). In the earlier years, his repertoire, never very large, was surprisingly varied. Ravel's *Mother Goose* Suite (a favourite of his), Debussy's *La Mer* and *Three Nocturnes*, Franck's Symphony and *Psyché et Eros*, Stravinsky's *Firebird* Suite, Berlioz's *Romeo and Juliet* (the suite) and *Nuits d'Été*, Mussorgsky's *Pictures* occurred in his programmes, along with certain Italians – Vivaldi, Rossini, Cherubini, Respighi, Casella, Petrassi. He was persuaded to do some Britten and, with the composer, conducted the *War Requiem* (in 1969). *Les Illuminations*, the *Serenade* and the first performance of the overture *The Building of the House* followed. (In the early 1960s he had conducted Wilfred Josephs' Requiem at La Scala). He did some big Romantic symphonies – Dvořák's Seventh, Tchaikovsky's Second, Schumann's Third, Bruckner's Eighth, Mahler's First. But he returned again and again to his first and abiding loves – Verdi, Brahms, Beethoven (the *Missa Solemnis* and the *Choral Symphony*) and Mozart.

In 1982, Giulini returned to opera with a production of *Falstaff* which originated in Los Angeles, where he was music director of the Philharmonic from 1978 to 1984. This production, subsequently seen in London and Florence, was controversial. He had supervised every aspect of it himself. He talked of 'stripping away *buffo* excess'. A Los Angeles critic wrote that 'the Giulini *Falstaff* is deficient in charm, wit and whimsy, but there are intelligence, elegance, suavity, profundity' – conspicuously Giulini's own musical characteristics. London expectations were on the whole disappointed: the performance was deemed an anticlimax.

There is a clue here to the man's nature. He was a deeply serious artist. As a young man he had conducted a Gershwin programme. 'I adore Gershwin, I love the music, but I cannot do it.' Similarly, 'I love and admire Puccini, but I cannot conduct Puccini.' (De Sabata had tried to persuade him to do *La Fanciulla del West*.) Though he had titanic physical energy in those long arms and wonderfully expressive hands he was, in general, slower than Toscanini and he did not have (or need) de Sabata's demonic character. In fact he was closer in style to Furtwängler, though he was delicate in Debussy and Ravel.

'Sempre cantare' and 'Staccato – ma sempre legato' were two of his quintessential concerns and they are beautifully illustrated in his 1959 recording of *Don Giovanni*. From the first bars of the overture it is clear that the orchestral sound will be full, rounded and big. Inner parts are always given proper value. Balance is admirable and tempi are, to my mind, virtually ideal – the slow ones never ponderous, the quick ones never rushed. Giulini had a fine, if not absolutely ideal, cast (Walter Legge saw to that) and with the exception of Giuseppe Taddei's occasionally wobbly Leporello he gets highly accomplished singing from Eberhard Wächter (Don), Joan Sutherland (Anna), Elisabeth Schwarzkopf (Elvira), Graziella Sciutti (Zerlina), Luigi Alva (Ottavio), Gottlob Frick (Commendatore) and Piero Cappuccilli (Masetto). Indeed, the singing is sometimes simply too beautiful. 'Là ci darem' is more bland than erotic, while Sutherland's recitatives are so smooth and quick that they often lack dramatic point. To what extent this is due to the fact that the performance was a studio creation and had not derived from a stage production, to Legge's no doubt firmly expressed wishes, or to Giulini's own obsession with legato it is hard to say. Either way – though now in one sense 'old-fashioned' – the set gives, and deserves always to give, enormous pleasure.

Giulini was a compassionate and exceptionally courteous man. At Edinburgh in 1955 he told me of Furtwängler's growing deafness and his distress, on behalf of a colleague, was palpable and touching. In February 1980, I visited him in Milan, with a Swedish colleague, on behalf of the European Broadcasting Union. He was solicitous, coming to the door himself and leading us on a stately walk to a favourite restaurant (a modest one) where he was clearly adored. He made us feel we had done him a favour; whereas he had undertaken to broadcast, live from Los Angeles, a programme comprising Webern's *Six Pieces*, Berg's

Violin Concerto (with Itzhak Perlman) and Bruckner's Ninth Symphony. The concert was heard throughout Europe on 8th November 1982. It was very fine.

A private man (it is said that it was part of his Los Angeles contract that he would never have to attend post-concert parties or to meet the blue-rinsed ladies' committees) he was deeply troubled, from 1982, by the illness and eventual death in 1995 of his wife, Marcella, to whom he was wholly devoted. She was a gifted painter and had organized his life. Partly paralysed by a stroke, she increasingly needed his presence and there came a stage when he would not leave Europe and insisted on being at home for two weeks between engagements. I think it is to this prolonged anxiety that one must attribute a certain loss of energy, of fire, in his later performances. Always a thinking musician, he had, when younger, combined and ideally balanced the physical with the cerebral. Latterly, the physical element was diminished and the performances, though never lightweight, were sometimes pedestrian.

So it is by those blazing earlier concerts and opera performances – notably the Verdi Requiem and *Don Carlos* – that we should now remember him; and for the nobility of his character.

The Independent, 16th June 2005

Rafael Kubelík

I wish I had known Rafael Kubelík better: he was an extraordinarily nice man, indeed rather too nice for his own good. He came to Edinburgh with the Philharmonia Orchestra in 1957, giving us Dvořák's *Symphonic Variations*, Martinů's Fourth Piano Concerto (with Rudolf Firkušný) and Beethoven's Fifth Symphony. The concert was memorably idiomatic.

* * * * *

Rafael Kubelík, the Czech conductor, was in every way a big man: tall and robust in physique, he was the most generous of human beings and he inspired devoted affection among his friends and colleagues.

The son of the violinist Jan Kubelík, he was born in Bychory, in Bohemia, in 1914. As a student at the Prague Conservatoire, he made his début with the Czech Philharmonic at the age of twenty, being appointed its principal conductor in 1936. In this capacity he appeared in London in 1937 (and Henry Wood noted that he was not yet to be compared with the great Václav Talich). From 1939 to 1941 he was director of the Brno Opera, where he began to explore Janáček and where he pioneered Berlioz's *The Trojans* – an amazingly original undertaking.

He then returned to the Czech Philharmonic, with whom he made such a reputation that in 1946 he was a guest with the BBC Symphony Orchestra – at the People's Palace (where Janáček's *Sinfonietta* had to be replaced with Dvořák's Seventh Symphony because the BBC had not budgeted for the extra trumpets) and in the studio. An internal BBC memo noted that he only needed 'a little more poise' to establish himself as an international star.

In 1948 Czechoslovakia turned Communist and Kubelík left, taking up residence in London. This was convenient because Glyndebourne had invited him to conduct *Don Giovanni* at the Edinburgh Festival that summer. (He was the first Glyndebourne conductor to use a harpsichord as continuo, Fritz Busch having always preferred the piano.) The performance, made unforgettable by Ljuba Welitsch's riveting Donna Anna, was richly romantic and it so greatly enhanced Kubelík's reputation that, next year, he was approached as a possible successor to Adrian Boult – who was to be retired at sixty – with the BBC Symphony Orchestra.

A rival offer from the Chicago Symphony, however (and his wife's preference for the United States to England), took him to Chicago, where he was musical director for three seasons, 1950-3. Though he premiered Roy Harris's Seventh Symphony among other works, his repertoire was thought to be unduly narrow, and he perhaps lacked the 'brilliance' by which that orchestra liked to identify itself.

The next landmark in his career came in 1954, at Sadler's Wells, when he revived *Katya Kabanová*, which Charles Mackerras had introduced three years earlier. The revival was a triumph and it was no doubt the main reason why, a year later, he was appointed musical director at Covent Garden.

At the Royal Opera House an introductory *Bartered Bride* (1955) led to *Otello* the same year, *Jenůfa* (1956) and *The Trojans* – which John Gielgud directed – in 1957, when he also appeared with the Philharmonia Orchestra at the Edinburgh Festival. But the Covent Garden years were not to be happy ones. Fiercely loyal to the principle of 'opera in English', to the native singers in his company and to the idea of a national ensemble, Kubelík was unwillingly involved in operatic politics. Attacked by, among others, Thomas Beecham, he characteristically and unwisely offered to resign (in a letter to *The Times*) 'since I do not want to be in the way as a foreigner'. His resignation was rejected, but a disappointing *Die Meistersinger* (a work he was gloriously to record in Munich in 1967) set the seal upon his future and he left Covent Garden in 1958.

George Harewood, then working at the Opera House, wrote of 'his ability to give unstintingly to colleagues, company, audience and above all to the music', and spoke of Kubelík's three years there as 'the best of my life'.

Between 1958 and 1961, when he was appointed to the Bavarian Radio Symphony Orchestra, Kubelík was a guest with many great orchestras, the Vienna and Israel Philharmonic among them. In Munich, *Die Meistersinger* apart, he recorded a complete Mahler cycle and worked often with Fischer-Dieskau – in Mahler songs, Franck's *Les Béatitudes* and Debussy's *Pelléas*. Together, too, they went to Milan to record *Rigoletto*. Elsewhere, as a guest, he offered Dvořák, whose complete symphonies he recorded with the Berlin Philharmonic, Smetana and Janáček, as well as the Schumann symphonies, Hindemith, Schoenberg (the concertos), Bartók and some Britten.

In 1971, Göran Gentele, Rudolf Bing's successor at the Metropolitan Opera, New York, invited Kubelík to become its first musical director. The two men had a similar vision of what could be done at the Met and Kubelík, perhaps anticipating a more sympathetic – and less xenophobic – attitude from the press than he had encountered at Covent Garden, accepted the invitation, though Klemperer, whom he had consulted in Switzerland (where both now lived), advised against. But Gentele was killed in a car crash in Sardinia in July 1972, a few weeks before their first season was due to open. So the partnership was dissolved and Kubelík, though he was to guest at the Met, returned to Europe.

Walter Legge, on hearing of his appointment, had written that 'much as I like Kubelík, I doubt if he knows his way about the repertoire...or has a firm enough way with him to get the desired and necessary results': a judgement characteristically negative but not without a grain of truth.

From 1972 Kubelík's career began to fade, though he worked here and there as a distinguished guest. He conducted the Otto Klemperer Memorial Concert at the Royal Albert Hall in January 1974 and he appeared at the Lucerne Festival, conducting his own *Sequenzen*, the following year. At the Prague Spring in 1990 he returned to Czechoslovakia, conducting an unforgettable performance of Smetana's *Vltava* at the opening concert of the festival, an occasion celebrating the collapse of the Soviet Union's hegemony over Eastern Europe. Thereafter he visited Prague from time to time, but only as a listener, for he was beginning to be ill and, for the sake of a warm climate, was spending some of his time in Florida.

Kubelík was twice married, first to the violinist Ludmila Bertlova, then in 1963 to the Australian soprano Elsie Morison, a member of the Covent Garden company during his regime there, who had sung for Glyndebourne at the Edinburgh Festival in 1953. They were a devoted couple.

Rafael Kubelík was the composer of two operas – *Veronika* given at Brno in 1947, and *Cornelia Faroli*, heard at Augsburg in 1972 – three requiems, various concertos, and a choral symphony. But he will be chiefly remembered as a magnificent interpreter of Dvořák, Smetana, Janáček and Martinů, and of late Romantic music – Wagner and Mahler in particular. He was a man of shining musical and personal integrity, perhaps ill-equipped for the cut and thrust of musical politics. He tended to wear his heart on his sleeve and was all the more loved for doing so.

Adrian Boult, a much more charitable man than Walter Legge, wrote of Kubelík, 'There is no one I would rather make way for.'

The Independent, 13th August 1996

Alexander Gibson

I owe a very great deal to Alexander Gibson, who coaxed me to Glasgow to manage the Scottish National Orchestra in 1964 and who taught me most of what I know about the psychology of orchestral musicians and their relationship with conductors. We first met when, newly appointed, he brought his orchestra to the Edinburgh Festival in 1959. Our friendship lasted until his death in 1994.

* * * * *

Alexander Gibson played nightingale in the performance of Haydn's *Toy Symphony*, which I conducted on the last day of my last Edinburgh Festival, 10th September 1960. Three years later he called on me in London (where I was working, unrewardingly, for the Independent Television Authority) and discreetly suggested that I might be interested in joining him in Scotland as the SNO's chief executive. I was flattered – but undecided; Glasgow seemed remote, uncouth, grimy. I had seldom been there and knew almost nothing about its considerable cultural resources, though I was well aware of the marked improvement in the SNO's standards which Alex had brought about since his appointment in 1959. In the end, it was his persuasive charm and the promise of scope that won me round. That decision was one of the best I ever made. Alex and his adorable wife, Veronica – 'V' to her many friends – were the hospitable hub of a circle (large enough not to be cliquey) of musicians, art-historians, lawyers, dons, journalists and broadcasters. A Sassenach administrator, albeit with Scottish connections, I was made immediately and warmly welcome when I began work in the spring of 1964. And it was Alex who unobtrusively steered me through the unfamiliar shoals of orchestral administration. His musicianship was pure bonus.

'I had facility,' he once told me. He meant it not boastfully, but almost apologetically: he was acknowledging an advantage which made things rather easier for him than for some of his colleagues. But he was certainly not facile. Instinctive, yes. And his instincts, always musical, were reinforced by serious study and a natural mastery of large-scale works. I think of *The Trojans*, *The Ring* and Mahler's Eighth Symphony in particular.

With facility went an extraordinary capacity for hard work. As the *supremo* of an opera company and a symphony orchestra he inevitably found that some of his energy had to be spent on planning, fund-raising, politics. He was gifted in all these fields and was a very persuasive diplomat in the board-room of a potential sponsor. His status, charm and sheer intelligence made him formidable. There were of course times when fatigue, or anxiety, brought out an irascible streak in him. Then he showed a pale, boot-faced look which I soon learned to recognise; it was best to keep a low profile until colour returned and the sun shone again, which it soon did. There were also times when he seemed – no, was – ill-prepared, as though learning his scores at rehearsal. I cannot explain this weakness, for Alex was the least lazy man I ever knew. Perhaps it was a reluctance to commit himself to a considered musical statement which inhibited him, just as, in non-musical matters, he was sometimes circumspect to the point of inertia where decision-making was concerned.

In this respect he was hypersensitive. I remember him phoning me one day and suggesting a walk at the Queen's View. Now this was very odd, for Alex rarely walked anywhere and I guessed he needed to discuss some mutual problem: perhaps I had unwittingly offended him. In any case, we toiled up the hill to the View. We admired it. We idled down. We returned to Glasgow. We sat in his garden – and *still* nothing was said. Eventually, some three hours after our initial meeting, he managed to broach the issue which lay between us. What it was I don't remember, but it had cost him dear in time and psychological effort.

Alex was a born performer; he could turn an apparently unpromising concert into an exhilarating success. Audiences adored him, as did the junior staff he encountered in opera-houses, concert-halls, colleges of music, hotels, restaurants and shops. 'You could die of thirst in this pub,' he would say if unreasonably kept waiting; but the rebuke was delivered with such charm that the barman was likely to be a friend for life. He was a gifted raconteur and a splendid mimic, Barbirolli being the most precise and the most affectionate of his portrayals. After an arduous programme-planning session there was nothing more entertaining than small-talk with Alex in some agreeable bar, often The Buttery in Argyll Street, or in his own home.

The eight years I spent in Glasgow were, without any doubt, the most satisfying of my career. This was essentially due to Alex. He motivated me to the point of inspiration. His ambition was rooted in an idealistic dedication to high standards – so Boult and Horenstein and Kletzki and Barbirolli were among our guests. He wanted the best soloists – so Janet Baker and Jacqueline du Pré, and Barenboim, Brendel, Curzon, Ogdon were 'regulars'. With Scottish Opera, Baker (memorable in *The Trojans* and *Così*), Elizabeth Harwood, David Ward, Geraint Evans were pre-eminent among a galaxy of fine singers. They came because of Alex's status, his professionalism and his musicianship: he was a superb accompanist.

After I joined the BBC in 1972, I naturally saw less of Alex, but I invited him to the Proms most years between 1974 and 1984 and his contributions were invaluably diverse: he contributed Haydn, Mozart, Schubert, Brahms, Sibelius, Rachmaninoff and Nielsen symphonies; vocal works by Berlioz, Verdi (*Falstaff*), Wolf and Elgar (*Gerontius*); and contemporary music by three Scots – Iain Hamilton, Thea Musgrave, Martin Dalby – and two English: Goehr and Birtwistle. This was all true Proms material.

Alex was by no mean a voluminous correspondent, but not much more than a year before he died I had a long letter from him, described, in it, as 'a few lines from your old (your *very* old) friend and collaborator'. I had sent him photographs of Strauss, Mengelberg and Toscanini rehearsing in the Musikverein, Vienna, along with a photograph I had taken (from much the same viewpoint) of him rehearsing there in 1967. He was grateful, of course, but, because I was then working for the

Musicians Benevolent Fund, he was full of the success of a concert he had conducted to mark the seventy-fifth birthday of the Scottish Musicians Benevolent Fund. This had involved four orchestras, the Royal Scottish National Orchestra, the BBC Scottish Symphony Orchestra, the Scottish Chamber Orchestra and the orchestra of Scottish Opera, which had been amalgamated into one huge band and had raised £35,000 for the SMBF. This amazing event had more or less coincided with the publication of Conrad Wilson's biography, *Alex*, which had given him 'a very curious feeling': he could not get used to 'the idea of somebody writing a whole book' about him. But, characteristically, he was looking ahead – to 'a new production of *Tosca* at the ENO'.

It was soon after the run of *Tosca* that he died, not in his own country but in London, which he had left thirty-six years before. His death was wholly unexpected and, for once, he was alone: a melancholy death for such a sociable being with so many friends in the music profession.

Rudolf Kempe

One of the string principals of the BBC Symphony Orchestra once told me that, at rehearsal, Kempe had made a mistake, giving a wrong lead to the section in question. At the concert he gave the right lead – and a collusive wink. He was that sort of conductor: the players were his collaborators. And he rarely made mistakes. I first heard him in Strauss's *Arabella* at Covent Garden in 1953.

* * * * *

When, on 6th July 1980, Charles Groves conducted the Verdi Requiem at the Royal Opera House in memory of Rudolf Kempe, the composite orchestra contained the elite of London's players, among them Raymond Cohen, Eli Goren, Frederick Riddle, Christopher van Kampen, Janet Craxton, Alan Civil and John Wilbraham. Such was the devotion that Kempe inspired among his instrumental colleagues. He had died on 12th May 1976, having recently assumed the chief conductorship of the BBC Symphony Orchestra. He would have conducted six Proms that year and his death, at the age of sixty-five, was a body blow to the orchestra.

Born on 14th June 1910, Kempe was a Saxon; he studied at the Dresden Musikhochschule. His conducting debut was at the Leipzig Opera in 1935 and, after military service, he was appointed music director of the Chemnitz Opera. He was promoted to the Dresden

Opera in 1949 and to the Bavarian State Opera, where he was Solti's successor, in 1952.

I had first heard him in 1953 when he brought the company to Covent Garden. His *Arabella* was memorable for its luminous clarity and rhythmic strength. He was soon engaged for Covent Garden itself and I heard his *Salome* later the same year when it was clear that he had absorbed Strauss's own by no means ironic advice to 'conduct my *Salome* and *Elektra* as if they were by Mendelssohn – fairy music'. Until 1960 he was a regular guest at the Garden, giving more Strauss, and in due course no fewer than ten *Ring* cycles. In 1956, my first Edinburgh Festival, he had opened the Hamburg State Opera's season with *Die Zauberflöte*, a performance I had to miss because Beecham – who was to name Kempe as his preferred successor with the Royal Philharmonic Orchestra – was exercising my diplomatic skills at the Usher Hall. But a later performance easily persuaded me to bring him back to the Festival, for concerts, in 1959.

By this time he had been offered, but had turned down, the music directorship at Covent Garden. But the RPO, happy to endorse Beecham's benediction, appointed him their principal conductor in 1961.

Coming to the BBC in 1972, I needed to find a successor to Pierre Boulez. I had my eye on a triumvirate: Kempe as principal, Boulez and Colin Davis as official guests. It seemed Kempe might consider a move and I met him regularly in 1973 and 1974. Eventually a contract was concluded. Kempe's agent was the astute and honourable Howard Hartog, who negotiated a very advantageous agreement. The price he paid, he told me, was that of long, brisk walks in Hyde Park when the portly Hartog had to keep pace with his slim and energetic artist.

Kempe began his BBC regime at the start of the 1975-6 season. He opened it with Haydn's *London Symphony* and Mahler's *Das Lied von der Erde*, but when he returned in February he was clearly unwell, though poor health did not affect his music-making. The last work he conducted for the BBC was a glorious Brahms Fourth. We did not see him again and his death came as a cruel shock because I could get no news of him during those last months. In my diary, on the day when word reached me, I noted that 'though I admired the musician, I hardly knew the man at all.'

He was a very private and a very simple person. Once, when I visited him in Munich, he did not appear immediately and, when he did, he explained that he had been repairing his model railway, which filled a large attic room. And he was immensely gifted. At eighteen he had been appointed principal oboe of the Leipzig Gewandhaus Orchestra; he was a very good pianist and had studied the violin – so he was ideally equipped. In rehearsal he talked little, but built up his conception of the music by adding cumulative detail. His left hand was very eloquent and his stick technique (he used a long baton) was immaculate. He rarely raised his voice and was never flustered; Fischer-Dieskau, after a stressful recording of *Lohengrin*, reported that Kempe 'stood there like a rock, quiet and kind.' As to repertoire, he recorded nothing later than Britten's *Sinfonia da Requiem* and was reluctant to undertake much contemporary music; but he once flummoxed me by offering to perform a work by Francis Burt, of whom I was then ignorant. So we compromised: he agreed to do Tippett's *Concerto for Double String Orchestra*, but he did not press me to sanction a 'comic' concert which I feared might fall short, in dotty but inspired wit, of Hoffnung's unique interplanetary galas.

Rudolf Kempe was a man after my own heart: modest to a fault but, as an interpreter, completely authoritative. Always at the service of the music, to which he brought a radiant clarity, he once wrote, 'One must not search, one must find. Searching implies conscious manipulation. Finding is the result of devotion to a composer and his music.' It was this devotion which the BBCSO found so winning. More than two years were to elapse before a worthy successor, Gennadi Rozhdestvensky, could be engaged.

BBC *Music Magazine*, September 2000

Jascha Horenstein

Though ten years younger than Adrian Boult, Jascha Horenstein had also studied with Arthur Nikisch and, like Boult and Kempe, he used a long stick: his beat was broad and very clear. The first work I heard him conduct was Mozart's *Prague Symphony* (1964), the last Bruckner's Fourth (1968), the latter particularly idiomatic.

* * * * *

When Alexander Gibson invited me to join him in Glasgow as general manager of the Scottish National Orchestra, he was offering me (I was later to discover) eight years of unforgettable musical enrichment. In those enlightened 1960s (we are in the dark ages now) the SNO could regularly engage the finest soloists – Argerich, Baker, du Pré, Ogdon, Ashkenazy, Barenboim, Brendel, Curzon, Menuhin, Tortelier among them – and some of the finest conductors. A specially grand guest was the Russian-Austrian conductor Jascha Horenstein, whom I had never met and whose now legendary London performance of the Mahler Eight I had missed. Learning my trade as a manager, I soon picked up allusions to the personality of a musician whose visits were anticipated by the orchestra with a mixture of veneration and alarm: it was unwise to come unprepared to a Horenstein rehearsal. And since his repertoire was unconventional, his concerts called for extra effort. Between 1964 and 1968 Horenstein gave ten programmes in Scotland, taking in Edinburgh, Glasgow, Aberdeen and Dundee. Reluctantly typecast as a Mahler and Bruckner specialist, he offered us works ranging from Mozart to the Argentinian Ginastera, whose *Variaciones Concertantes*, an effective piece, preceded a Beethoven concerto and Schumann's Fourth Symphony. On another occasion Schumann's Third was followed by his *Manfred* music, with the splendidly ham Michael MacLiammoir as narrator. Horenstein and MacLiammoir were chalk and cheese but the collaboration worked well. A safer work was Mozart's last piano concerto, the K595, which Barenboim decorated differently on each of the four nights, as the mood took him. Rarities included *Verklärte Nacht* – Horenstein had attended Schoenberg's lectures in Vienna – and the Busoni Violin Concerto (with Sam Bor). And, of course, there were Mahler and Bruckner: the *Kindertotenlieder*, with Janet Baker, and the fourth symphonies of both composers. But, for me, the crowning glory of all Horenstein's concerts was the Glasgow performance of Bruckner Eight. The setting was not auspicious. Since the burning of the acoustically magnificent St Andrew's Hall, the SNO had performed in a squalid and badly converted cinema. But the performance was a triumph, wonderfully paced and delivered with a loving authority which I have heard matched only by Günter Wand.

During his visits, Horenstein and I ate together regularly. I was mesmerized by his memories of Arthur Nikisch, by whom he was strongly influenced, and of Furtwängler, for whom, at the 1927 ISCM (International Society for Contemporary Music) Festival, he had prepared works by Janáček (who, he said, was 'very easy-going'), Bartók (who was 'not very human') and Nielsen (who was 'nothing but human').

Some of his recollections may be heard on the BBC Legends release of the Mahler Eight which is preceded by an interview with Alan Blyth. In the interview Horenstein says that Strauss advised him that 'you should hold your baton at the same height as your eyes so as to force the musicians to look into your eyes.' Another lesson he had learned from

Rachmaninoff: 'I was the conductor for the Paris premiere of his Fourth Piano Concerto and he was the soloist. It was a great chance for a young man; I had a Beethoven symphony in the second half. The concerto went well, but instead of going to Rachmaninoff's room to thank and congratulate him I went to my own room to prepare for the Beethoven. The time came and I began. I had not gone far when I noticed a tall, stern figure standing discreetly behind the double basses. It was Rachmaninoff. He had come to hear me when he could have been drinking champagne. And I had not been to thank him! I was mortified.'

Horenstein was born in Kiev in 1898, and took American citizenship in the 1940s after the Nazis forced him to leave Germany. His eyes strongly resembled Bartók's, and he could appear positively baleful; nor did he possess much obvious charm. But Maurice Murphy, then principal trumpet of the BBC Northern Symphony Orchestra where Horenstein regularly guested, penetrated his rather austere exterior, if not without effort: 'It took me three days to crack him, to make him smile. He was really a nice man.' On the rostrum his style was four-square (and it irritated Clifford Curzon when he emphatically beat out bars of orchestral silence accompanying the soloist). But William Glock should perform a special penance for describing him as 'the cultivated butcher'. Cultivated, yes. Just listen to that Mahler. Butcher? I think not. Student of Furtwängler, pupil of Adolf Busch and close friend of Berg, he was of the old school – good-hearted, undemonstrative, modest, a servant of the music. His recordings deserve to be treasured.

BBC *Music Magazine*, September 1999

Norman Del Mar

Glasgow, always a lively place, was specially stimulating in the 1960s. Alexander Gibson was successfully developing the Scottish National Orchestra and Scottish Opera. At the BBC, Norman Del Mar was in charge of the Scottish Symphony Orchestra, exploring, with colossal energy, some unusual repertoire.

* * * * *

'That's the sort of thing.'

Countless British orchestral players will remember Norman Del Mar's much-imitated comment, habitually made at the end of the first run-through of an unfamiliar piece.

Then the hard work would begin, and nobody worked harder than Del Mar himself. His energy was prodigious, his knowledge of the score comprehensive and meticulous. The sheer number of works he had mastered was mind-boggling and his curiosity infinite: among the rarer names whose music he promoted can be found those of Blomdahl, Bacewicz, Havergal Brian, Don Banks, Dennis Aplvor, Lord Berners and Balfe, whose *The Bohemian Girl* he conducted for Beecham in 1951 – Festival of Britain year. He launched (and often re-launched) an amazing number of works by British composers. He loved extravagant projects: the Busoni Piano Concerto, Granville Bantock's *Omar Khayyam*, d'Indy's *La Forêt Enchantée* with the full complement of harps. Above all he loved Richard Strauss, and his three-volume critical commentary on the composer's life and works is definitive.

As a horn-player (with Dennis Brain) in the Royal Philharmonic, Del Mar played some Strauss for Beecham and it was in 1947, when he was twenty-eight, that the latter arranged his professional debut. He conducted *Macbeth* and the Symphonic Fantasia from *Die Frau ohne Schatten* as part of a Strauss Festival presented by Beecham in the Theatre Royal, Drury Lane. Strauss was present and during the rehearsal of the Fantasia (in Del Mar's own words) 'came up to the podium, glumly regarded the score for a few moments, muttered "All my own fault", and went away'.

As Beecham's associate with the RPO Del Mar acquired both experience and repertoire, though it was as founder, in 1944, of the Chelsea Symphony Orchestra that he was best placed to explore some of the riskier parts of the repertoire: for example, Hindemith, Poulenc, Stravinsky and Mahler's Second and Ninth Symphonies. In 1949 he was appointed principal conductor of the English Opera Group and made – not least because of his own histrionic gifts – a considerable personal success of Britten's *Let's Make an Opera*. The association continued for several years.

In the mid-1950s Del Mar began to work with the BBC Symphony Orchestra, mainly undertaking, it has to be said, the studio programmes which Sargent found too great an effort. However, this valuable apprenticeship led to his appointment as chief conductor of the BBC Scottish Orchestra which, in five years, he put firmly on to the map as an ensemble of fine quality. Naturally, too, he explored new parts of the repertoire, especially the music of Scottish composers including Iain Hamilton and Thea Musgrave, whom he greatly admired and to whom he dedicated his encyclopaedic *Anatomy of the Orchestra*. From time to time he crossed the road in Glasgow to conduct the Scottish National Orchestra and I can clearly remember performances of Bloch's

Schelomo with the very young Jacqueline du Pré: the energy given off jointly by soloist and conductor was formidable. His Scottish connections continued over many years and, as recently as 1985, he conducted Strauss's *Capriccio* for Scottish Opera.

During the 1960s and 1970s Del Mar was more and more busy and successful. He conducted all the major British orchestras and gave some memorable Elgar with the Philharmonia. (Boult greatly admired his *Enigma Variations*.) He travelled extensively, often for the British Council, and made many recordings, among them works by Gerhard, Rawsthorne, Lutyens and Maw with the BBC Symphony Orchestra. With the same orchestra he gave premieres of music by Rainier, Wood, Crosse, LeFanu, Bennett and Dalby among many others. His championship of British composers continued in the early 1980s with a series of four EMI records on which he conducted the Bournemouth Sinfonietta.

His connections with the BBC also continued. After the musicians' strike in 1980, during which he joined the picket-line outside Broadcasting House, he took over the Academy of the BBC – previously its Training Orchestra – and was distressed (as I was) when it became clear that the orchestra was not fulfilling the purposes for which it had been established and was not always, by its very nature, of an acceptable broadcasting standard. Del Mar found himself torn between loyalty to a group of committed young players and an objective understanding of the BBC's requirements. It was a wretched dilemma and it brought out his most sensitive and human qualities.

A happier occasion was a Far Eastern tour by the BBC Symphony Orchestra in 1981 which he shared with Gennadi Rozhdestvensky, who was forbidden by the Soviet authorities to visit China. Del Mar had a huge success in Peking and Shanghai, conducting programmes which included music by Maw, Britten and Elgar. I shall long remember his quizzical delight when the encore provided by the Chinese turned out to have been written by two composers jointly, and his professional outrage when Rozhdestvensky, conducting *Also Sprach Zarathustra* later in the tour, omitted the bells at a critical climax.

It sometimes seemed that fate was needlessly hard on Del Mar and it was characteristic that an expedition from Tokyo to Mount Fuji was an unmitigated disaster: low cloud and heavy rain obscured the mountain and there was a monstrous traffic jam on the return journey. He once refused to strike a match in the kitchen, explaining that he had only struck one match in his life and it had been 'a ghastly failure'. There was indeed a certain boyish clumsiness about him and it was odd, I always thought, that though he had watched Strauss at work and had observed his extraordinary economy of gesture, he seemed quite unable to emulate it. Like Strauss a very big man, his physical style was also very big, sometimes extravagant and not always helpful where tricky leads were concerned. One trembled when an emphatic down-beat gave him complete lift-off. Not for nothing was he affectionately known as 'The Mass of Life'.

He was a man who inspired affection and loyalty, as well as exasperation. But those who knew Norman Del Mar best were aware, latterly, that despite his achievements and his popularity (he more than once conducted the Last Night of the Proms) he was in some sense a disappointed man. He had certainly hoped to inherit the BBC Symphony Orchestra. In 1985 he was appointed principal conductor, and later Conductor of Honour, of the Aarhus Symphony Orchestra in Denmark, where he did excellent work with a fine ensemble. But he would have loved a major British orchestra and, on grounds of musicianship, experience and enthusiasm, he no doubt deserved one.

The Independent, 7th February 1994

Djura Jakšić

Djura Jakšić appeared at the Glasgow Proms in 1965 and 1966, and in the Scottish National Orchestra's 1967 Edinburgh/Glasgow series. He was well liked by the orchestra and his English was excellent. A most cultivated and hospitable man, Jakšić's welcome to Jane Glover, when she appeared in Belgrade, was characteristic.

* * * * *

In Belgrade, on 12th September 1952, I was introduced – over slivovitz and Turkish coffee – to the young conductor of the Belgrade Philharmonic. Djura was twenty-eight, dark and handsome, a Belgrade-born Serb. On a picnic at Avala a day or two later he astonished me not just by his fluent English, but by his acquaintance with the music of – among others – Vaughan Williams, Bliss, Rawsthorne and Gordon Jacob. He revered Purcell.

Nearly forty years later, in July of 1991, when Yugoslavia was breaking up and I was concerned for him, I phoned his home, only to learn from his wife, Seka, that he had died a few days before. Though a heavy smoker, his death had been accelerated, Seka was sure, by his anguish over the future of his country and of his two sons, Tichon and Dušan.

Djura came to the Edinburgh Festival in the late 1950s as a journalist and in 1958 he took part in the Liverpool International Conductors Competition. Zubin Mehta was the winner, but it was generally agreed that the American jury chairman, William Steinberg, had been unreasonably prejudiced against Djura who, coming from a Communist state, he presumed to be a Communist. John Pritchard, then in charge of the Liverpool Philharmonic, generously – and characteristically – offered him an associateship but Djura, though flattered and a little tempted, was doubtful about the ultimate advantage of such an appointment and determined to make Belgrade his professional base.

The decision, which he occasionally regretted, assured his eminence in Yugoslavia (he was successively principal conductor of the Belgrade Philharmonic, director of the State Conservatoire and intendant of the State Opera); and with his own chamber orchestra, Pro Musica, which he founded in 1967, he toured extensively – and not only in Eastern Europe. But his career in the west was limited. In 1967 I invited him to conduct the Scottish National Orchestra and he gave us a wonderfully idiomatic Dvořák Six (he had studied in Prague). The following year he was a guest with the BBC Northern (now Philharmonic) and he wrote to me afterwards:

> It was a few months after the invasion of Czechoslovakia...and Yugoslavia was threatened also. The leader, Reginald Stead, and a trombone player...were extremely nice to me...They both came to me...and then – to my utmost surprise – expressed their worry about the future of Yugoslavia, asking me not to hesitate to call on them (in case I should be forced to leave the country), offering their homes as a refuge – for me and my family. I could cry.

In 1991 he wrote to tell me that Belgrade Radio, which had pointedly neglected him for political reasons (he was never a Party member), had announced that they wished to celebrate his forty years as a conductor with a special concert. Djura declined the suggestion but agreed to the preparation of a retrospective CD and asked if I could help him find tapes of one or more of his Manchester recordings. Sadly, none survived, but Djura himself had a few unedited tapes and these would have been issued had not political turmoil engulfed Yugoslavia.

In October 1990 he had written to say that:

> I had an unexpected phone call this morning. Miss Glover (?) rang me up and said she had a note for me beside a bottle of whisky. I had no idea that an English (lady) conductor was coming...

Later, he wrote:

> Miss Glover had a very good success here. The orchestra liked her, she was warmly received by the audience and got very positive press... We had her here in our flat and enjoyed her company very much.

After her return, Jane phoned me. It had been a tough week, she said, but her visit to Djura and Seka had been memorable. Their flat, in a depressingly featureless Soviet-style block, had turned out to be full of icons, pictures, books and music – the home of a deeply cultivated couple. There was a 'glow within'; they had courteously served her a beautiful meal and had offered her all kinds of help. But she left them with a strong feeling of sadness: Belgrade was depressing, and they were full of anxiety about the future.

In fact, Djura had less than a year to live and he had already written:

> You know, when I was younger, I looked forward to my retirement, believing that I would be able to afford every year a trip to a place or to people I wished to see: once to you, another time to Prague, then to Switzerland and Holland, even to Moscow, etc. I never imagined that it would be beyond my means. After all, it didn't seem to be an extravagant luxury.

In what turned out to be his last letter to me, written on 3rd May 1991, he thanked me for an offer I had made to help his children (should the worst come to the worst) and added,

> We are on the brink of a civil war which easily can end in a mutual slaughtering of tens of thousands of people from both sides. *That* is the real danger. Shall Europe remain unconcerned?...We all hope that reason shall prevail, but we see not much reason in heads of our republican leaders...Obviously such tension as it is now cannot last for ever!

I am glad he did not live to witness the bombing of Belgrade and the realization of his worst fears.

I don't think Djura died a disappointed man. His achievements were considerable: his conducting apart, he founded and edited a serious music magazine; he translated (with a little help from me) Bernard Shaw's music criticism into Serbo-Croat – an amazing feat. But he was deeply sensitive and, latterly, he worried endlessly about his family and his country. So I prefer to think of him as I knew him when we met: enthusing about English music on a picnic outside Belgrade, laying out for me the beauties of Dubrovnik, explaining his love for a tiny retreat he had on the Croatian coast at Tribunj, chuckling about music gossip over a bottle – at least a bottle – of whisky in Aranno, near Lugano, where for many years his chamber orchestra was in residence at an open-air festival of Mozart's rarer works.

Adapting E.M. Forster, I ended my obituary:*

> Djura Jakšić was without doubt a member of that international aristocracy among whom integrity, loyalty, generosity, humanity and modesty are the golden characteristics.

*In *The Independent*, 12th July 1991

Charles Groves

Charles Groves, though oddly uncertain of his own gifts, was undoubtedly a very fine conductor. If he had a failing it was to take on too vast a variety of work, so that he deprived himself of a reputation as a superlative interpreter of a particular composer or school of composition. But his contribution to our musical life was outstanding.

* * * * *

When Charles Groves conducted the Last Night of the Proms in 1974 he bravely – and characteristically – seized the chance provided by the presence of BBC radio and television to remind the government of the day that politicians neglect the arts 'at their peril'. He created a healthy stir and was widely applauded by musicians and music-lovers.

Throughout his life, Groves espoused musical causes: he served on the council of several music colleges, was president of the Incorporated Society of Musicians and of the National Youth Orchestra. In 1980, during the musicians' strike, he was prominent on the picket line outside Broadcasting House, and when the strike ended he generously agreed to 'mind' the BBC Scottish Symphony Orchestra while it was being reorganized and a chief conductor found. He served on innumerable committees, bringing unrivalled experience and a natural, modest wisdom to their discussions. He was in every sense a good man, a Christian with Christian qualities. But he was no prude and he enjoyed bawdy as much as anyone, provided it had some wit.

The range of Groves's achievement was extraordinary. He had had the ideal background. A chorister at St Paul's Cathedral, he then studied piano and organ at the Royal College of Music. In 1937, at the age of twenty-two, he accompanied the choral rehearsals for Toscanini's broadcast performance of the Brahms Requiem and this no doubt led to his joining the BBC the following year as chorus master. Learning all the time, he advanced via the BBC Theatre Orchestra and BBC Revue Orchestra to the conductorship of the Manchester-based BBC Northern Orchestra, a post he held for seven years from 1944.

The demands upon broadcasting orchestras thus brought him, during the early years of his career, a rare chance to lay down a huge stock of repertoire which was to stand him in good stead when it matured. And it was in Manchester, at the BBC, that he met Hilary Barchard, whom he married in 1948. She was to prove, quite simply, the perfect conductor's wife.

From the BBC he moved, in 1951, to Bournemouth, where during his ten-year appointment the orchestra graduated from Bournemouth Municipal to Bournemouth Symphony Orchestra. As in Manchester, he left it a finer and more professional ensemble than when he arrived. In 1960 he went to Cardiff, as resident musical director of Welsh National Opera, and during his two seasons there conducted, among other things, *The Marriage of Figaro*, *William Tell* and *Lohengrin*.

It was with the Liverpool Philharmonic, however, that Groves discovered his métier most completely. He was appointed, in 1963, musical director and resident conductor and he fulfilled both roles with deep commitment. He made his home in Liverpool and became a popular figure there. With Stephen Gray, the Philharmonic's chief executive, he developed a true programme strategy, building a strong and devoted local following. This enabled him to undertake audacious projects on a grand scale: the complete Mahler symphonies (including Deryck Cooke's realization of No.10) which, excepting No.2, he conducted himself; Messiaen's *Turangalila-symphonie*; the Busoni Piano Concerto; the Berlioz *Te Deum* (complete with twelve harps) at the opening of Liverpool's Metropolitan Cathedral; a concert performance of *Pelléas et Mélisande*.

Groves played the music of at least twenty living British composers, including John McCabe, Daniel Jones, Graham Whettam, Kenneth Leighton, Peter Fricker, Hugh Wood and Gordon Crosse. His programmes included Lutosławski, Henze and Berio as well as all the major British figures. He made fine recordings of Delius, Elgar, Walton and Bridge. He arranged four seminars for young conductors, in which Andrew Davis, Mark Elder and John Eliot Gardiner took part; and he was a strong influence on a very young musician who sometimes played extra percussion with the Philharmonic. 'Keep an eye on him,'

Groves said to me at one of the seminars. 'He's extraordinary. His name's Rattle.'

Between 1977, when he left Liverpool, and last February, when he suffered a stroke, Groves was in constant demand as a conductor. His brief spell as musical director at English National Opera in 1978-9 was a period of anxiety and stress: he found the combination of conducting and administration too demanding and his health began to deteriorate. But thereafter he devoted himself to concerts (he was for many years associate conductor of the Royal Philharmonic Orchestra), and he was never without a crowded diary, and often worked overseas.

Perhaps as a result of sharing a BBC Symphony Orchestra tour in the Far East with Pierre Boulez in 1975, Groves was later a regular visitor to Tokyo, to which city he introduced Delius's *A Mass of Life*, one of his finest interpretations. On that tour his programmes complemented those of Boulez and when it was over he admitted that he had grown 'dissatisfied with my programmes. Schoenberg, Berg and Mahler seemed such giants compared with our composers, except Elgar and Tippett...and I longed to have different things to conduct.' This was characteristic for, despite his straight back, strong chin and stocky build, Groves was not privately a confident, let alone a ruthless man. (Indeed he was sometimes too soft-hearted for his own good.) Watching Boulez rehearse in Tokyo, he said to me, 'How *does* he do it? And without a stick!'

There were times when nervousness or uncertainty, or some absence of the fire of conviction resulted in lacklustre, prosaic performance. Arguably, too, Groves simply did too much. But he never produced anything sloppy or ill-prepared and he was deeply hurt when, after the concerto finals of the Young Musician of the Year Competition, a young critic condemned him for slipshod accompaniments. In fact he had consulted all the finalists before rehearsing with them and he was acknowledged as a fine accompanist, in demand by artists as fastidious as the pianist Alfred Brendel.

Charles Groves will be remembered for his comprehensive professionalism, his championing of living composers, his excellence in twentieth-century British music and his mastery of much of the German classical and romantic repertoire. In the mould of Wood or Boult, rather than Beecham or Boulez, he enriched the musical life of Britain in many ways and brought to his profession the most admirably selfless qualities.

The Independent, 21st June 1992

Günter Wand

If invited to name the Bruckner interpreter I most admired I would unhesitatingly choose Günter Wand, whose mastery of the architecture of those massive symphonies was unsurpassed in my hearing. He was a difficult man, but his Bruckner, his Schubert, his Brahms demanded one's forbearance.

* * * * *

The conductor Günter Wand was a most idiosyncratic man. Fastidious to a fault, he shunned any publicity that was 'glamorous', let alone gimmicky, and led a life that, while by no means spartan, was simple and intensely private. He did not care to join the jet set – though opportunities to do so came his way and, late in his life, he appeared in Chicago, Boston and Cleveland. He spent over thirty years in the relative obscurity of Cologne.

Though well-read and well-informed, he was single-minded, to a degree I had rarely encountered, in his devotion to music and to the service of the composer. The ideally truthful performance was for him the Holy Grail. He returned again and again to scores he had known for decades. And he liked to quote Klemperer, 'Ich bin jetzt alt, muss Beethoven lernen.' Indeed, such was his passion for music that he once said, 'For me, those geniuses – Mozart, Schubert and Bruckner – are proof of the existence of God.' And he was, surely, the finest Brucknerian of his generation.

Wand was born in 1912 in Elberfeld. There were no musicians in his family, but he learned the piano as a child and his parents had season tickets at the State Theatre. There, in his early teens, he heard *The Magic Flute*, the *St Matthew Passion* and Richard Tauber in *The Gypsy Baron*. He was bewitched; and he took up the piano with a vengeance, till his mother had often to beg him to stop. But there was no stopping him and at sixteen he was playing Bruckner symphonies from the full score and learning parts of them by heart so as to avoid the problem of turning the pages. Bruckner was already embedded in his musical system.

Before long he entered the Hochschule in Cologne and such were his gifts that at the age of twenty-two he was engaged for four years at Allenstein, where he conducted over 500 performances, both opera and concerts. After a year in Detmold he was appointed Kapellmeister at the Cologne Opera. There, in his first year, he had to learn and conduct fourteen operas, together with the six he knew already. Only

Parsifal he refused: he had an aversion to religious subjects in opera.

He was in Cologne throughout the Second World War, working steadily, often in appalling conditions, and in 1946 he was invited to become the city's general music director, for opera and concerts. He rebuilt the Gürzenich Orchestra, with which he was regularly to work for twenty-eight years. Later, he was a frequent guest with the Cologne Radio Symphony Orchestra.

Nowadays we associate Wand with the central German classical tradition, so it is surprising to discover that in the years after the war his repertoire contained much Schoenberg, Webern, Hindemith, Bartók and Stravinsky. He was a champion of Bernd Alois Zimmermann and of Frank Martin. He programmed Messiaen, Henze and – astonishingly – Vaughan Williams (Fifth Symphony) and Britten (*Les Illuminations*). Like Furtwängler and Klemperer, he was himself a composer and he occasionally offered his own works, including *Odi et Amo*, a concertino for soprano and chamber orchestra, written for his devoted wife, Anita Westhoff, a gifted coloratura soprano.

He began to make recordings with the Gürzenich Orchestra in the mid-1950s: a complete Brahms cycle, a nearly complete Beethoven one, a Bruckner Eight, some late Mozart and some Schumann. With the Cologne Radio Symphony Orchestra there are complete Schubert and Bruckner cycles, recorded between 1974 and 1984. In 1982, at about the same time as he came to the BBC as chief guest conductor of the Symphony Orchestra, he was appointed to the North German Radio Symphony Orchestra in Hamburg, where he repeated his Brahms cycle and issued a complete Beethoven one.

Wand first worked with the BBC Symphony Orchestra on 27th January 1982. I had gone to hear him rehearsing in the radio studio in Cologne and had encountered for the first time his nice, if somewhat waspish, sense of humour. During a pause in the proceedings he remarked to the orchestra, 'The gentleman sitting at the back is Herr Ponsonby. He is from the BBC and he has come to see if I can conduct.'

He had appeared in London soon after the war but was apparently dissatisfied with his reception and by 1982 he was unknown as a public figure, though not as a recording artist. I booked the Albert Hall, engaged Margaret Marshall and alerted the press. Because it was a 'trial' engagement I was happy to give Wand all the rehearsals he asked for – I think five in all – which in other circumstances might have seemed excessive for a programme comprising Schubert's *Unfinished Symphony*, Strauss's *Four Last Songs* and Beethoven's *Pastoral Symphony*. But the orchestra needed a master of the classical style and Wand was almost uniquely qualified in this respect.

His rehearsals were a revelation, so intense was his concentration, so meticulous his attention to detail. The players – at that time accustomed to the genially relaxed methods of Rozhdestvensky and Pritchard – were stunned, but they accepted Wand's rigour because of his authority, his clarity and his modesty. And, of course, he immediately became 'The Magic Wand'. The concert was excellent, as were the press notices. It was clear that Wand would bring to the orchestra a comprehensive regrounding in German classical style.

Wand did some superb things for the BBC, but nothing better, I think, than the Bruckner Eight at the Proms in September 1992. His mastery of this immensely complex work was absolute. From the first pianissimo violin tremolando it seemed clear that he knew precisely how he would handle its sweep and scope, how contrasting tempi would be related, how detail would be integrated in the overall design and how each climax would punctuate the music's development.

Throughout, Wand sustained complete physical poise, a very slight rhythmic flexing of one knee being the only obvious movement other than those of eyes and head, hands and arms. His beat was large, elegant and perfectly clear. His left hand was never fussy or otiose. His whole posture was economical and restrained. And, despite his absolute control and meticulous rehearsal, the music emerged completely fresh. At the end he accepted the applause with a shy smile, immediately inviting the orchestra to share the reception.

He was generous towards his orchestral colleagues but he was not always an easy man. He was hypersensitive and his sensitivity extended to concern for his physical well-being. I believe he could have detected a draught in a vacuum. In studio and concert-hall he almost invariably complained that one was playing on the back of his neck.

He was equally demanding where his accommodation and meals were concerned. In London, he liked to stay at the Hyde Park Hotel and to eat well there. A well-meaning agent once took him to supper in a popular, crowded restaurant near the Festival Hall. The food was moderate. There was a good deal of noise and – of course – there were draughts. As the evening wore on, Wand slid lower and lower in his chair, his collar rising up his neck, an expression of resentful misery on his face. The party was not a success.

Difficult he certainly could be, but he won the admiration, and often the affection, of orchestral musicians by his technical mastery, his profound concern for the music as set down by the composer and his pride in his own profession. (He would not engage as a soloist any artist who had also taken up conducting.) After one particularly fine performance a distinguished singer said to Wand, 'It was wonderful to hear the music reaching us so truthfully and directly.' Wand's reply was characteristic: 'But that is why we are here.'

Last August, at the age of eighty-nine, he conducted the North German Radio Symphony Orchestra at the Proms in performances of the unfinished symphonies of Schubert and Bruckner, 'so measured', in the words of one critic, and 'spiritually crystalline – each phrase with a lifetime of reflection behind it – that there was no countenancing other ways of making music'.

The Independent, 16th February 2002

Hans-Hubert Schönzeler

When, after leaving the BBC, I worked for the Musicians Benevolent Fund, there were calls, from time to time, from Hans-Hubert Schönzeler, then only a name to me. In due course I visited him and was his guest at the Savage Club. He was enjoyable company, opinionated, sometimes outrageous; he was also generous.

* * * * *

The conductor and musicologist Hans-Hubert Schönzeler was an engagingly paradoxical man and he would have been tickled by the notion that an important Bruckner exponent and scholar was specially mourned among the membership of the Savage Club, that louche but friendly fraternity of musicians, actors and artists whose company he so much enjoyed. Indeed, I was to have been his guest at a dinner there six days before he died.

Schönzeler, who was an only child, was born in Leipzig to parents neither of whom was a professional musician. He took up the violin at the age of five and this instrument always had a prime place in his affections. Sent to Brussels by his father – who was not Jewish, but who strongly opposed the Nazi regime – so as to avoid contact with Hitler Youth, he returned to Germany in 1938. A year later, first his father, then he and his mother, emigrated to Australia where, on the outbreak of the Second World War, his father was interned.

Schönzeler went to Sydney Boys High School, but after two years, and quite irrationally, he and his mother were also interned. During the four years of his incarceration he continued to study the violin, music theory and, with a former director of the Vienna Boys Choir, conducting.

Released in 1946, he became a naturalized Australian – and hence a British subject – the following year. At the New South Wales State Conservatorium he studied with Eugene Goossens, a musician for whom he retained the warmest admiration, and began to direct student orchestras and choirs. But it was clear that he needed to be in Europe and so, with the help of Rafael Kubelík, he settled in London in 1950, securing a job with Eulenburg Edition, of which he later became a director. From 1957 to 1962 he led the Twentieth Century Ensemble.

Adrian Boult and Wilhelm Furtwängler – the tenth anniversary of whose death was marked by a concert which Schönzeler conducted at the Royal Albert Hall in 1964 – encouraged him, and he was a successful participant in a number of important conductors' courses, among them the Paris Conservatoire and the Accademia Chigiana.

Schönzeler worked as a freelance all over the world and guested with a majority of the British orchestras. His repertoire was catholic (he premiered new works in Britain, Germany and Australia) but his special strengths lay in the German romantics, notably Bruckner. For the BBC he gave the world premiere of the first version of the Eighth Symphony (in 1973) and for the Adelaide Festival the world premiere of the authentic first version of the Third Symphony (in 1978). He had already in 1970 published an authoritative book on the composer and he was later honoured by the Bruckner Society of America and the International Bruckner Society, Vienna.

Another of Schönzeler's specialities was the music of Dvořák; he visited Prague both for research and for recordings of Janáček and Martinů. In 1974 he appeared at the Prague Spring Festival and, in 1975, was made an honorary member of the Antonín Dvořák Society.

Illness curtailed Schönzeler's career but he remained passionately interested in music and musicians; he was not above some cheerful gossip and a visit to his Chelsea home was always stimulating, occasionally bibulous. He was pugnaciously argumentative, but his sometimes outrageous dislikes were generally tempered with a beady humour. He idolized Furtwängler and it was hard work to persuade him to change his mind about one's own heroes. I failed lamentably where the admirable Günter Wand was concerned. But we were generally of one mind about the charlatans and show-offs.

Schönzeler was hospitable and generous, as was his devoted wife, Wilhelmina ('Helmi'). For some years he had supported the Musicians

Benevolent Fund in various ways, donating – for auction – his own violin and the complete *Urtext* of Hugo Wolf. He was a man of impressive musical and personal integrity. German by birth, he became an estimable Englishman; his last recording was of music by Edmund Rubbra.

The Independent, 9th May 1997

COMPOSERS

Hans Gál

Joining the staff of the Edinburgh Festival in 1951 and still wet behind the ears, I found Festival Committee meetings daunting (and the formidable Lady Rosebery simply terrifying), so that Hans Gál's friendly helpfulness was very welcome.

* * * * *

I must first have met Hans Gál in 1951 when, as assistant to the Director of the Edinburgh Festival (then Ian Hunter) I attended the meetings of the Programme Committee, of which Hans was a lively and authoritative member. He was one of that distinguished band of mostly Jewish musicians who so enriched our cultural life in the late 1930s. Fleeing the Anschluss in 1938, he became, thanks to Donald Tovey, a music lecturer in Edinburgh University; already forty-eight when he arrived, he lived on in Edinburgh till his death at the age of ninety-seven.

Slight and lean, he reminded me of a sparrow, so sudden were his movements, so cheerful his demeanour. From the start he was helpful and sympathetic, saving me from more than one bad musical gaffe. When I was appointed to succeed Hunter he expressed himself 'inexpressibly delighted'. It was only gradually that I learned of his successes in Austria and Germany during the 1920s. His opera, *Die Heilige Ente*, which George Szell had premiered in Düsseldorf in 1923, was staged in at least twenty cities. Three other operas were produced, among them *Die Beiden Klaas*, which was given (as *Rich Klaus, Poor Klaus*) in York in 1990. But he was prolific and I was delighted when, in 1976 – by which time I was at the BBC – Colin Davis offered to record his *Idyllikon*, an orchestral piece whose performance Hans found 'superb'. Later the BBC Scottish Symphony Orchestra recorded a whole programme of his music. But, all in all, not much was heard, probably because his idiom was post-Brahmsian, with a flavour of Richard Strauss. Inevitably the music of an elderly Austrian immigrant writing in a conventional style was not accorded a high priority among promoters.

But Hans was not, I believe, embittered. He continued to compose, to teach and to perform and it was in the last capacity that I was most specially indebted to him.

Noting that during the 1952 Festival Irmgard Seefried, Kathleen Ferrier and Julius Patzak would all be present, I persuaded Ian Hunter to programme the Brahms *Liebesliederwalzer*, which I adored then, as I do now. I consulted Hans, who was later to publish an excellent book about Brahms, and he offered not only to play one of the two piano-duet parts but also to coach the singers. I had, before consulting him, engaged the bass-baritone, Frederick Dalberg, for the bottom line of the quartet. Dalberg was a Wagnerian, busy at Covent Garden, and I reckoned he had the necessary weight to 'anchor' Seefried's bright soprano and Patzak's curiously plangent tenor. There remained the question of the second pianist – or, rather, the first, for Hans insisted on playing 'secondo' (which made sense: he, a Viennese, would establish the tempo of each waltz). 'I suppose,' said Hans, 'that Clifford Curzon would not do it?' It was a thrilling idea, but I doubted if Clifford would want to find time for it. I was wrong: he knew and admired Hans and was happy to play 'primo'. It seemed I had the perfect cast.

But there was a hiccup. Coaching Dalberg, Hans discovered that he lacked both charm and style (vital ingredients). This was embarrassing, but Hans then revealed another aspect of his remarkable character: by the subtlest of suggestive means – for example, 'Are you *sure* the part is not too high for you, Mr Dalberg?' – he persuaded the singer that he would not do himself justice, and he withdrew, to be more than adequately replaced by Horst Günter from the Hamburg State Opera.

The performance went wonderfully and in the green-room afterwards I found Seefried and Ferrier waltzing together, enraptured. Many years later the BBC issued a recording on CD and the fruits of Hans's idiomatic coaching – and the sheer pleasure of the artists – are captured, though, not surprisingly, the recording quality is not all it would be today.

Hans was an amusing companion and correspondent. Though a devoted husband, he was susceptible to pretty women and during the Brahms rehearsals confessed to me how much he would have liked to be Seefried's husband 'for just one night'. Of another soprano, Inge Borkh, a slim Aryan giantess who was singing the *Fidelio* Leonora with the Hamburg State Opera, he remarked, 'There is no *colossal* bosom. Generally one cannot get away from that bosom. But, poor girl, she will end her days a Brünnhilde; there is no escaping it.' More seriously, when the curtain went up on Scene 2 of the Hamburg *Fidelio*, he hissed,

'Ach! Der first signs of German re-armament.' (Ita Maximovna's sets were indeed forbiddingly austere).

His letters were quaintly affectionate. When I was appointed to the BBC he wrote,

> My dear R.P.,
> With a tear in one eye, and smiling with the other, I get to offer you my warmest congratulations.
> Well, if the BBC were a person, I would congratulate the BBC.
> Lots of kindest wishes!'

At the age of eighty-six (in what connection I can't remember) he wrote,

> My dear Robert,
> Lots of thanks for your very kind letter! Well, at my age one knows that one is on leave of presence, that can always be cancelled at short notice. As to my way of living, I have raised the principle of Descartes, saying 'musico, ergo sum'. That's all!

I liked that dog-Latin tag. Hans did indeed live music.

William Walton

Acquaintance with Walton's music began in 1951 when I heard some of his songs at Morley College. The following year I enjoyed *Façade*, with Edith Sitwell. And at about the same time I discovered the Viola Concerto, in Frederick Riddle's fine recording, the composer conducting.

* * * * *

William's first letter was distinctly formal:

> April 22, 1955
> Dear Mr Ponsonby,
> First, I should like to congratulate you on your new appointment.
> I am still thinking about a Cello Concerto, and if I can finish it in time, I should be delighted for Piatigorsky to give the first performance in Edinburgh in 1956. But I can give no guarantee that it will be ready by then.
> With kind regards…

In the event, the world premiere took place in Boston on 25th January 1957, the European premiere in London on 13th February 1957. The latter was a Royal Philharmonic Society concert by the BBCSO, under

Sargent, and I made it my business to be present and to introduce myself. As luck would have it, I was able to find William a taxi after the concert and this (together with the remote coincidence that my father had played a march by him at the wedding of Henry Ley at Christ Church, Oxford, in about 1925) marked the beginning of what turned out to be a friendly relationship.

In 1959 William conducted the Royal Philharmonic Orchestra at the opening concert of the Edinburgh Festival, sandwiching the Cello Concerto (with Pierre Fournier) between his *Partita* and the First Symphony. Both conductor and soloist were nervous, so that the concert lacked the ultimate *élan*, but Fournier's immaculate elegance and William's efficient, economical conducting secured performances that more than adequately matched the importance of the occasion. But I still wanted a Walton premiere for the Festival and I was aware that the Second Symphony, commissioned by the Royal Liverpool Philharmonic Orchestra for performance in 1958, was not yet complete at the end of 1959. When I approached John Pritchard, then music director of the orchestra and well known for his Musica Viva concerts there, he jumped at the chance of bringing his orchestra – and the Symphony – to the 1960 Festival. (In Liverpool itself, some angry voices complained that John had allowed 'their' symphony to be kidnapped by Edinburgh.) William, naturally enough, was entirely happy for the Festival to present the premiere.

The symphony (preceded by Haydn, Berg and Ravel) had been well rehearsed and was very well received but, by and large, the critics were lukewarm. William, they said, had produced the same mixture as before – a complaint he was to encounter with growing frequency, and dejection, as the years went by.

William's and my paths did not often cross during the 1960s, but my appointment at the BBC soon brought an invitation to visit him and Susana in Ischia. Taking advantage of a BBCSO tour which included Rome, I visited them in May 1973. *Conceivably* because of my new and influential position, I received red-carpet treatment and a personally guided tour of the remarkable garden. William was in characteristic form. When I asked if Gillian Widdicombe, who was meant to be writing his biography, carried a tape-recorder, he replied, 'Yes, I think she is discreetly bugged.' Of the peculiar upright piano whose upper parts had been adapted to accommodate orchestral manuscript paper, he said, 'I found it in Harrod's; it makes a *horrid* sound.'

We discussed the 1974 Proms, my first season, and I eventually programmed the Second Symphony, *Scapino* and, on the Last Night, *Belshazzar's Feast*. This he attended, having written in advance:

> Thank you immensely for finding room in your box for the Last Prom. The five consists of our two selves, Lord Goodman, Prue Penn and Gillian Widdicombe. Except for Lord G,[1] the rest won't occupy an undue amount of space.
>
> (9th August 1974)

Belshazzar, conducted by Charles Groves, brought the house down and the Promenaders gave William an ecstatic ovation. His popularity with that unique audience gave me the greatest pleasure.

In the summer of 1976 he wrote to me about *Troilus and Cressida*, which was to be revived (with Janet Baker) during November:

> The pest is at you again, but only to find out if any of the perfs. of 'Tro. & Cress.' are going to be put on the air...*The Bear* is becoming quite a 'hit'...now Hans [Werner Henze] really does know how to manage things. At his Montepulciano Festival he managed to get it televized by the Italians, the Germans and the BBC TV among others...I've been trying to cope with 'Boulez on Music Today' and find I just can't. Most depressing.
>
> (20th August 1976)

'Tro. & Cress.', sadly, was not the success he had prayed for. (No other work caused him such anguish.) But he told me he hoped to come over to hear Kyung-Wha Chung play his Violin Concerto ('Much more sexy than the Viola Concerto,' he once told me) on the Last Night in 1977. By then, though, his health was beginning to fail and he did not make it. Similarly, in 1978:

> I'd like to come over to hear 'In Honour'[2] (I can't remember when I last heard it) but the journey is a deterrent...Hans H [Henze] as you probably know is not too well after his heart attack in Vienna, but I talked to him the other night and he seemed to be rather better. I tried to persuade him that it was quite unnecessary for him to write more music – he [has] done already enough for two lifetimes, and certainly not to organize further festivals. I don't expect him to pay any attention!

William and Hans got on well, but William was undoubtedly envious

1 Arnold Goodman resembled, in his own words, an enormous 'cuddly toy'.

2 In Honour of the City of London

of his younger colleague's astute manipulation of the media, let alone his compositional facility. Almost as an afterthought he wrote:

> Maybe Sinf. 3 will eventually appear – but it's very much maybe, though there's a great big Scherzo, not much of a 1st. mov. and nothing of a slow mov. which will end it – or at least ought to and will too.
>
> (29th June 1978)

Whether this was wishful thinking, self-delusion, or whether the 'great big Scherzo' and other fragments were destroyed, it seems we shall never know.

Later that year William wrote to say he had visited Henze and found him 'seemingly quite recovered'. He added, apropos the possibility, of which Sir Vivian Dunn had told me, of a wind-band piece:

> Don't believe Sir V. Dunn. There will be no wind-band piece until the dollar recovers...
>
> (3rd September 1978)

This was characteristic, for William's commercial sense was well developed and he was an astute negotiator. In the same letter he thanked me for entrusting to Gillian Widdicombe (who, he said, was 'very volatile these days') tapes of Liszt's *Christus* which I had recently programmed at the Proms. And this, too, was characteristic: he retained his curiosity about unfamiliar music into his old age, though he was often violently dismissive of new works, telling me that there was 'not a note of music from beginning to end' in *Bomarzo*, an opera by a kinsman of his wife Susana, Alberto Ginastera.

In 1982 William's eightieth birthday was celebrated in Westminster Abbey (among many other places) with a programme of smaller works, most of them, including the *Coronation Te Deum* ('my Tedium'), liturgical. One, the very early '*Where Does the Uttered Music Go?*', he once told me was his favourite work. I guess this was a capricious, passing preference, but it was enough to persuade me to include it in the 1983 Proms, when it was sung by the BBC Singers from the top gallery, a magical effect.

His friends and admirers were back in the Abbey (where he is buried) on 20th July 1983 for an imposing Memorial Service at which I had a privileged stall in the Choir. Susana and Gillian Widdicombe were prominent – and superbly dignified – among the mourners; '*Where Does the Uttered Music Go?*' was heard again and William's progression from the Witty Young Man of *Façade* to the Grand Old Man (he had the OM) of English Music was celebrated in a manner unique to the Established Church of England.

I had, almost accidentally, included at least one work of William's in every season of Proms between 1974 and 1986 – because I loved his music. I wondered, all the same, whether, on his last day, he regretted his self-imposed exile on Ischia, the relative failure of *Troilus and Cressida*, the self-evident inertia of his musical idiom.

Michael Tippett

Michael Tippett's *Corelli Fantasy*, commissioned by Ian Hunter for the 1953 Edinburgh Festival, was the first major work of his that I heard. Then came the *Midsummer Marriage*, which John Pritchard conducted at Covent Garden in 1955. In due course I got to hear all his published music. Unlike Britten, who had prodigious facility, and Walton, whose idiom, brilliantly used, was traditional and stable, Tippett audibly struggled to express himself. At his very best he found a uniquely beautiful radiance – but sometimes there were too many notes, there was too much going on. Personally, though, he was, of all my musician-friends, the most infectiously and mischievously life-enhancing.

* * * * *

> I'm still somewhat aloft, on cloud 9, after that fine performance and marvellous reception. In the words of the text: I'd like to name each one in turn – but not to mourn, to praise and thank; yourself especially. Love Michael.
>
> (27th July 1984)

Michael's letters, always scrawly and often breathless, began to come in 1980 and continued for more than ten years. This one arrived a day or two after the first London (and European) performance – at the Proms – of his cornucopian *The Mask of Time*. The concert, on 23rd July 1984, had been an amazing occasion, the work is *abend-füllend* and I had been fearful of a small audience. But I need not have worried: the hall was comfortably full, and full of Tippett enthusiasts. The reception was indeed 'marvellous' and BBC forces under Andrew Davis (Colin Davis had given the world premiere in Boston) had done a superb job.

At the pre-Prom talk, a series I had inaugurated in 1974, I had interviewed Michael and, nervous about a public encounter with a nearly-eighty-year-old creator of formidable eminence, I had fallen victim to his tendency to 'tease'. Aware that *The Mask of Time* had had a very long gestation and that it embodied some, if not all, of its composer's most profound thoughts about man's place in the universe, I ham-fistedly framed an initial question along the lines of 'Did you feel you had to compose this great testimony *before it was too late*?' Michael raised his head, opened his eyes so wide I feared his eye-balls would pop out, tipped back his chair, grinned and said – *nothing!* Our audience let out a great roar of laughter (in which I could not but join) and in due course the interview proceeded, Michael speaking of the influences which had contributed to *The Mask*, notably Jacob Bronowski's *The Ascent of Man*, but also writers as diverse as Milton, Shelley, Rilke, Yeats, Anna Akhmatova and Mary Renault, whose 'novel' of classical Greece, *The Mask of Apollo*, provided the image of a young actor being told by Zeus to 'make peace with his mortality'. Not always easy to follow because of a sometimes stumbling allusiveness, Michael was nevertheless deeply impressive: the range of his thinking and his transparent sincerity combined irresistibly with an impish self-deprecation. The interview was memorable, notwithstanding my no doubt jejune promptings.

We had first met (though he would not have remembered) at the 1953 Edinburgh Festival for which my predecessor and mentor, Ian Hunter, had commissioned the *Fantasia Concertante on a Theme of Corelli*. Malcolm Sargent, then the BBC Symphony Orchestra's chief conductor, had characteristically declined to conduct the new work (he detested Tippett's music) and Michael had done so himself, more than adequately. I was in the offing, heard the work, and was introduced to its composer afterwards. I found the lean, boyish figure, with roguish eyes, a surprising source for music which was both brilliant and deeply felt, rooted in tradition, but unmistakably 'modern'. To my shame, the only Tippett work which I scheduled at Edinburgh between 1956 and 1960 (my tenure as director) was *The Heart's Assurance*, which Richard Lewis and Gerald Moore gave in 1959.

Similarly, but for different reasons, there was not much I could do for him during my years managing the Scottish National Orchestra (1964-72): the orchestra was Scottish *and* National – so that composers like Thea Musgrave, Iain Hamilton, Robin Orr, Thomas Wilson and Martin Dalby claimed a higher priority and were – gladly – accorded it. In 1966, though, Michael conducted an Elgar/Tippett programme in Edinburgh and Glasgow which comprised the *Introduction and Allegro* and *Enigma Variations*; arias from *A Midsummer Marriage* and *A Child of Our Time*, and the *Ritual Dances*. I found fascinating the implicit evidence of a recognizably 'English' style linking the two composers, and Michael's apparently rather wayward stick-technique was actually very effective.

To listen to the *Ritual Dances* (of which I had once heard Charles Groves say, 'That *has* to be great music') interpreted by their composer was a special thrill. Michael was then just over sixty, still slim and boyish, his only apparent frailty a 'nervous tummy' which caused him nausea and was, no doubt, in part psychosomatic.

At what point I became, conversationally, 'love' (or maybe 'luv') I don't now remember, but it pleased me: I was now, as it were, an acknowledged pal, a trustee, a supporter. And I was bona fide. At Covent Garden in 1970 I had heard Colin Davis conduct *A Midsummer Marriage* and *The Knot Garden*, wonderfully cast, and luminously directed by Peter Hall. Then, in 1972, when I was on the brink of joining the BBC, I heard the Third Symphony with the superb Heather Harper and, again, Colin Davis. I was comprehensively hooked (though not always comfortable, later on, with – for example – *The Ice Break*). So that when, in 1974, I took over the Proms, I had not only the will, but also the opportunity, to promote Michael's music. I find that, for what statistics may be worth, I scheduled twenty-five performances of sixteen works over thirteen years. And, surely, I could have done more? Be that as it may (and bearing in mind that Britten, to whose music I had not always warmed, and Walton, to whose I certainly had, had both to be 'accommodated' at a comparable level), Michael's music was present every year, whether by the massive *Mask of Time* (1984) or the minuscule *Severn Bridge Variation* (1976).

Generally, Michael's letters came after particular performances. At the 1987 Canterbury Festival I had programmed a concert which began with Tallis's *Spem in Alium* (the forty-part motet) and ended with Michael's own *The Vision of St Augustine*. Though the cathedral's acoustics did not ideally suit either piece, Michael wrote:

> What a marvellous concert! The great Tallis had me soon in tears of joy. And, surely, the music was fine to the very end. Thanks and love, Michael.
>
> (undated)

This semi-objective reference to his own music was characteristic: I had once heard him, during a rehearsal of his Piano Concerto (with John Ogdon as soloist) exclaim, at a particular point, 'How *beautiful*!' Apparently he could detach himself from his role as creator and express his wonder at his own music.

But sometimes a letter would relate to a non-musical issue. Such a one – and it was very astute – reached me towards the end of July 1980.

The musicians' strike, which very nearly broke my spirit, had cost us universal opprobrium and had lost us the first fourteen Proms. Michael wrote:

> It's somewhat [I snorted at that 'somewhat'] distressing...that things got to such an impasse. Heartening, too, in some odd way, that the concern for music has been so public and wide. Disheartening that the BBC has not been thought of as at the head of such concern. Failure of PR, surely.
>
> Problem of communication between producers of programmes and managerial bureaucrats are not new! Long before your time. Morale descends with the lessening communication.
>
> Sorry – how pompous and obvious that sounds.
>
> (21st July 1980)

(He was right about the BBC's failure of PR: Aubrey Singer, Radio's managing director, adopted from the start a deeply offensive, sabre-rattling posture which could hardly have been more counter-productive; and he was brutally dismissive of my objections to his tactics.)

Leaving the BBC in 1985, but handing over to John Drummond much forward planning (including the virtually complete 1986 Proms), I had scheduled a performance of the *Concerto for Orchestra* on 29th July.

A few days later, Michael wrote:

> I don't think even you, when you fixed the date, imagined there would be such a superb performance to a full house. Quite extraordinary. I am still utterly demolished by it, and doing just nothing till I recover enough poise to return to work!! I write now, in this letter, only about musical things. With deep affection as always, Michael.

What non-musical things may have been in his mind I did not discover. I had graduated from being a conversational 'love' to one of those kissed full on the lips – a surprise on the first occasion, but neither lascivious, nor unwelcome: simply, for him, a natural means of expressing affection and received, by me, absolutely in the same spirit. Later, he dedicated to me, 'with esteem', his *Tippett on Music*. I was proud and delighted (but not *absolutely* sure I was glad to be thought of as estimable). And I was invited to become a trustee of the Michael Tippett Musical Foundation which, though by no means wealthy, did good work with small organizations promoting music (and not only 'serious' music) in deprived areas. Sadly, after Michael's death, there were difficulties with the Trustees over his Estate, which turned out to be a good deal smaller than expected, and the Foundation had to be moth-balled temporarily.

Where Michael's music will stand in the annals of eternity it is too soon to say. Though I love much of it (and not only because I loved the man), viewed overall it is uneven, Michael's insistence upon writing his own opera libretti handicapping some – not all – of the operas, the innate, sometimes positively tortured, intricacy of his own idiom rendering some of the non-vocal works hard to penetrate. But he had a special radiance (the *Corelli Fantasy*, the *Triple Concerto*) and a unique compassion (*A Child of Our Time*): qualities in himself which made him lovable. And, of course, he had a 'wicked' sense of humour: Vaughan Williams's *Flos Campi* became 'Camp Flossy', which, coming from an unabashed homosexual, was at least cheeky. So that to visit him, as I did, at his Wiltshire home was to experience a complete spectrum of communication, from matters deeply philosophical to shop-talk of delicious (sometimes scandalous) triviality. Either way, one was enriched.

Robin Orr

A near-contemporary of Tippett, Robin Orr was already the first chairman of Scottish Opera when I was appointed to manage the Scottish National Orchestra in 1964. Under Orr, Alexander Gibson, its musical director, and Peter Hemmings, its administrator, the company developed with faultless professionalism.

* * * * *

Robin Orr's entertaining, if personally somewhat reticent, autobiography has the title *Musical Chairs*, which suggests the career of a conventional academic. In fact, Orr's achievements outside his own composition and his teaching were, if complementary, perhaps even more important: Scottish Opera's initial years and Cambridge University's new Music Faculty both owed a large debt to his energy and wisdom.

Born in Brechin, he went to Loretto School in Edinburgh and, at seventeen, to the Royal College of Music, where he became an organ pupil of Sir Walter Alcock, a piano pupil of Arthur Benjamin and a composition pupil of Henry Moule. Elected Organ Scholar of Pembroke College, Cambridge, in 1929, he there came under the influence of Cyril Rootham and Edward Dent. Later, in Siena, he studied with Casella and, later still, with Nadia Boulanger in Paris.

In 1933 he was appointed music master at Sidcot School, but he found that music was 'the Cinderella of all subjects' and, after three years, he was glad to move to Leeds University as assistant lecturer. He spent the war years as a photographic intelligence officer in the RAF after a very brief spell as Rootham's successor as organist of St John's College, Cambridge. Returning there in 1945, he was soon appointed a lecturer at the university and it was at this time that he began seriously to compose.

Professorships, at Glasgow University in 1956 and at Cambridge in 1965, followed. Scottish Opera had been brilliantly launched by Alexander Gibson, under Orr's chairmanship, in 1962 and he continued in this role until 1976, a period which encompassed many of the company's finest achievements.

At Cambridge he set about fundraising for a new and much-needed music school, encountering much frustrating prevarication from the university authorities. However, after twelve years of effort, the new building, in the design of which Orr himself had a hand, was opened by the Duke of Edinburgh in 1977.

Orr's compositions, mostly in a traditional idiom, are extremely well crafted, effective and concise. The first symphony, *Symphony in One Movement*, was given at the 1966 Proms by Alexander Gibson and subsequently recorded by him (with the Scottish National Orchestra) for EMI. Two more symphonies followed, in 1971 and 1978. For Janet Baker he wrote a song cycle, *From the Book of Philip Sparrow*, which she premiered in Glasgow in 1969. His opera, *Full Circle*, to a text by the Scottish poet, Sydney Goodsir Smith, was produced in 1967 and well liked by press and public. Other operas were *Hermiston*, heard at the 1975 Edinburgh Festival, and *On the Razzle*, derived from Tom Stoppard's eponymous play, which was presented – though to a mixed reception – in 1988. The large-scale works apart, Orr wrote a good deal of chamber music. His church music is often heard in Anglican and Episcopal cathedrals.

Although, to the unwary, Orr sometimes gave an impression of vagueness, he was, in fact, one of the shrewdest of men. He had a tremendously effective way of dealing with authority, whether real or pretended, and was adept at discovering the poseur and the bore, then avoiding them. He himself was the best of company, a knowledgeable epicure and an amusing raconteur.

He was twice married: first to Margaret Mace, with whom he had a son and two daughters, who survive him; later to Doris Meyer, whose house in Switzerland became their second home, Cambridge being their first.

Orr was appointed CBE in 1972. He had honorary degrees from Glasgow and Dundee. He was very loyal to the land of his birth and used his gifts as teacher and animateur to Cambridge's considerable advantage.

The Times, 17th April 2006

Iain Hamilton

Iain Hamilton and Thea Musgrave, who studied with Hans Gál, were Scotland's leading composers from the 1960s onwards. Hamilton's music sometimes has a rather Hindemithian 'greyness', but his operas, presented by English National Opera as well as Scottish Opera, have obvious dramatic force.

* * * * *

In the summer of 1958 I encountered Iain Hamilton in St James's Street where the Edinburgh Festival had its London office. On the spur of the moment I asked him if he would write something to celebrate the bicentenary of the birth, in 1759, of Robert Burns.

We agreed that it should be a substantial work for symphony orchestra, to be performed by Alexander Gibson with the Scottish National Orchestra at the 1959 festival. The piece that emerged was Hamilton's sharply astringent *Sinfonia for Two Orchestras* – a work which left the conservative audience, in Peter Heyworth's words, 'slightly stunned', and which the president of the Burns Federation (whom I had persuaded to share the commissioning fee) described as 'rotten and ghastly'. It was certainly uncompromising and it was characteristic of the composer's current idiom.

Hamilton was already an established figure, whose Op.38 (the *Light Overture, 1912*) he had himself conducted at Morley College, where he was teaching, the previous year. Born in Glasgow in 1922, but largely educated in London, he was a late starter in music, which he studied in his spare time while pursuing a career in engineering. This he abandoned in 1947, when he won a scholarship to the Royal Academy of Music.

Here he made prodigious progress. In 1951, his Clarinet Concerto was awarded the Royal Philharmonic Society Prize and his Second Symphony won a Koussevitsky Foundation award. The concerto was performed by Frederick Thurston and the RPO, under Clarence

Raybould, in the Royal Festival Hall in 1952, the symphony by the Hallé Orchestra under Adrian Boult, at the Cheltenham Festival the following year.

Hamilton had arrived. Commissions began to flow in – from the Dartington Summer School (at William Glock's perceptive instigation), from the Scottish National Orchestra (at Alexander Gibson's) and from the BBC: the *Concerto for Jazz Trumpet*, for the Light Music Festival, and *The Bermudas*, a big choral work partly written in a twelve-note idiom.

This had a mixed reception, but there could be no doubt that here was a substantial composer and one who had considerable range: he could turn his hand to *Scottish Dances* (a work the Burns Federation would no doubt have much preferred to the *Sinfonia*) as successfully as to the *Symphonic Variations* which Barbirolli premiered in 1956 or the *Sonata for Chamber Orchestra* which John Pritchard included in his Musica Viva series at Liverpool. Hamilton had a very high opinion of Pritchard: 'A consummate, natural musician...John did remind me of Boult.'

With success as a composer came calls upon his administrative and diplomatic skills. He was soon serving as chairman of the Composers Guild, chairman of the music section of the ICA and a member of the BBC's Music Advisory Panel. He organized concerts of contemporary music, continuing to teach at Morley College and London University. He was much in demand, but composition always came first and by 1961 he had produced a Violin Concerto, a Piano Concerto (which Pritchard was to take to Berlin), *Five Love Songs for Tenor and Orchestra* (first heard at Cheltenham) and a *Sonata for Cello and Piano* in which Hamilton himself accompanied Joan Dickson, at Glasgow University.

But in 1961 he migrated to New York on being appointed Mary Duke Biddle Professor of Music at Duke University. Here he was to live for twenty years, commuting weekly to North Carolina.

His new life suited him. He enjoyed the high voltage of New York, and he was an avid theatre-goer. At Duke University he could teach and work in relative tranquillity. Nor was he forgotten in Britain (as was his contemporary, Peter Racine Fricker, with a professorship at UCLA). He himself, with his publishers – Schott's in London, Theodore Presser in New York – saw to that. His first commission for the Proms, the *Cantos for Orchestra*, came in 1965, by which time he had already had five works performed at that great summer festival.

Hamilton was well read and he now began to be drawn towards opera. The year 1968 saw the completion of a 'dramatic narrative',

Agamemnon; a 'dramatic commentary', *Pharsalia*; and a full-scale opera based on Peter Shaffer's play *The Royal Hunt of the Sun*. This was given (and later revived) by English National Opera. It caught the ear of Alexander Gibson, a loyal champion of Hamilton's music, who was embarking upon a programme of commissions for Scottish Opera. Four composers – Thea Musgrave, Thomas Wilson, Robin Orr and Iain Hamilton – were approached and in due course Hamilton produced *The Catiline Conspiracy*. This derived from Ben Jonson (whose *Bartholomew Fair* he had already used as the inspiration for an overture) and it provided a nice vehicle for implicit commentary upon the latter days of Edward Heath's government. It was launched on 16th March 1974 at Stirling University, where it received a total of ten performances. The public found Hamilton's language austere but *The Scotsman*'s music critic, Conrad Wilson, hailed the opera as a masterpiece (a view he later modified) and, in *The Times*, Bill Mann evoked comparisons with Verdi and Puccini.

It was certainly a taut and powerful piece but the singers found the idiom awkward: the vocal line, one told me, was often 'shadowed' by a woodwind solo, but at an unsettling interval rather than in unison. Whatever its failings, *The Catiline Conspiracy* was successful enough to be revived for four performances in the Theatre Royal, Glasgow, in 1978, when, in a more spacious acoustic, it 'sounded' more effectively and was better liked.

By this time Hamilton had completed another major work, a BBC commission which, as Controller Music, I was in the happy position of being able to offer. My colleague Stephen Plaistow and I had for some time been concerned to commission a dramatic work for voices and orchestra which would be composed essentially for the medium of stereophonic radio and which would not necessarily transfer to the stage or the concert platform. We believed Hamilton would understand this requirement and he was enthusiastic about it, choosing Marlowe's *Tamburlaine* as the basis for what he called a lyric drama. The piece turned out to contain much beautiful music and, when broadcast in 1977, worked well on radio, but it was not the radiogenic revelation for which we had hoped and Hamilton clearly had a stage picture in his mind. Perhaps we were asking too much of someone so steeped in the theatre as he was.

Tamburlaine was followed by *Anna Karenina*, which ENO commissioned and performed in 1978, later reviving it. Hamilton always spoke warmly of the collaborative attitude of the ENO team and of the singers in the company and it was one of these, Lois McDonall, who sang his fine *scena*, *Cleopatra*, at the 1978 Proms. This work marked a perceptible change in Hamilton's idiom: an almost conventional tonality was now apparent and I was able to tease him about 'overt passion in downright D major'.

Hamilton returned to London in 1981 and, after the sudden death of a beloved partner, immersed himself in composition: two operas, a 'lyric comedy', two symphonies, a *St Mark Passion* and other smaller works all appeared between 1981 and 1983. I was not the only one to begin to feel that he needed a sabbatical, time out from the routine of what Vaughan Williams once referred to as 'compo' and, over a lunch in Soho, I suggested that he was writing too much. He was hurt by my well-intentioned though no doubt inept proposition, but, for whatever reason, he did begin to write less, and mostly on a smaller scale.

His seventieth birthday, in 1992, was barely noticed by Radio 3 – which wounded him – though his *Commedia* (the revised *Concerto for Orchestra*) was heard at the Proms that year. In 1993, thanks to an imaginative initiative on the part of a well-informed official, he was invited to Bermuda, whose capital is Hamilton, to hear his *The Bermudas*. In Britain, though, not much of his music was heard. Younger composers, among them the 'minimalists', were more accessible. Easy listening was increasingly fashionable. Someone of Hamilton's intellectual seriousness and literary associations was likely to be too taxing for the average listener, whose attention-span was manifestly shrinking.

Hamilton's last years were sombre. A friendly man, with a pawky sense of humour, he increasingly sought privacy and, though he once told me that it was vitally important to him to be able to 'care for' another human being, he never established a relationship to replace that with his much-loved Cass. And it grieved him that from bright beginnings he had come to see his music unreasonably neglected.

The compositions of his last years include *The Transit of Jupiter* (first performed by the BBC Scottish Symphony under Jerzy Maksymiuk in 1995), *Bulgaria Invocation: Evocation for Orchestra*, *The Wild Garden* (five pieces for clarinet and piano) and *London: a Kaleidoscope for Piano and Orchestra*, written this year.

His death provides the belated opportunity for a selective revival of the best work of a serious and accomplished composer.

The Independent, 27th July 2000

Luciano Berio

When I saw the score of Luciano Berio's *Bewegung*, which had its premiere at Glasgow in the Musica Nova concerts of 1971, I thought it sparse – and so it turned out to be, for it was soon extended and later acquired a partner-piece, *Still*. I found its composer modest, wryly humorous and quietly opinionated.

* * * * *

Asked what he understood music, and his own music in particular, to be, Luciano Berio declared, 'I have no vocation for oracular pronouncements. I have seen other people trying to explain their music but all too often they end up producing delirious verbal arabesques, which may well tell us some interesting things about the author's personality and neuroses, but not much about what he does, or has done.' His reply absolutely typified the man, down-to-earth, self-deprecating and humorous, but it gave no hint of the quite extraordinary range of his curiosity or the variety and originality of his musical thought. Though Italian, Berio composed music which was not in any recognizable sense Italian.

Born, on 24th October 1925, into a family of musicians, Berio was taught by his grandfather, Adolfo, and his father, Ernesto; both were composers and keyboard players. Their home was in Oneglia on the Ligurian coast, and their standards were provincial. But there was chamber music in the house and the young Berio was developing as a gifted pianist until an accident to his right hand during military service turned him towards composition.

He had already written works for piano and a *Preludio* for string orchestra. At twenty he joined the Milan Conservatoire, in due course entering the class of Giorgio Ghedini, whom he described as 'a great musician'. During the same period he attended Giulini's conducting classes, also acquainting himself with much of the opera repertoire by conducting in provincial theatres. He also occasionally played the timpani, but when he attempted this from the full score, he soon discovered it was impractical: the pages had to be turned too often.

In the early 1950s important encounters came thick and fast. He met and soon married the American mezzo, Cathy Berberian, in 1950; he fell under Dallapiccola's influence in 1951; and two years later he formed a close friendship with Bruno Maderna: 'from 1953 to 1959 it was almost as though we were living together,' he said.

In 1954 he met Boulez and Stockhausen at Darmstadt. Already

interested in electronic music – he had been in New York for the first public concert in America to include any – he began to plan an electronic studio for Italian Radio (RAI), a project in which Maderna soon joined him. Together they composed *Ritratto di Città* for single-track tape. Later, though, he was to assert that music consisting solely of synthetic sound was 'absurd'.

The year 1955 saw the opening in Milan of RAI's Studio di Fonologia Musicale and the composition of Berio's first stage work, *Mimusique No.2*. This 'mime-piece' re-emerged at the Venice Biennale of 1959, somewhat reworked, as *Allez Hop*, and it was further revised in 1968, a cannibalistic procedure to which Berio sometimes resorted when a deadline was imminent.

In 1956 Berio edited and published the first issue of *Incontri Musicali*, a periodical devoted to contemporary music, and, with Maderna the following year, he arranged a series of concerts with the same title. A second series was promoted in Naples in 1958, the year in which he completed the first of his thirteen *Sequenzas*, short pieces combining extreme virtuosity with a dramatic element. With one exception, that written for the voice of Cathy Berberian, these are for a solo instrument, and in most cases Berio had a particular player in mind: a player with, in his own words, 'a virtuosity of knowledge'.

Berio had studied with Dallapiccola in 1952 at the Berkshire Music Festival in Tanglewood, and he returned there in 1960 to teach and to supervise the premiere of *Circles*, a seminal piece based on poems by e. e. cummings, for Berberian, harp and two percussion instruments, the music and the poetry invading one another, the singer moving among the instrumentalists, who, in the case of the percussion, had an aleatoric role.

At the Dartington Summer School the following year Berio was assisted, as translator, by the young Peter Maxwell Davies, and in 1962 he replaced Milhaud at Mills College in Oakland, California. Two years later he taught at Harvard, one of his principal subjects being 'arrangement', an apt topic as he had begun to compose a series of *Chemins*, which were elaborations of and commentaries upon earlier *Sequenzas*.

At various times he was to arrange, either literally or creatively, works by Monteverdi, Bach, Boccherini, Mozart, Schubert, Brahms, Falla, Hindemith and Weill. And what became Berio's best-known work, *Sinfonia*, is underpinned by the scherzo of Mahler's Second Symphony. It was premiered in 1968 by the New York Philharmonic (for whom it was written), and was soon followed by *Opera*, a chronically complex piece involving actors as well as singers, which was premiered in Santa Fé in 1970 and was, Berio conceded, 'one of the biggest disasters in my life'.

The year 1971 saw a surge of interest in Berio's music in Britain. His *Bewegung* was heard in the Scottish National Orchestra's first Musica Nova series and later at the Edinburgh Festival (in a 'definitive' version), when *Sinfonia* was also in the programme. At the Proms, where *Sinfonia* had already been performed, Berio conducted his *Laborintus* II, using texts by Sanguinetti, a 'musical catalogue' in which there is a jazz episode and the voices are amplified. 'I am rather pleased,' the composer said, 'with the sound of *Laborintus* II.' The promenaders welcomed it with a predictable shout: 'Berio in stereo!'

Between 1971 and 2000 his music featured at the Proms almost every year, most memorable being Cathy Berberian's *Recital* I (1974) and *Coro* with Cologne Radio forces (1977). Pierre Boulez was often the conductor (he recorded *Sinfonia*), a natural arrangement since from 1974 to 1980 Berio had been in charge of the electro-acoustic department of IRCAM, Boulez's research studio in Paris.

In January 1990 the BBC promoted a four-day Berio Festival at the Barbican. This well-attended event featured not only *Coro* and *Sinfonia* but also the British premiere of *Ofanim*, a setting of Biblical texts involving a female voice, two children's choirs and two instrumental groups, the music 'treated' by a sophisticated electro-acoustic system which Berio had developed at his own IRCAM: Tempo Reale in Florence. The instrumental element was provided by the London Sinfonietta, with which he had regularly worked. As early as 1976 he had given with them what he believed was the first concert ever heard in his birthplace, Oneglia.

The BBC's Berio Festival came just a year after the production at Covent Garden of his *Un Re in Ascolto* (A King Listens). This remarkable and moving work – an *azione musicale*, not an opera, the composer insisted – has a text by Italo Calvino and Berio jointly, with roots in Shakespeare and references to Auden and others. (The King/Prospero is struggling to realize his vision of 'another theatre' before he dies – as he does, alone on the empty stage.) The Royal Opera House did Berio proud, and the complexity of the production was apparent in the multifarious list of credits, among them 'Flying' and 'Vultures supplied by'.

During the 1990s the torrent of Berio's output abated a little. A *Sequenza* for accordion emerged, as did *Kol Od* (from *Sequenza* X via

Chemins VI) and *Récit* (from *Sequenza IXb* via *Chemins* VII). Much more important, though, were two more *azioni musicali*. The earlier, *Outis*, heard at La Scala in 1996, was a powerful indictment of materialist society. A supermarket, said Berio, could obliterate human personality as effectively as a concentration camp. The second, *Cronaca del Luogo*, was produced at Salzburg in 1999. In 2001 his completion of Puccini's *Turandot* was very well received and seemed likely to supplant Alfano's version.

Though Berio's marriage to Cathy Berberian was dissolved, her extraordinary vocal virtuosity continued to inspire him after his subsequent marriages to the Japanese psychologist Susan Oyama and later the Israeli musicologist Talia Packer. In 1972 he had bought farm buildings and land in the Tuscan hills near Siena, and after much restoration and cultivation, he moved there in 1975, as if to affirm his Italian roots after more than ten years when the centre of gravity of his activity was in the United States. Radicondoli became his settled home and it was there that he wrote *Requies*, in memory of Berberian, who died in 1983. Ten years earlier he had written *Calmo* in memory of Bruno Maderna. He was generous and loyal to those he loved, but could be acerbic where an earlier generation was concerned. Mascagni, he said, was 'a troglodyte' by comparison with Puccini. As to Bellini, 'By all means pulverize [him], frankly, I reckon he deserves it.'

Berio never committed himself wholeheartedly to the Darmstadt ethos, but he is likely to be thought of as one of a triumvirate, the other two being Boulez and the slightly younger Stockhausen. Examination of his music should dispel this assumption. For one thing, electroacoustics play a relatively small part in his output. For another, his originality is rarely systematic. The layering of his music and its frequent self-derivation are highly personal, generally depending upon a fundamentally simple harmonic structure. Most strongly characteristic is the theatrical dimension, which is evident in a majority of his works, whether a solo *Sequenza* or a complex *azione musicale* such as *Un Re in Ascolto*.

The colours of Berio's compositional voice, the vividness of his imagination, his remarkable technique and the compassion evident in many of his verbal works entitle him to a special niche in the musical pantheon of the second half of the twentieth century.

He is survived by his third wife and by the two daughters and three sons of his three marriages.

The Times, 28th May 2003

John Buller

Liking and admiring John Buller, whose *Proença* had been a hit at the 1977 Proms, my wife, Lesley, and I personally commissioned a setting of *Three Shakespeare Sonnets* (Nos.15, 61, 27) for performance by the Nash Ensemble.

* * * * *

A composer who goes to Aeschylus, Euripides and Thucydides, to Shakespeare, Dryden and Dante, and to James Joyce for his inspiration, is likely to be a man of broad culture and of gravitas. But John Buller, though described by one commentator as 'austerely perverse', was by no means a cerebral composer. Indeed, William Mann of *The Times* deemed one of his Joyce pieces 'sympathetic music, witty and lyrical and brightly coloured'.

Buller's career was unusual. Born in London in 1927 to parents who recognized and encouraged his musicality, he was a chorister at St Matthew's, Westminster, and began to compose in his teens, having a work accepted by the BBC before he was twenty, while serving in the Royal Navy. But he then decided against a career in music and took up work as an architectural surveyor. In due course, however, his first love beckoned irresistibly and in his early thirties he turned back to it, studying with Anthony Milner and taking a London University BMus.

Progress was nevertheless slow. The Nash Ensemble accepted Buller's *The Cave* and performed it on the South Bank in 1970. This eight-minute piece for five musicians employed a taped element, a tool which was to recur in a much larger work, *Le Terrazze*, first heard at a BBC Invitation Concert in 1974. By this time his obvious capability and good sense had earned him the chairmanship of the Macnaghten Concerts Committee, a position he held for five years until 1975, when he was appointed composer-in-residence at Edinburgh University.

There, his *Familiar*, for string quartet, was heard in May of the following year. Already, though, he had dipped into Thucydides with *The Melian Debate* (1972) and into Joyce with *Two Night Pieces from Finnegans Wake* (1971), *Finnegans Floras* (1972) and – on a large scale – *The Mime of Mick, Nick and the Maggies* (1976). The pianist and writer Peter Stadlen reckoned that Joyce and Buller 'turn out to have been made for one another.' The BBC had broadcast the second and third of these Joyce pieces, and they had caught the ear of Stephen Plaistow, head of the corporation's commissioning unit.

As a consequence, two major works emerged, both premiered at the

Proms and both conducted by Mark Elder with the BBC Symphony Orchestra (in 2003 they were issued together on a single CD). They were *Proença* (1977) and *The Theatre of Memory* (1981). The former, which uses Provençal verse of the twelfth and thirteenth centuries, is concerned with the age and ethos of the troubadours, the flowering of their songs and the ultimate suppression of their liberal attitudes.

The 'singing' protagonists are a mezzo-soprano (at the first performance the splendid Sarah Walker) and an electric guitar, which perhaps represents masculinity: certainly there are passages which are strongly erotic. The work was warmly received by the Proms audience; its composer – hitherto unfamiliar to them – a diminutive figure apparently unfazed by his reception.

Buller perhaps was a little 'austerely perverse' in choosing as the subject of his next orchestral work the memory theatre, itself deriving from the Greek theatre, which Giulio Camillo built for Francis I of France in the sixteenth century. He described it as 'a vast memory bank or Renaissance computer'; but 'it was this Greekness that became the other source of the piece'.

The orchestra is thus laid out, as in a Greek theatre, in seven radial wedges, each led by a soloist. The public reacted with intrigued puzzlement (the conductor enters after the work has begun) but David Cairns described it as 'a vast and glittering orchestral score of riveting power'.

Buller's last major work, his only opera, again looked to classical Greece for its inspiration. *The Bacchae*, or Βάκχαι (which the composer preferred, since most of the text is in the original Greek) was an ENO commission first performed, in a less than ideal production, on 5th May 1992.

Its success was nevertheless such that a revival was planned. But it did not materialize, which grieved the composer of a work which had been described, in the periodical *Tempo*, as 'the finest British opera since Britten's *Curlew River*'. There was, however, a by-product: *Bacchae Metres*, heard at the Proms in 1993.

John Buller was married to the painter Shirley Claridge, who was his immaculate copyist and who, in the late 1980s, designed a Christmas card for the Musicians Benevolent Fund. There were four children.

The family's life was not always easy; Buller's output was small and rarefied. For a while they lived in France, eventually returning to rented accommodation in Dorset. In 2003 signs of Alzheimer's manifested themselves; a bitter conclusion for a composer with a muscular mind.

His voice was fresh, colourful and energetic, and his music now richly deserves revival.

He is survived by his wife, three sons and a daughter.

The Times, 18th September 2004

György Ligeti

I met György Ligeti only once – and then very briefly – at the Royal Academy of Music in 1995. But I had been intrigued by his music since 1976 when Pierre Boulez had conducted his *San Francisco Polyphony* at a BBC concert and, in Budapest, I had heard his *Aventures* in a brilliant puppet production.

* * * * *

György Ligeti was two years older than Boulez and Berio, and five years older than Stockhausen, but there was no concurrence between him and them in his formative years.

He was thirty-three before he escaped from the tyranny of the Iron Curtain, itself closely preceded by the Nazi tyranny. Moreover he was a Jew. His father and brother died in concentration camps. He himself was one of a Jewish group, used by the Nazis as slave labour, which handled high explosives close to the front line.

He deserted in the confusion of battle and evaded capture by the Russians. Eventually he walked home – the trek took two weeks – to Cluj, in north-west Romania, only to find his family vanished and their apartment occupied by strangers.

He was called up by the Romanians, now under Soviet control, but a tubercular infection put him in hospital. He had been exceedingly lucky; and he was lucky again in 1956, when the Red Army invaded Hungary. He dodged the invaders and escaped to Vienna, making part of his hazardous journey in a mail train, where he lay hidden under the mailbags.

Ligeti was born in 1923 of Hungarian parents in Dicsöszentmárton (now Tirnaveni), a country town in Transylvania, by then part of Romania. His family were cultivated people; the eminent violinist Leopold Auer was a great-uncle.

In 1929 they moved to Cluj, which became briefly Hungarian under the Nazis. Here Ligeti learned Romanian, but he was soon aware of both anti-Hungarian and anti-semitic prejudice. In his early teens he discovered the cinema – in particular Charlie Chaplin and Buster Keaton – and Lewis Carroll's Alice books. Both discoveries fed his vivid imagination in ways which emerged as comedy and fantasy in his music. At sixteen he began to compose, Weber, Wagner and Strauss being his chief models, and, about a year later, he first heard Bartók and Kodály.

In 1941 he had a song published by a Jewish organization and on the strength of this and other compositions he was admitted to the Cluj Conservatoire. There he was a pupil of Ferenc Farkas, a conservative teacher who insisted that he study Bach and Mozart. Privately, he investigated Hindemith and Stravinsky, and in 1945 he was accepted (as was Kurtág) by the Franz Liszt Academy in Budapest.

It was a blow that Bartók, due to return to Budapest that autumn, died in New York, but for three years Ligeti enjoyed a rich musical diet. There was no restriction on the performance of Bartók or Stravinsky; and *Peter Grimes* was presented just a year after its world premiere.

But in 1948 Moscow issued the infamous diktat accusing Prokofiev and Shostakovich of 'formalism' and banning, in its satellites, all 'degenerate' Western music. This silenced, among others, Debussy, Ravel, Schoenberg, Stravinsky and Britten. Even Bartók was largely proscribed, and Ligeti's own Cello Sonata was also banned.

Fortuitously he won a scholarship to study folk music in Romania. In 1949 his *Cantata for Youth*, which he said was in a 'sort of Kodály-Handel-Britten style', was performed in Budapest. In the mid-1950s he began 'to come towards a Ligeti style', and his *Six Bagatelles* for wind quintet, written in 1953, were heard in 1956, though the last was omitted because of its excessive dissonance.

Then, on 7th November 1956, during the Soviet Union's invasion and against a background of gunfire, he listened to a Western broadcast of Stockhausen's *Gesang der Jünglinge*, the first electronic piece he had heard and an apt prelude to his own escape to Vienna in December.

Once free, Ligeti contacted Stockhausen, who gave him access to West German Radio's electronic studio in Cologne. There he 'soaked up things like a sponge', discovering Webern among much else and himself composing three electronic works. But, despite his regular attendance at Darmstadt from 1957 to 1966, he did not eventually pursue electronics as a medium, though its possibilities inspired him, as did Bartók, to explore clusters and what he called micropolyphony.

His first big public success came in 1958 with *Artikulation*, a very short piece which explores the acoustics of the voice and is also funny. It led directly to *Aventures* (1962) and *Nouvelles Aventures* (1966), but before them came two big orchestral works, *Apparitions* (1959) and

Atmosphères (1961); the latter quickly achieved multiple performances despite its complexity – a mirror canon in forty-eight parts which uses both clusters and micropolyphony.

Volumina (1962), for solo organ, uses similar means and it was memorably performed at the 1978 Proms: the Albert Hall organ wheezed admirably when switched off, as required, over a sustained cluster.

That Ligeti was capable of self-ridicule is proved by his account of the first performance of the ironically titled *Poème Symphonique*, a work for 100 metronomes which did not amuse the pompous audience in Hilversum City Hall for the final civic reception of the Gaudeamus Music Week.

Aventures and *Nouvelles Aventures* are quintessential Ligeti, an *opera buffa* for three singers and small ensemble. The 'text' consists of nonsense words and sounds, often anarchic and bizarre. Instead of slowly moving clusters there are abrupt changes and sudden silences. The effect, as in much of the best of Ligeti, is both comic and serious.

Wholly serious, however, was the Requiem, first heard in Stockholm in 1965, whose impact was so powerful that William Mann, *The Times*'s chief music critic, declared that he would 'gladly have forgone Beethoven's Ninth Symphony after the interval.' First contemplated before the war, the work had passed through two earlier attempts and had drawn upon the composer's own vision of the Day of Judgement, upon Flemish polyphony and Bach, upon Bruegel and Bosch – sources of inspiration which would also nurture his opera, *Le Grand Macabre*.

Exceedingly difficult to perform accurately, it has had relatively few performances. But it was a milestone in Ligeti's development for it caused him to 'distance' himself from clusters, a change apparent in *Lux Aeterna* (1966) and the Cello Concerto (also 1966). This new idiom became even more manifest in a big orchestral piece, *Lontano* (1967).

Ligeti's international status received a backhanded compliment when, in 1968, Stanley Kubrick appropriated, without the composer's knowledge or consent, large parts of three recently recorded works for the soundtrack of his film, *2001: A Space Odyssey*.

Eventually Ligeti was paid a paltry sum by MGM, but he undoubtedly benefited from the publicity attendant on the success of the film, and Kubrick used more of his music in later films, paying appropriately.

Also in 1968 Ligeti completed what he would later describe as the most important work in his oeuvre, the Second String Quartet, which was described by one pundit as 'livid, hectic and freakish'. Ferociously difficult to play (its preparation took the Lasalle Quartet a year), it makes extensive use of harmonics.

After a number of orchestral works – *Ramifications* (1969), *Melodien* (1971), the *Double Concerto* for flute and oboe (1972), *Clocks and Clouds* for female voices (1973) and *San Francisco Polyphony* (1974), there came *Le Grand Macabre*, premiered by the Swedish Royal Opera in 1978 under the British conductor Elgar Howarth. Its underlying theme is death, but its message is 'gather ye rosebuds', through politics, drunkenness and sex. Ligeti described the style of the piece as 'some kind of flea market half real, half unreal…a world where everything is falling in'. In a revised version it was heard at the Salzburg Festival in 1997.

Works on a small scale followed, among them the Horn Trio (1982), which was inspired by Brahms, and, in 1985, the beginning of the piano *Etudes* which, by 2001, had reached eighteen in number. Formidably difficult (one proved unplayable, even by Pierre-Laurent Aimard, and had to be rewritten), they nod in the direction of Chopin and Schumann and owe something to the most advanced pieces in Bartók's *Mikrokosmos*.

Meanwhile, the Piano Concerto (1988) and the Violin Concerto (1993) had appeared. The *Hamburg Concerto*, for horn (1999), was heard in London, with Michael Thompson and the London Sinfonietta, before it was revised in 2002.

All of Ligeti's major compositions have been performed in England. Regular promoters have included the BBC, at the Proms and elsewhere, and the London Sinfonietta. The Philharmonia, under Esa-Pekka Salonen, was involved in a massive Sony recording project, but it foundered (for want of rehearsal time) and was taken over by Teldec, which brought in the Berlin Philharmonic, under the young English conductor Jonathan Nott. But the Philharmonia did salvage a mini-festival entitled *Clocks and Clouds*.

ENO presented *Le Grand Macabre* in 1982, though the production, by Elijah Moshinsky, did not please the composer, who described it as 'an absolute misunderstanding'. He was happier, not surprisingly, about a grand manifestation mounted by the Royal Academy of Music in 1995, when, in his presence, thirty-two works were performed at eight concerts, the conductors including Stephen Barlow, Nicholas Cleobury and the ever loyal Howarth.

At the Huddersfield Festival of 1993 the King's Singers gave the first complete performance of the *Nonsense Madrigals*, some of which set words by Lewis Carroll. And in 2003, Nicholas Kenyon marked Ligeti's eightieth birthday by scheduling no fewer than eight works at the Proms.

Ligeti was a bewilderingly complex personality. Born Hungarian in Transylvania, he eventually became Austrian. For a time he lived in Hamburg. He taught in Sweden and the USA. His first wife, Brigitte Löw, he probably married because she was on hand when he returned to Cluj to find his family gone. His second, Vera Spitz, he married in 1952; he divorced two years later and remarried, partly for practical reasons, in 1957. She was for many years his 'closest friend'. He was undoubtedly a 'difficult' man, so demanding that neither Karajan nor Abbado would admit him to their recordings of his music.

And his idiom was constantly in flux. Before 1956 he was influenced by Bartók and by Balkan folk melody. Encountering Boulez in 1957 he rejected serialism and flirted with electronics. Next came clusters and micropolyphony and 'mechanic' music. But in due course he rediscovered the value of melody; and he became fascinated by the music of South-East Asia and of the Banda-Linda tribe in the Central African Republic

Arguably he was a magpie: he shopped, as he himself put it, in the 'marché aux puces'. And there were those who, admiringly, called him 'mad'. But there was method in his madness: he moved on when he perceived that a particular vein was exhausted; he knew what he could use and what he could not; the 'layering' of his music was a constant, as was its theatricality. He knew that to be torn between tears and laughter is the best experience the theatre can offer. He loved the absurd, was a born outsider, witty and self-deflating. He was unique, both quite impossible and very endearing.

He is survived by his wife Vera and by their son Lukas, a composer and percussionist.

The Times, 13th June 2006

PERFORMERS

Sena Jurinac

It is obvious – from what follows – that I idolized Sena Jurinac: there is nothing more to be said on that score. But I have found since writing this piece that she was First Lady, not Pamina in Karajan's 1950 recording of highlights from *Die Zauberflöte*; and her *Frauenliebe und -leben* has been issued on a Westminster CD.

* * * * *

September 1947 was a miracle month for music in Britain. At Edinburgh, the first Festival closed gloriously and endowed London with recitals of Schubert and Brahms by a magisterial quartet comprising Szigeti, Primrose, Fournier and Schnabel. In the Royal Opera House, the Vienna State Opera paraded a cast of superb singers in Mozart, Beethoven and Strauss. The men included Hotter and Schöffler, the women Schwarzkopf, Seefried and Sena Jurinac. Of this trio Jurinac, at twenty-six, was the youngest and though she sang Cherubino and Dorabella she did not quite hit the headlines as did Schwarzkopf – Elvira – and Seefried – Fiordiligi. Both roles are more showy and in both Jurinac was later to excel. But, if outshone, she was certainly not out-sung. Ljuba Welitsch, Salome in the same season, had already noticed that 'This Croatian girl is really something.'

Glyndebourne's talent scouts recommended her for Dorabella and this role she sang at Edinburgh in 1949, not, as Grove 6 states, at Glyndebourne, where Fiordiligi, in 1950, was her first role. Meanwhile, George Harewood had heard her at Salzburg in 1948, as Amor (*Orfeo*) and Cherubino. With Josef Krips in Vienna, and now Fritz Busch, she became a Mozartian of excellence, graduating from Dorabella to Fiordiligi and from Cherubino to the Countess. (A recording of *Zauberflöte* apparently exists but I have failed to trace it so do not know if she was the Pamina or one of the Ladies.) In *Idomeneo*, under Busch, she was the serenely poignant Ilia, while in the second version of *Ariadne* she created, as the Composer, a characterization so touching that, in memory, it still brings tears to my eyes.

The role is quite short – about 350 bars – but it covers an extraordinary range of emotions, and Sena brought to them all an immediacy which I do not think even Callas surpassed. The (nameless) young Composer's opera, mutilated at the whim of a wealthy patron, is her own flesh and blood and, despite the consoling concern of Zerbinetta, she cannot be reconciled to it and rushes off, disconsolate, fervently declaring that 'Musik ist eine heilige Kunst'. After that heart-melting scene, those of us – and we were innumerable – who were in love with her fell even more deeply into that agonizing state.

Sena herself gave her heart and hand to Sesto Bruscantini who, during her 'reign' at Glyndebourne between 1950 and 1956, sang Don Alfonso and Guglielmo to her Fiordiligi, Figaro to her Countess and the Music Master to her Composer. (John Christie, always endearingly innocent, was heard to ask, 'What happens if Sena has a baby?') Their marriage, initially very happy, did not for very long survive the strains unavoidable when the partners are successful singers. For Sena was soon a regular guest at Salzburg, and Karajan, while directing the Vienna State Opera, gave her Desdemona (*Otello*) among other roles. Of him she could not speak too highly: 'It was fantastic to sing for him... I remember the scene where I had to begin the Amen. Karajan was standing there in the pit, his arms folded. He looked at me, nodded "please", I began, and the orchestra was there. How wonderful.' (Not naturally unkind, she nevertheless said of Bernstein, 'I hate to look down and see flailing...he is like a dervish in the pit.') During Karajan's Vienna regime she also sang Cio-Cio-San (*Madame Butterfly*), of which George Harewood thought her 'the most honest, most heroic and in the end the most touching interpreter'. Other Italian roles included Tosca and Elisabeth (*Don Carlos*). But it was in the German field that she was generally most at home: Elvira and Anna in *Don Giovanni*, Elisabeth in *Tannhaüser* and Eva in *Meistersinger*, in which, apparently, the quintet scared her more than any other passage she ever sang.

Sena's recordings are not many and are by no means all available. The classic film of *Rosenkavalier*, in which she was Octavian (she later graduated to the Marschallin) will surely remain in the catalogue. Like the Composer, Octavian is a trousers role to which her Strauss style – not to mention her admirable legs – ideally suited her. The Marschallin was Schwarzkopf and the two appeared together many times in international houses, including Covent Garden, with Solti, in 1959. Years later she recalled the necessity of insisting that her Marschallin wore less perfume, particularly during the embraces of Act I: 'Elizabeth, *please*; I cannot breathe!' Her first sound recording was made, so far as I can discover, in 1948, when she sang 'Voi che sapete' in a small *Figaro* anthology with Seefried and Cebotari. There followed, in 1950, some oddments, including a touching 'Endlich allein' (*The Bartered Bride*) and arias from *Eugene Onegin*, *Aida* and *Tosca*. Also from 1950 came *Così* excerpts from Glyndebourne, whose *Figaro* (with Gui) appeared in 1955, followed by *Idomeneo* (with Pritchard) in 1956. She is Donna Anna in Fricsay's *Don Giovanni*. Strauss's *Four Last Songs* she recorded twice, most memorably with Busch in 1951. And to some reprehensible person (but whom?) I have lent an LP of Schumann's *Frauenliebe und -leben*, full of passion and tenderness. There must be other recordings around in the sound archives of radio stations, including the BBC, and we must pray that they include, in *Jenůfa*, both the title role and her formidable Kostelnička; above all her Leonora in *Fidelio* at Covent Garden, with Klemperer, who thought her 'very good'. A recording followed, but Walter Legge preferred another singer, perhaps agreeing with Montague Haltrecht's assessment of her Leonora as 'unabashedly feminine, a human, not a heroic figure'. Another critic found her Donna Anna 'not quite as thrilling as in the flesh' – and indeed, if you could not see Sena's eyes there was a dimension missing. She could by her presence transform an unpromising occasion: Moran Caplat recalled her singing 'Vissi d'arte' at a Highland Ball in Edinburgh's Assembly Rooms and finding it 'shatteringly beautiful'.

In 1988, Sena accepted my invitation to give master-classes in Mozart and Strauss at the Canterbury Festival and for five days she coached ensembles from the National Opera Studio, the Royal College, the Royal Academy, the Guildhall School and the Royal Northern College, who brought scenes from *Così* and *Rosenkavalier* and, among their singers, the very young Amanda Roocroft. Authoritative, energetic, practical and funny, she was irresistibly watchable, and George Harewood, who wrote a profile in *Opera* of her as early as 1950, came with his wife from Leeds to watch her. Always extraordinarily beautiful, short grey hair had given her an extra dignity without compromising her sense of fun. One evening at supper there was talk of her Covent Garden debut in 1947 and of her colleagues, notably Schwarzkopf, whose technique we agreed had become obtrusive. 'Dear Elisabeth,' said Sena, 'she get one note from her elbow, another from the back of her neck.' She sprang up and demonstrated, hilariously. Moran Caplat remembered meeting her at the Astoria Hotel in Vienna after a period during which he had grown a beard. When she saw it 'she burst into laughter and went two or three times round in the revolving door before falling into the hall.'

At work she was the complete professional: 'one of the most sympathetic colleagues one can ever meet', as Michael Langdon, an eminent Baron Ochs, said of her. George Harewood found her voice 'thrilling' and it did indeed have an unusual intensity, less creamy than Schwarzkopf's, less bright than Seefried's. She was always accurate and she phrased with wonderful sensitivity. Above all she was moving in a quite special way.

These days – she was eighty-five on 24th October 2008 – she lives quietly, near Augsburg, with her second husband, Josef Lederle, a retired surgeon, quite content to be off-stage, a private person enjoying her garden, her small dogs and her cats – and her cooking which, like her voice, delectably combines Croatian spice with Viennese cream.

Opera, October 2006

John Kentish

I first heard John Kentish's excellent Don Basilio (in *Figaro* at Sadler's Wells) in 1949, never dreaming that a year later I would be sharing the stage of Oxford's Town Hall with him in *The Trojans*. He was the gallant Aeneas, I the barely adequate Narbal.

* * * * *

John Kentish was a versatile lyric tenor with a fine voice and an attractive stage presence.

Born in Blackheath, London, he was educated at Rugby School and Oriel College, Oxford, where he joined the opera club and in 1928 scored a success in Weber's *Der Freischütz*, conducted by Reginald Jacques. The following year he took the role of Vašek in Smetana's *The Bartered Bride* conducted by Sir Hugh Allen. He got rave reviews and, as a result, went down before taking his finals. He studied seriously, in Vienna and elsewhere, and had begun to make a career in opera and as a recitalist when the Second World War intervened.

A junior officer in the Royal Navy throughout the war, he saw action in the Mediterranean and on convoys to North Russia. Soon after the war ended, Kentish joined Sadler's Wells Opera.

His lyric roles included Don Ottavio in *Don Giovanni*, Ferrando in *Così fan Tutte*, Alfredo in *La Traviata* and Almaviva in *The Barber of Seville*. He repeated Vašek and sang Tichon in *Katya Kabanová* for Rafael Kubelík in the legendary performance in 1954.

By that time he had begun to appear at Glyndebourne where his roles included Malcolm in *Macbeth* (1952), Sellem in *The Rake's Progress*, Scaramuccio in *Ariadne auf Naxos*, Valzacchi in *Der Rosenkavalier* and Mauer in Henze's *Elegy for Young Lovers* (1961). Meanwhile he appeared in two Handel Opera Society productions: as Ulisse in *Deidemia* (1955) and as Oronte to Joan Sutherland's Alcina (1957).

His versatility and courage were self-evident when, in 1950, he returned to Oxford to sing Aeneas in Berlioz's *The Trojans* on three consecutive nights in the first English performances, under Jack Westrup. As the years passed he moved from lyric to character roles. Harold Rosenthal, in *Opera* magazine, thought his Basilio (in *Figaro*) 'the best I can remember'.

During the 1960s Kentish taught privately and at the Guildhall School, and in the late 1970s he became director of studies at the London Opera Centre. He was then director of opera at the Royal College.

In 1983 he retired from professional activity and moved to Wells in Somerset where he continued to teach privately.

Properly, but never aggressively, ambitious, John Kentish made the very most of a beautiful voice of medium size, which he enhanced with exceptional musicality, intelligence and charm. He was also a good colleague: a friend described him as a 'gentle, handsome, romantic man'.

He is survived by his wife, Leigh, and three of his four children.

The Times, 23rd November 2006

Clara Haskil

Clara Haskil, whom I venerated, was an extraordinary link with great figures from the past. Fauré, Albéniz and Enescu were on the jury which awarded her first prize at the Paris Conservatoire in 1910. She played with Enescu, Ysaÿe and Casals; Busoni and Paderewski praised her. I am immensely proud of her single appearance, in 1957, at the Edinburgh Festival.

* * * * *

In August 1950, having sat my finals, I drove to Salzburg with friends in a state of relaxed euphoria. Hans Keller had asked me to review Strauss's *Capriccio* and a double bill of Britten's *The Rape of Lucretia* and Blacher's *Romeo and Juliet* for *Music Survey*. Otherwise, we had no tickets; we took pot luck. And what luck we had: Mozart's Mass in C Minor with Schwarzkopf and Patzak; and Mozart's E Flat Concerto, K271, with a pianist I had barely heard of: Clara Haskil.

Then fifty-five, Haskil was a curious figure on the platform. She had contracted scoliosis, a curvature of the spine, when quite young and had spent 'four interminable years' in plaster; her body remained unnaturally bowed, her hair was rather grey and wild. Her general demeanour was shy, even tentative. But when she played she was transformed and, inexperienced though I was, I knew that I was listening to a Mozart performance of memorable distinction. The slow movement, surely a touchstone, was magical.

I was ignorant of her pedigree. Romanian like Dinu Lipatti, with whom she had a close, affectionate relationship (he called her 'Clarinette'), she had gone to Vienna as a child and there studied with Richard Robert, the teacher of Rudolf Serkin and George Szell. Then she moved to Paris to study with Cortot at the Conservatoire. There, at the age of fifteen, she won the premier prix, the jury including Fauré, then head of the Conservatoire, who took a solicitous interest in her career. It is often said that she also studied with Busoni, but this is not so. He had heard her play and she did attend master-classes with him, but she turned down – to her later regret – his invitation to work with him in Berlin. She preferred to teach herself and, once the years of her illness were over, she began in about 1921 to be sought after by the grandest of older colleagues. With Ysaÿe she played the Beethoven violin sonatas; Enescu was a regular partner; Casals once had to drag her on to the platform to acknowledge the audience's applause.

With the Second World War came another medical crisis: fearful headaches and failing vision turned out to be caused by a tumour on the optic nerve. From this, too, she recovered, soon afterwards moving to Switzerland and becoming a Swiss citizen. Her neighbours, in Vevey, included Furtwängler and Hindemith.

The last ten years of Haskil's life (she died in Brussels, after a bad fall, on 7th December 1960) were crowned by many triumphs, but she was often surprised by them, sometimes even doubting their validity. Having never forgotten her K271, I was elated when she accepted my invitation to appear at the Edinburgh Festival in 1957. We agreed three concerts: Mozart's last concerto (K595) with Barbirolli and the Hallé on 21st August; the K459, in F, with Jochum and the Bavarian Radio Symphony Orchestra on 26th August; and, between them, on 23rd August, a recital comprising sonatas by Mozart (K330), Beethoven (Op.31/3) and the great B Flat (D960) of Schubert – a programme which matched her gifts to perfection.

Both the concertos went very well, particularly the one with

Barbirolli, with whom she had already collaborated. But the recital gave rise to a nerve-racking crisis. That morning (the recital was at 11 am) I was told she needed to see me urgently, and at the Freemason's Hall, about an hour before she was due to play, she announced, firmly, 'Il faut supprimer le recital.' I was aghast and we sat down, side by side, she fearful of playing, I desperately fearful that she would not. Very tenderly, I probed her anxiety (which, I believe, stemmed from a combination of nerves, an unfamiliar piano and the echoing acoustics of an empty hall) and described the bitter disappointment of a capacity audience. I longed to hold her very beautiful hand, but guessed she would find such a gesture intrusive. Gradually it emerged, unspoken, that she would play. She did, and though I had to miss the Mozart and Beethoven, the Schubert was a revelation for its luminosity and truthfulness.

It is very hard to say precisely what made Clara Haskil's playing so wonderful. 'Inspired simplicity' is the nearest I can get. Listen to the Mozart sonatas with Arthur Grumiaux; to Schumann's *Abegg Variations*, which, in her hands, glitter for Florestan and dream for Eusebius quite unforgettably. (Lipatti thought them 'perfection'.) I have heard it said that she couldn't 'cope' with Chopin, but I disagree: the F Minor Concerto is masterly – and wholly idiomatic.

Of all the 'classical' pianists I have heard she is the one I would most love to hear again, if possible at the stage before her illnesses, when a melancholy facial beauty was added to her innate modesty and her dazzling gifts as a musician.

BBC *Music Magazine*, July 2002

Yehudi Menuhin

In 1975 I was a guest speaker at a meeting in Canada of the International Music Council of which Yehudi Menuhin, whom I had first met at Edinburgh in 1953, was then president. One day there was informal talk about pop concerts, Menuhin and I utterly at a loss to understand them. So we agreed to attend one together – but the plan did not materialize!

* * * * *

'They listen more intently if one doesn't shout.'

Yehudi Menuhin's observation, made apropos an orchestral rehearsal he was conducting, could have applied equally well to his way with the whole of life. No musician can have been listened to so intently, or raised his voice so little. For seventy years he was an international personality, worth listening to well beyond the sphere of music, a voice all the more eloquent because of its essential innocence. He once said of Elgar's music that it was 'never crude, never aggressive, never vulgar'; and that was true of Menuhin himself.

As his career unfolded, he was listened to in different ways. At first, he was simply the breathtakingly gifted child prodigy; then, as he matured, the master violinist. With the Second World War, he became a tireless public servant, giving innumerable concerts for Allied troops, often in hazardous conditions. With peace, he emerged as a legendary figure, in world-wide demand. At the same time he began to be known for his boundless curiosity, not only within music but also about man's responsibility both for his own body and to the planet he inhabits. He took to conducting and, though by no means a 'born' conductor, he was listened to because of the conceptual integrity of his interpretations. Latterly he acquired a status verging upon sainthood, such was the idealism of his views. There were those who mocked him for his fads – 'his yoga and his yoghurt' – but they missed the point.

By his own account, Menuhin's parents, both of them teachers of Hebrew, took him to a concert by the San Francisco Symphony Orchestra when he was two and he begged for a violin for his fourth birthday. At the same time, he asked for lessons with Louis Persinger, leader of the orchestra. Initially, Persinger was unresponsive, so the boy went to another teacher, whose sole instruction into the technique of vibrato was to shout, 'Vibrate! Vibrate!' In due course Persinger relented.

However, 'He demonstrated and I imitated...Never having taught me a method, Persinger allowed me to beget my own.' Vibrato came to him at the age of six or seven, but it remained a problem and he relearned it as an adult. At eight he had prepared the Mendelssohn Concerto, and the Tchaikovsky, concertos by de Beriot, Spohr and Lalo, and the Bach Sonata in G Minor. He longed to play the Beethoven and, to 'earn' it, he learned the Mozart A Major in eight hours. Persinger was furious and his father 'laid a strap' to him.

At about the same time he first heard Enescu and conceived a passionate desire to study with him, so, in 1926, when Menuhin was ten, the family sailed to Europe. Before settling in Paris to work with Enescu, he went to Brussels to play to Ysaÿe. The audition was instructive. Having listened to the first movement of the Lalo *Symphonie Espagnole*, Ysaÿe asked for an A major arpeggio in four octaves. Menuhin 'groped all over the fingerboard' (his own words) and Ysaÿe remarked, 'You would do well, Yehudi, to practise scales and arpeggios.' Enescu, whom the family followed to Romania in 1927, had similar advice: Menuhin, he believed, should study as well with Adolf Busch, pre-eminent among German 'classical' violinists and a teacher who would be likely to counteract his tendency to over-expressiveness, what Menuhin himself later described as his 'too passionate playing'.

This too passionate element is apparent in parts of the wonderful first recording of Elgar's Concerto (though Elgar himself defended the interpretation with the memorable comment, 'Austerity be damned! I am not an austere man, am I?'). The collaboration between the sixteen-year-old Russian-American Jew and the seventy-five-year-old Roman Catholic Englishman was entirely happy but, curiously, accounts of the run-through which preceded the concert differ sharply. Popular legend has it that Menuhin and Ivor Newton had barely reached the soloist's second entry when Elgar declared himself satisfied and announced that he was off to the races. Newton's more circumstantial account is to be preferred: 'We played right through the concerto except the *tuttis*...Menuhin and Elgar discussed the music like equals but with great courtesy...on the boy's part. Most of the time Elgar sat...with his eyes closed, listening intently.'

The Elgar recording was made in 1932. Meanwhile, Menuhin had had a phenomenal success in New York, playing, at last, the Beethoven Concerto with Fritz Busch who, until the boy had auditioned for him, had scornfully dismissed the possibility with the remark, 'Man lasst ja auch Jackie Coogan nicht den Hamlet spielen' ('one wouldn't let Jackie Coogan play Hamlet')! A comparable success followed in Berlin, where he played the Bach E Major, the Beethoven and the Brahms with Bruno Walter. He was not quite thirteen. He now took lessons with Adolf Busch and though he accepted the need for classical rigour, he found Busch's fastidiousness irksome: 'While Busch developed in me a sense of discipline, precision and authority...it was Enescu who fired my imagination.'

Meanwhile, more recordings had been made, initially with Persinger at the piano. Mainly trifles, they included a Mozart concerto movement, which is very elegant. More important is the first recording with orchestra, Bruch's First Concerto, with Landon Ronald and the LSO. This has all of Menuhin's virtues at the time – freshness, a loving concern for the music and complete technical assurance.

A year later, in June 1932, came the famous Bach *Double Concerto*, with Enescu playing second violin and Pierre Monteux conducting, a collaboration wildly unfashionable by purist standards but nevertheless unarguably convincing and, in the slow movement, very moving. Between 1929 and 1936 all the unaccompanied Bach sonatas and partitas were recorded, while, with his sister, Hephzibah, Menuhin recorded Bach, Mozart, Beethoven, Schumann, Brahms and Enescu sonatas. Just before the war came the Franck and Pizzetti sonatas, also with Hephzibah, and the Schumann Concerto with Barbirolli (who remarked upon his 'very Jewish talent') and the New York Philharmonic. All in all, Menuhin never played more immaculately than in his late teens and early twenties.

Who can tell what effect his experiences during the war may have had upon him? He had married in 1938 (unsuccessfully as it later proved) and when Pearl Harbor was attacked in December 1941 he was twenty-five.

Over the next four years he gave over 500 recitals for Allied forces in the Americas, in the Pacific theatre and in Europe. The stresses of this, the anguish of playing to troops who might shortly lose their lives in battle, combined with separation from his children and discord with his wife, must surely have disturbed him fundamentally. He went through a period of personal dejection, tension and fatigue. His playing, based upon inspired facility rather than a rock-firm technique, self-evidently suffered and the critics began to comment upon his unpredictable standards.

In private, he embarked upon a thorough-going review of his technical resources. This, together with three unrelated but in different ways inspiring events, brought him back to a point at which he was again capable of the superlative performances which had come to him before the war. Indeed, he sometimes surpassed those earlier standards: he was, after all, a more deeply experienced and mature artist.

Menuhin had met Bartók for the first time in November 1943, and Bartók had remarked of his performance of the Second Concerto, 'I did not think music could be played like that until long after the composer was dead.' Impulsively, Menuhin asked him for a work for violin alone and, in March 1944, the Sonata was ready. Menuhin was shaken; it seemed 'unplayable'. But after some minor technical adjustments he performed it at Carnegie Hall in November the same year.

Bartók, who had less than a year to live, was overjoyed and the two men developed a deep friendship. Two months before Bartók's death (from leukaemia) Menuhin met Benjamin Britten in London and the latter urged him to take him on tour in Europe, where recitals for war victims had been arranged. Gerald Moore generously withdrew and so it was that the two eminent figures played at Belsen – twice in one afternoon – to those who had survived the horrors of that most vile of concentration camps.

It was for both a deeply haunting experience. Coming to terms with it, Menuhin was consoled by the evident healing power of music. He was perhaps also fortified by the growing warmth of his feelings for the dancer Diana Gould, and hers for him. In any case, he married that remarkable character in 1947 and, despite the prickly but humorous badinage to which she not uncommonly subjected him, there is no doubt they lived happily ever after.

Bartók, Britten and Belsen, his marriage to Diana – these restored Menuhin to his former interpretative glory, while his controversial support of Wilhelm Furtwängler, a public declaration of very great courage, led him to some of his finest achievements: the Brahms, Mendelssohn, Beethoven and Bartók second concertos, all recorded with Furtwängler between 1949 and 1953. It is clear that the two men had a profound spiritual and emotional affinity, and the Beethoven, as Menuhin himself would have wished, is probably the best thing he ever did.

His sheer range is easily forgotten. At the Edinburgh Festival of 1958 he played the Mozart G Major Concerto, the Brahms *Double* (with Cassadó) and the Shostakovich First; with his brother-in-law, Louis Kentner, the Mozart Sonata in A, K526, the Beethoven in G, Op.96 (a magical performance) and the César Franck; and, with Cassadó and Kentner, trios by Mozart, Beethoven, Schubert, Mendelssohn, Brahms and Ravel. (The Beethoven and Mendelssohn they took to a suburban cinema. The recital – for local people who were charged a shilling – was a sensation.) Bloch, Enescu, Bartók, Martin, Walton and Panufnik wrote works for him. His repertoire included music by Berg, Chausson, Delius, Nielsen, Sibelius, Debussy, Fauré, Poulenc and Vaughan Williams, much of it idiomatically and lovingly performed.

It is not clear when Menuhin began to conduct. Robert Magidoff's biography has a photograph of him conducting, apparently in 1944. But it seems likely that he did not take up the baton regularly until he established the Gstaad Festival in 1956. In Britain, as artistic director of the Bath Festival between 1959 and 1968, he developed the Bath Festival Orchestra (later the Menuhin Festival Orchestra) and made a number of recordings: notably Bach's Brandenburg Concertos and the four Suites, performances which have more than stood the test of time.

In 1967 he recorded Mozart's *The Seraglio*, a notoriously difficult piece to bring off. In due course he began to play less and to conduct more.

By the late 1980s he had formal appointments with the Royal Philharmonic, the Warsaw Sinfonia and the English String Orchestra. He was appearing with the Berlin Philharmonic and the English Chamber Orchestra. And his repertoire was steadily growing, sometimes in unexpected directions. In 1990 he undertook Walton's *Belshazzar's Feast* and, though the performance lacked *élan*, the dramatic spirit of the work was realized. A recording of Beethoven's *Choral Symphony* made the same year was more successful. Mozart's G Minor Symphony, recorded with his Polish forces a little earlier, was rated the best of innumerable versions by at least one critic.

The truth is that Menuhin had little natural aptitude as a conductor. His bowing wrist could not adapt to the need for darting flexibility; his elbow seemed the last flexible joint in his arm. As a consequence what he did looked laboured. Players unfamiliar with his method found him hard to follow, but those who knew him well learned to interpret his wishes by that mysterious form of communication which exists between instrumentalist and conductor. In any case, there can be no doubt that because of his innate musicality and his imaginative grasp he was sometimes able to convey the essence of a piece of music at least as successfully as some of his technically better-equipped colleagues.

Menuhin was both a polymath and a perfectionist, but one who sometimes fell short of perfection. Compare him, as a violinist, with Heifetz or Haendel, and, as a conductor, with Toscanini or Kleiber, and his uneven technical standards are easily perceived. But for sheer generosity of spirit, for the range and infectiousness of his enthusiasms and for the profound nobility of his finest achievements he was *nonpareil*. As Adrian Boult, writing in the early 1970s, put it: 'It is impossible not to feel that Yehudi Menuhin is now the greatest man in the profession.' And that he remained until his death.

The Independent, 13th March 1999

Evelyn Rothwell

I much regret that, though I knew some of her recordings, I never heard Evelyn Rothwell (Barbirolli) at a concert: by all accounts her elegant platform manner and her self-evident warmth of character were compelling.

* * * * *

During the summer of 1931, Lehár's *The Land of Smiles* was playing at the Theatre Royal, Drury Lane. In the orchestra were Peter Barbirolli, a viola-player, and Evelyn Rothwell, the principal oboe. Although Rothwell was then only twenty years old, she was already so impressive that Peter recommended her to his brother John Barbirolli, who was conducting Verdi and Puccini round the corner at Covent Garden and looking for a sub-principal oboe.

On 13th July, Rothwell received a note from someone apparently signing himself 'John Barkworth', who invited her to play for him. Two days later, she went for her audition, and John Barbirolli and Evelyn Rothwell first met: Evelyn recorded in her diary that he 'didn't behave like a foreigner in the least'. She joined the Covent Garden orchestra on 7th September and within days was playing Ethel Smyth's *The Wreckers*, *La Bohème*, *The Bartered Bride* and *Die Walküre*.

For the next two years Evelyn Rothwell was regularly busy in a number of orchestras. In 1933 Barbirolli was appointed conductor of the Scottish Orchestra (now the Royal Scottish National Orchestra) and at the start of the 1933-4 season he brought her to Glasgow as principal oboe; she was soloist in a Handel concerto. It was at about this time that John's brief marriage to the singer Marjorie Parry collapsed and his feelings for Evelyn Rothwell began to grow in warmth. He was a copious correspondent, and she a copious diarist: his letters to her are touchingly affectionate. They were eventually married at a civil ceremony in 1939 (and towards the end of his life their marriage was confirmed by the Roman Catholic Church at a private service in Dublin).

Meanwhile Evelyn Rothwell's career went from strength to strength. Because the Scottish Orchestra was then part-time, she was also able to work at Glyndebourne, from 1934 to 1938, and with the London Symphony Orchestra, in which she was the first woman, from 1935 to 1939. In 1936 Henry Wood noted, of his Queen's Hall Orchestra, that 'the woodwind was remarkably fine with...Miss Rothwell and Miss Boughton (oboes).'

That same year, John Barbirolli took over the New York Philharmonic as Toscanini's successor; he and Evelyn were often separated, though they managed a holiday together in France during the summer of 1938 and they honeymooned in Normandy the following year. When the Second World War broke out, on 3rd September 1939, John was on a liner in the mid-Atlantic but Evelyn – because of a difficulty over her visa – was left behind. Until she joined him in New York six weeks later, he was very miserable. He was also deeply concerned about her safety: 'You must only travel on a neutral ship', he wrote.

There now began a marriage which lasted for thirty-one years until John Barbirolli's death in 1970, and in which, it is clear, Evelyn was a pillar of loving strength. But she was certainly no doormat and her own career as a soloist, which Barbirolli nurtured with a quite proper professionalism, developed impressively.

In 1940, Evelyn Rothwell (she continued to perform under her maiden name) played the Pergolesi concerto, which Barbirolli had arranged for her, in Vancouver. Concertos by Corelli (arranged by Barbirolli), Cimarosa (Arthur Benjamin), Handel (Barbirolli and Charles Mackerras) and Marcello (arranged by Evelyn herself) emerged in due course. In 1948, during an Austrian tour by the Hallé Orchestra, she gave the first performance of a newly-discovered Mozart concerto in the Salzburg Mozarteum. Later, she was to play, and record, concertos by Albinoni, Haydn, Strauss, Castelnuovo-Tedesco and Vaughan Williams, as well as the baroque concertos already cited.

John Barbirolli was named conductor of the Hallé Orchestra in 1943, and he was knighted in 1949. For the next twenty-five years until 1968, when her husband was made its conductor laureate, Evelyn's life was inextricably bound up with the Hallé. She often toured with it, sometimes appearing as a soloist, and she accompanied her husband to Houston, Texas, when he took on the additional role of principal conductor of the Houston Symphony Orchestra in the early 1960s. He had meanwhile returned to the New York Philharmonic, as a guest, in 1958. Both Evelyn Rothwell and Barbirolli were fêted and there was a memorable dinner at which Eleanor Roosevelt and Danny Kaye were guests.

In England, Evelyn had already published in 1952 *Orchestral Studies* and *Bach Studies* followed by *Oboe Technique* (1957). She contributed to the *Journal of the International Double Reed Society* and was to publish *The Oboist's Companion* in 1977. She was in world-wide demand as an adjudicator.

In 1971 Evelyn was appointed a professor at the Royal Academy of Music. She was also honoured by Leeds University, the Royal College of Music, where she had studied under Leon Goossens, Trinity College and the Royal Northern College, to whom she in due course presented her own large collection of wind music. This included works she had commissioned from Gordon Jacob and Arnold Cooke, among others. To the Musicians Benevolent Fund, for sale at auction, she presented John Barbirolli's uniforms as a knight and two lots which she had inherited from Kathleen Ferrier, a close and beloved friend: Kathleen's own copy of Gluck's *Orfeo* (the last work she sang) and a still life by the singer, a painting known as her 'opus 2' which was signed, characteristically, 'Klever Kaff'. At one auction Evelyn bought back, for herself, a full miniature score of *Pelléas et Mélisande* which had once been her husband's property.

Evelyn Rothwell's last years were filled with adjudicating and giving good advice. She was president of the Incorporated Society of Musicians in 1981 and from 1983 served the Musicians Benevolent Fund for many years as a committee member. In 1993 she launched the Isle of Wight International Oboe Competition, an event, now moved to the Isle of Man, which stands as a lasting memorial to her.

Tall – much taller than her husband – and dignified, Evelyn's patrician nose belied a character both warm and refreshingly down-to-earth. Endlessly generous with her time and energy she was, despite increasingly unreliable knees, wonderfully hospitable. Lunch at her flat near Swiss Cottage was always memorable for good food, which she cooked herself, for friendly laughter and, if one was lucky with the weather, for the pleasure of sitting in the ravishing garden which she had created behind it.

Evelyn and John Barbirolli chose not to have children, but she will be remembered by innumerable wind-players, many of them students, as fulfilling, ideally, the qualifications of parenthood: exacting but considerate, loving but not sentimental, direct and above all, shiningly honest.

The Independent, 29th January 2008

Mstislav Rostropovich

Like Paderewski, earlier, and Daniel Barenboim, later, Mstislav Rostropovich had immense political courage. His gifts were superhuman, but he retained to the end of his life an adorable humanity: '*Pon*sonbee!' he shouted when he spotted me at Paul Sacher's party. I was at once warmed and enriched.

* * * * *

When the Leningrad Philharmonic Orchestra came to the Edinburgh Festival in 1960, its conductors were Evgeny Mravinsky and Gennadi Rozhdestvensky. Its only soloist was Mstislav Rostropovich who contributed Shostakovich's First Cello Concerto and, in recital, Brahms, Bach and Prokofiev: impassioned, bravura performances, all technically immaculate and glowing with the warmth of his personality.

He was a star of the festival and I asked him to play in the *Toy Symphony* which I was to conduct on its last day. He happily agreed and suggested that Rozhdestvensky join him. So I allocated them the triangle, though which of them held the instrument and which hit it I do not now remember. They were of course note-perfect (as were Leonid Massine on rattle and the conductors Vittorio Gui on drum and Alexander Gibson on nightingale). Slava was enchanted and asked for the score and parts to take back to Moscow.

He subsequently came to the Glasgow Proms and delivered a marvellous Dvořák Concerto. It was a Saturday night and when I took him to his train, he could not but notice the unbridled conduct of Glaswegian youth. 'Kissing?' he said, with a kind of benignly quizzical curiosity.

Then, in 1984, I was the guest of Paul Sacher at a concert in Basel when Slava again played the Dvořák concerto. Self-evidently he was in terrific form, and at dinner afterwards announced that he wished to demonstrate that you could get a champagne cork out of the bottle with a sabre, if you had one. And it so happened that he did. It hung from his waist in a military scabbard.

Within a minute, by dint of downward slashing and hacking, the cork was out (with much champagne). The demonstration had been so rapturously received that, at the brandy stage, Slava announced that he would repeat it. I held my breath as the second cork came out during a slightly tipsy, rather sentimental, quintessentially Russian, monologue in praise of Sacher. As before, those precious hands survived, and I was in due course embraced in a tremendous bear-hug.

His humanity matched both his musical eminence and his political bravado. He was often impulsive, boyish, mischievous, on one occasion muddling up all the shoes left outside bedroom doors for polishing in the hotel where he was staying. This was, I think, during a holiday he arranged for Peter Pears and Benjamin Britten, whom he venerated. Pears's diary, published privately as *Armenian Holiday – August 1965*, paints an enchanting portrait of a glorious musician and a glorious man.

The Guardian, 28th April 2007

Jacqueline du Pré

I first heard – and met – Jacqueline du Pré in December 1964 when she played Bloch's *Schelomo* with the Scottish National Orchestra under Norman Del Mar. She was nineteen, but already her exuberant personality, her commitment and her technical assurance marked her out as a future master.

* * * * *

Jackie, which was how she signed herself, was not a great letter-writer: she was, after all, a supremely good communicator in music. But an inscription in a book about the Meistersingerhalle in Nuremberg was worth any number of letters. It read,

> For Robert
> Love from an impossible teenager!
> Jackie.

It was dated 26th October 1967. The previous evening she had played the Dvořák Concerto in the Meistersingerhalle with the Scottish National Orchestra under Alexander Gibson. We were on tour in Austria, Germany and Holland. Our two soloists were Jackie and Janet Baker. We travelled – from Vienna, to Graz, Linz, Salzburg, Innsbruck, Munich, Nuremberg and Rotterdam – in three coaches: 'smokers', 'smokers tolerated' and 'non-smokers'. Jackie and I went in the 'non-smokers' (Alex and Janet in 'smokers tolerated') and such was Jackie's surplus energy that when most of us were inclined to doze, she prattled brightly on, demanding conversation. The point came when, my patience exhausted, I said, 'For God's sake, Jackie, shut up. You are an impossible teenager.' (She was actually twenty-two.)

By the end of the tour she had played the Schumann, Dvořák and Elgar Concertos in seven cities, among them Vienna, Nuremberg and Rotterdam. At Aschaffenburg, near Schweinfurt, the twin-town of Motherwell, Alex Gibson's birthplace, the local spokesman, whose English was primitive, but whose sincerity was touching, told her, 'There is poetry in your instrument...*inexplicable* diminuendo,' then lapsed into inarticulate silence. The concerto that night had been the Schumann, with which on 14th October she had made her Vienna debut. The Dvořák followed in Graz and Nuremberg, the Elgar in Leverkusen and Rotterdam.

Jackie had married Daniel Barenboim in Israel on 15th June (Janet Baker had been present) and he joined us when his engagements permitted. Similarly, Jackie abandoned us, to join him, on days when Janet was our soloist or we were on the road. In January that year Dannie had played the *Emperor Concerto* for us in Edinburgh and Glasgow. Just before the Edinburgh concert was due to begin I encountered Jackie in the Usher Hall.

Unaware of the developing love-affair between them, I said, 'Jackie, what are you doing here?'

'Oh, I thought I'd like to hear Dannie play the Emperor.'
'Where've you come from?'
'Well, Moscow, actually,' she replied.

The following evening, after the Glasgow concert, they came to my flat with Alex and Sam Bor. Dannie and Alex played Schubert duets; Sam, Jackie and Dannie played trios: Beethoven and Schubert. It was a magical evening: Jackie and Dannie exuded happiness, Sam and Alex were in their element, I had the most thrilling guests. The music stopped in the small hours, Dannie finishing up sitting on the floor with Jackie's cello across his knees, guitar-fashion.

Sadly, Jackie did not return to the orchestra during my time in Glasgow: she was in relentless demand internationally. Then, in 1972, she became a tragic victim of MS. I was never one of her intimate circle, but she was a welcome guest in my box in the Albert Hall during the Proms and she generally came when special friends were appearing, Zubin Mehta conducting or Pinchas Zukerman playing.

To have known her, and her playing, in her prime was a golden privilege. Her heaven-sent talent was strikingly 'physical', as was her temperament, and I found odious the publication of her sister's book, *A Genius in the Family*, which I did not read.

Happily, she lives on in some documentary footage and in some superb recordings.

John Ogdon

John Ogdon's first serious teacher, now almost forgotten, was Iso Elinson, whom, as a prep-school boy, I heard play in, I think, 1938. He also had lessons with Egon Petri and Gordon Green. So his credentials were immaculate and his technique, which included an astounding ability to sight-read, formidable, despite the fact that his fingers rather resembled small bananas.

* * * * *

Dear Sir Robert,
Thank you so much for the copy of my Concerto – hope all is well with you; I have found the Balakirev-Tausig Waltzes and will return them to the Library. Brenda and I had a lovely time playing Mozart's K365 with the BBC Scottish Orchestra, with Jerzy Maczymiuk. Brenda joins me in

sending deepest good wishes and kindest good hopes. As always,
John (Ogdon)

4 February 1986

This letter, the only one I ever had from John, was completely characteristic of its writer. I *could* not persuade him I was a commoner, but his ennoblement of me was also a reflection of his own profound modesty, as was the addition of his bracketed surname. It wasn't likely, was it, that another John had borrowed the Balakirev-Tausig Waltzes from the BBC's Music Library or that this other John was married to another Brenda, also a pianist!

I loved his 'deepest good wishes and kindest good hopes'. And I loved the man; it was impossible not to, so gentle, so unassuming and so vulnerable was he.

I first met him in Edinburgh on 9th October 1964 when he had come to play the Liszt E Flat Concerto and Stravinsky's, to my mind, arid *Movements* with the Scottish National Orchestra. (Other pianists that season included Ashkenazy, Arrau, Curzon, Cherkassky and Denis Matthews, so he was in good company.) Very popular, he returned most seasons and over seven years gave us, as well as the Liszt and the Stravinsky, the Schumann, the Tchaikovsky B Flat Minor (a brilliant performance), the Ravel *Left Hand* with Ronald Stevenson's *Faust Triptych* – just John's sort of music: virtuosic, complex – Rachmaninoff's Fourth (which he persuaded us all was better than it is) and, with his wife, Brenda, the Mozart K365 and Bartók's *Sonata for Two Pianos and Percussion*. One of his visits fell on my wife's birthday and after supper in the Gibsons' house he improvised, effortlessly and with panache, 'Happy Birthday to You' in the styles of Bach, Chopin, Rachmaninoff, Gershwin, and others. He was utterly relaxed, genial and beaming.

But in the early 1970s the mental instability which he had inherited, and which was surely hastened by the sheer pressure of his professional commitments, overcame him and I saw no more of him for several years. I kept in touch with his very sympathetic agent, Nina Kaye, however, and when it seemed that his confidence had been restored and as soon as *he* expressed a wish to return to the Proms, I invited him to do so. He appeared on 13th September 1983 in the Liszt E Flat Concerto – and had a hero's welcome. In the green-room afterwards I found him no less shy and (I *must* use the word; there is no other) obsequious, but clearly also happy and relaxed.

So it was a special pleasure for me when I asked him to give masterclasses at the 1987 Canterbury Festival, and he accepted. To be honest,

I was not sure whether he would turn out to be a born master-tutor, but I reckoned his name would bring us a good audience. In the event, he did boost our box-office takings; but his classes were hardly models of articulacy: he simply could not bring himself, so gentle was he, to utter more than the merest hint of criticism. A young pianist would perform a Rachmaninoff Prelude averagely well. It would come to an end and a long silence, ruffled only by John's heavy breathing (he was miked), would ensue. Eventually, '...*wonderful* Rachmaninoff playing...' would emerge. Another long silence, as John searched the music for a point of comment. Then, '...here' (pointing) '...I wonder if you could...hold back...just a little...*wonderful* Rachmaninoff playing...' Finally, he would take over and illustrate, unforgettably, what he wanted but could not find words to convey. His own recital was memorable for a towering performance of the Liszt Sonata, not immaculate, but intense and passionate.

When planning his contributions to the Canterbury Festival I had visited him in his home in Earl's Court and had been surprised to discover that his wife, Brenda, appeared to occupy the lower floor, where there was a grand piano and French windows to the garden, while John's 'space' seemed to be upstairs, where there was no sign of a piano of any kind. When we had finished he urged me to 'come and see Brenda' and we went downstairs. She asked what he would be playing and when he mentioned Rachmaninoff she exclaimed, to my astonishment, '*My* repertoire!'

In 1988, about a year before his death, I learned that the BBC were making a 'factional' film, *Virtuoso*, about John's career and his schizophrenia. I have always disliked the portrayal of living persons by actors and I discovered that several colleagues were so portrayed, but had not been consulted. So I acquired a copy of the script – and was appalled. It was novelettish and prurient. 'He embraces her...She responds. The telephone starts to ring. Brenda grimaces...John reluctantly rolls off...' Moreover, it shed little or no light on the professional life of a 'virtuoso', or upon schizophrenia. And I felt sure it would be hurtful to John. So I wrote to the director-general and phoned John Drummond, who was wholly sympathetic to my conviction that *Virtuoso* should be cancelled. Finally, I found myself speaking to Bill Cotton, managing director of BBC TV. I said I thought the film was disgraceful and asked whether John and Brenda had authorized it. 'Oh, yes,' said Bill, 'we have their signatures on the contract.' And that was that. But I have little doubt that it was not John who led the signing, and the odd fact that

Brenda herself emerged unattractively seems to me not to mitigate her own willingness to authorize a project which only diminished, and perhaps unsettled, a stupendous pianist and an adorable human being.

Sidonie Goossens

At the age of nineteen, Sidonie Goossens had a solo spot in *Chu Chin Chow*. The Shah of Persia, in the audience one night, was desperately smitten by her beauty and sent round an offer not only for her harp but also for her person. About eighty years later she confirmed to me the essential truth of this story. She remained very beautiful.

* * * * *

'In a wheel-chair one only gets a worm's eye view,' Sidonie complained in a letter posted not long after her hundredth birthday concert at the Wigmore Hall. 'Why didn't I see you, you usually tower above everyone.' The truth is that there was a great scrum around her and the scrum contained many who knew her better than I did, so that I stole away and wrote to her. Hence her letter.

I had seen her many times playing in the best London orchestras but I did not meet her, to talk to, until I took charge of the BBC Symphony Orchestra, of which she had been a founder-member in 1930. From the first I realized that she was *hors concours* among orchestral musicians, a close personal friend of Adrian Boult and of Pierre Boulez, the doyenne of her profession. She was already seventy-three and it struck me that it was high time her services to music were acknowledged. Ian Trethowan, managing director, BBC Radio, agreed and said he would put the matter in hand. And so he did, but I had not realized that the award she would receive, if any, would be linked to her 'grade' in the BBC. When in due course the Honours List appeared I was utterly mortified, for she was listed under the MBEs – and several of her peers, recommended independently, had an OBE, one or two a CBE. She later told me she was in two minds whether to accept her modest MBE. But she did. Later, however, when George Howard became chairman, I consulted him and suggested that it would give the entire profession – she was universally loved and admired – enormous pleasure, and would enhance the status of the profession itself, if she were to be made a Dame, a DBE. George was enthusiastic and undertook to organize an independent recommendation. But it failed and some years later, the Cabinet Secretary told me why: the highest honours had to have Prime Ministerial approval and when Mrs Thatcher inspected the proposed list of Dames, she said, 'We can't give a DBE to an orchestral musician.'

Such was the perception of that lady, so far as I am aware a comprehensive philistine, of a profession demanding exceptional talent, long training, stringent discipline, arduous preparation, emotional commitment and nerve-racking execution: all for a generally paltry remuneration. (Things changed a little in 2000 when the admirable Thea King, clarinettist, was made a Dame.)

Sidonie's MBE had come in 1974; she was promoted to OBE in 1980. Not nearly good enough, but better than the initial MBE. Between the two awards she was with the BBC Symphony Orchestra, under Pierre Boulez and Charles Groves, when the orchestra toured Japan in 1975. The tour was strenuous, as were the programmes. She was seventy-six, but never once failed in musicality or cheerfulness. She was an example to us all, and I was a lucky witness of her conduct.

Her last public appearance came in 1991 when she emerged from retirement to accompany Dame Gwyneth Jones in her own arrangement of *The Last Rose of Summer* on the Last Night of the Proms. To her hundredth birthday concert on 20th October 1999 I have already referred, but it should be recorded that there were six harpists among the many performers, who all gave their services, and that the music included works by her first husband, Hyam Greenbaum, and by her brother, Eugene.

In the summer of 2001 I found myself staying not far from her home near Dorking and one hot afternoon I visited her for a cup of coffee. She was in her 102nd year and could walk only with a zimmer, but her sitting posture was upright, her elegant hair a silky white, her voice strong (if a little hoarse), her memory completely lucid: she gave me, on the phone, faultless instructions how to reach her rural farmhouse. We fell immediately to gossiping and were talking about Pierre Boulez when John Bird dropped in, with an enormous, friendly French sheepdog. She had told me that he lived nearby and called on her most days to see that all was well. I had read a piece by John in (I think) *The Guardian* which was, in effect, a eulogy on the occasion of Pierre's seventy-fifth birthday and he now confirmed his enchantment with his music. He had recently been to hear the first performance of *Notations 7*; he had been present in Edinburgh, as I had, at the first performance of *sur incises* and – much earlier, in London – of *Répons*. Now he said that *Le Marteau sans Maître* had opened up a new and refreshing sound-world for him. Knowing him only as a comic actor of genius and having laughed helplessly at his duologues with John Fortune, I was very glad – and distinctly tickled – to make *him* laugh with a story about Malcolm Sargent's snobbery, originally told me by Sidonie's brother, Leon.

Sidonie now said that she had always found Sargent perfectly agreeable and reports of his womanizing hard to believe (I begged to differ). She could not remember who had succeeded him with the BBC Symphony Orchestra, so we went through the succession: Rudolf Schwarz, Antal Dorati ('Ah yes,' she said, 'Dorati always looked round the orchestra and said, "Oh good, we have a Goossens today"'), Colin Davis, Pierre Boulez ('We write to each other twice a year and he hopes to come to see me when he's here for the Proms'), Rudolf Kempe ('Poor man, he hardly began'), Gennadi Rozhdestvensky ('I loved *him*') and John Pritchard ('Such a good musician'). Then, to change the subject, and out of natural curiosity, I asked her why her first husband, Hyam Greenbaum, had been known as 'Bumps'. 'Well,' she said, 'he was very interested in…you know, the head…' 'Phrenology,' said John. 'Yes – and so Greenbaum, Greenbump, bump, Bumps.' (Later she told me he had died of drink.) 'Was he,' I said, 'related to the pianist, Kyla Greenbaum?' 'Yes – and she was remarkable; she gave the first British performance of the Schoenberg Piano Concerto, in Bedford, from memory: she knew *every* orchestral entry.' John then remarked that the pianist Pierre-Laurent Aimard had, a night or two before, played Messiaen's *Turangalîla Symphony* from memory at a televised Prom – an amazing feat, we all agreed. But Sidonie confessed that tinnitus prevented her from listening to much music since the sounds were all distorted, though from time to time the complaint receded, only to return.

John now withdrew and I sensed she was tiring. But, before leaving, I asked her about her domestic arrangements, for there was no sign of anyone else in the house. 'Well, there are two nice girls, one of whom always sleeps here. And in the daytime I have this alarm [an electronic 'bell' round her neck] which rings in various nearby houses. If nobody's in – well, too bad! But I *won't* go into a home. T*his* is my home and I'm going to stay here!'

I was awe-struck by her courage and her resilient good humour. After the death of her second husband, Norman Millar who, he had said, 'adored' her, she had replied to my letter (though I had told her not to),

> Yes Robert, we had a wonderfully happy forty-five years together and forty of those years spent here in this little Paradise – Norman never

wanted to leave this place...I am alone now – I don't want anybody to live here with me – I prefer to be on my own with my thoughts and memories.

At Christmas 2001 her card told me that, 'I have been rather ill and frightened everyone around me – I'm glad I survived because I have all my cards to write – but it was a nasty shock.' A few weeks later, when I visited her, she said it had been a small stroke, but there was no sign of any after-effects: she was completely lucid, her speech and handwriting as clear as ever, her attitude cheerfully fatalistic. Her only complaint was of a chronically painful shoulder. When I recommended cannabis she told me, with naughty glee, that she would certainly try to obtain some. At a mere seventy-five, I found her quite simply rejuvenating; the sheer warmth of her personality ensured that, even at 102, she had innumerable friends and admirers.

A great lady – who should have been a Dame.

Philip Jones

From time to time one hears on Radio 3 brass ensemble playing of astonishing brilliance and unanimity. It is likely to be by the Philip Jones Brass Ensemble, whose eponymous founder I guess I met soon after joining the BBC in 1972.

* * * * *

Philip Jones was one of those musicians who set standards for a generation: under his influence the trumpet and the brass ensemble acquired a status previously denied them. He insisted, by his own impeccable standards, by his energy and his charm, that the trumpet be taken as seriously as any other instrument, not as an accident-prone, raffish poor relation. When he gave up playing he embarked upon a second career as conservatoire principal, later taking up charitable work on behalf of musicians.

Philip Mark Jones was born in Bath, to a family of brass musicians: his father was to join the BBC Symphony Orchestra in 1939. By the age of nine Philip was playing the bugle as a sea cadet. At eleven he was promoted to trumpet and cornet in the Battersea Grammar School Brass Band and a year later he embarked upon lessons with Ernest Hall, the doyen of orchestral trumpeters. In 1944 he won a scholarship to the Royal College of Music.

His professional career took off when he was engaged, at the age of twenty, as fourth (bass) trumpet in the Royal Opera House Orchestra; at twenty-one he was appointed first trumpet, playing for Erich Kleiber among others. His name was made, and, remarkably, he became, in succession, principal trumpet of the major London orchestras: the Royal Philharmonic (1956-60), the Philharmonia (1960-4), the London Philharmonic (1964-5), the New Philharmonia (1965-7) and the BBCSO (1960-71). As an extra player with the Philharmonia in the early 1950s he was booked by the orchestra manager, Ursula Strebi, who later remarked that 'I engaged Philip Jones and Philip Jones then engaged me.' The couple were married in 1956 and Ursula, a woman of phenomenal mental and physical energy, proved to be the ideally devoted support to one whose profession was inherently stressful. Principal trumpets occupy a very hot seat.

In 1947 Jones heard by chance a BBC broadcast by a Dutch ensemble, all brass members of the Concertgebouw Orchestra, and it fired his imagination. Work in the opera pit did not inspire him, nor was he interested in endlessly performing baroque concerto arrangements. So, in 1951, he formed the Brass Ensemble that bore his name. Initially its members all came from the Royal Opera House Orchestra.

Initially, too, there was almost no natural repertoire for a brass quintet. They started with the *Theme and Variations* of John Gardner, a Covent Garden colleague, and simultaneously began to explore the early repertoire, Giovanni Gabrieli and Johann Pezel in particular. Their first broadcast, in April 1952, included the Gardner piece and a specially commissioned *Scherzo* by Gordon Jacob.

Gradually a flexible group was developed which often worked with the 'early music' choirs of Paul Steinitz, John Eliot Gardiner and Roger Norrington. Later it became a fixture at David Willcocks's Christmas Carol Concert at the Albert Hall. But Jones remained deeply committed to the idea of brass chamber music in its own right. He began to commission both new works and arrangements of existing repertoire, so that complete concerts of brass music became viable.

In the early 1960s Jones began to involve Elgar Howarth, a trumpet-player who shared his views about contemporary music. (The two were the soloists in Iain Hamilton's *Circus*, a hair-raisingly difficult work premiered by the LPO in 1969.) Howarth was to play an important part in the Ensemble's development and, in 1977, he conducted the recording of his own arrangement of Mussorgsky's *Pictures at an Exhibition*. This was acclaimed as worthy to stand beside Ravel's version and it became a staple of the Ensemble's repertoire. Thanks to its now well established reputation and to Jones's persistence, original scores were commissioned from, or offered by, Hans Werner Henze, Richard Rodney Bennett, Toru Takemitsu, Harrison Birtwistle and Witold Lutosławski among many others.

Ceremonial dates came the Ensemble's way. And they toured – all over the UK, and to more than thirty countries overseas.

Jones had declared that he would retire at fifty, in 1978, but, always remarkably fit, he continued until June 1986, his decision oddly hastened by an accident in which he ran over and crushed his own trumpet-case. For more than ten years he had interested himself in teaching and had promoted brass summer schools in Canterbury and Lincoln. He had been head of wind, brass and percussion at the Royal Northern College of Music and had held a similar post at the Guildhall School of Music and Drama. So it seemed a natural progression when, in 1988, he was appointed principal of Trinity College of Music.

Trinity College, when he took it over, was rather dim; it had neither the perceived nor the official status of the other London conservatoires. Jones quite simply turned it round, by vigorous reorganization and innovation. His reforms were not only musical but also practical. He converted the college's examinations department into a successful commercial company whose profits returned to the college through a trust. But it was the musical standards which meant most to him, and his success in this area was such that, a few months after he retired in 1994, the college was awarded an 'excellent' grading, an achievement which simultaneously gave it the same status, officially, as its Royal competitors, the College and the Academy.

Before retiring from Trinity, Jones served for a number of years on the awards and trusts committee of the Musicians Benevolent Fund, latterly as chairman. Then, in 1995, he took on the chairmanship of the fund itself. In this role he was energetic and involved, once memorably demonstrating one of six antiquated trumpets commissioned for Covent Garden's *Aida* in 1894 and donated to the Fund for an auction a hundred years later. The trumpets, notoriously, did not 'blow well', but Jones's well-preserved skill was equal to their capriciousness.

Philip Jones was a refreshing personality. He had no side and always spoke his mind, sometimes so impulsively as to disconcert his colleagues. Scornful of increasing commercialism in the performing arts, he was once heard to declare that a well-known musicians' agency was creating 'new standards of greed'. But where young artists were concerned he was solicitous and thoughtful, if uncompromising.

In constant demand for competitions and auditions, he was highly respected as a top-class performing musician whose teaching and leadership skills were exceptional. Appointed OBE in 1977, he was advanced to CBE in 1986.

His wife Ursula survives him.

The Times, 19th January 2000

ADMINISTRATORS

Moran Caplat

When, in 1949, Rudolf Bing moved to New York to administer the Metropolitan Opera, his deputy, Moran Caplat, inherited the management of Glyndebourne Opera. He and Ian Hunter (see page 102) were my first tutors in the skills of arts administration.

* * * * *

As its general administrator for more than thirty years, Moran Caplat, who has died aged eighty-six, brought continuity to Glyndebourne Opera. He joined the company on his twenty-ninth birthday in 1945 and retired on his sixty-fifth in 1981, showing, in the meantime, a single-minded loyalty to the Glyndebourne ethos.

Early on, while still serving as assistant to the then general manager, Rudolf Bing, Caplat was head-hunted by the English Opera Group; but it was as well that he stayed put, for he succeeded to the top administrative job in 1949.

The following year, with admirable diplomatic finesse, Caplat coaxed back as musical director the great Fritz Busch. After Busch died in 1951, he was followed, successively, by Vittorio Gui, John Pritchard and Bernard Haitink, of whom Caplat said, 'Every time he leaves the stage door at Covent Garden, he feels glad that he is one day nearer Glyndebourne.'

On the production side, Carl Ebert was succeeded by Günther Rennert, Franco Enriquez and John Cox. Such sharply differing personalities represented powerful modulations in Glyndebourne's musical strategy, and Caplat supervised the changes with tact and sympathy.

More fundamental to the opera's future was the death, in 1953, of Audrey Christie, the admirable singer, hostess and wife of Glyndebourne's owner, John Christie. She had been her husband's ideal complement: she made his often wild ambitions workable, and her absence threw an extra responsibility onto Caplat, who became adept at handling the idiosyncrasies of the grieving widower. When John Christie himself died in 1962, Caplat's role became even more central.

Not that he was ever simply a co-ordinating presence. Far from it. He brought, for example, Peter Hall to Glyndebourne, and encouraged Raymond Leppard's enthusiasm for Monteverdi and Cavalli. And the wonderfully successful, semi-staged Proms performances were, in effect, redirected by Caplat himself so that they worked in the Royal Albert Hall.

Caplat was born on the north Kent coast, to a French architect father and an English mother whose own father had been a theatre manager of some status. Such music as he heard was bandstand stuff; his love of opera came later. But he grew up within sight of the sea, and was sailing dinghies solo in his early teens. Then, at fifteen, he saw *Twelfth Night* and was stage-struck. He went to RADA, where he did well – Bernard Shaw saw him as the Lion in *Androcles and the Lion* – graduating to Margate Rep and, later, to the Unity Theatre.

Somehow he combined sailing with acting and, as a member of the Royal Ocean Racing Club, took part in some big races. The threat of war forced him to abandon a plan to sail round the world in 1939, and when the threat became a reality, he enlisted in the RNVR, serving on the northern patrol, and later navigating a paddle steamer to Dunkirk. He trained as a submariner, but near Malta his boat was depth-charged and had to surface; the survivors were imprisoned in Italy.

Caplat's nerve suffered during this period and, on returning to submarines, he found that he had developed claustrophobia – characteristically, he recorded that he was ashamed of being 'shit-scared' – and was posted ashore. By then, he had already made contact with Glyndebourne, which he had visited with an uncle who worked there. Uncertain of his future as an actor, he was glad, if surprised, when, after quite casual interviews with Bing and the Christies, he was appointed as Bing's assistant. Glyndebourne had its downs as well as its ups, but to criticize it in Caplat's presence was to incur a fearsome wrath, in which both the sea-dog and the actor played their parts consummately: the beard was an important cosmetic aspect of his persona.

He was always elegant in coiffure and stance, dapper in dress, diplomatic in negotiation, a peacemaker when rows erupted. He could be formidable; he was often very funny. In other words, he was ideally equipped for a job whose various demands called for a versatile touch: a round peg in a round hole he occupied almost by accident. He was lucky. So was Glyndebourne.

Caplat called his dashing memoirs *Dinghies to Divas* (1985), reflecting his twin passions of opera and the sea. When the company was in

Liverpool in 1956, he had the idea of uniting the two through touring performances on an aircraft-carrier. But though the proposal was widely aired, no such vehicle could be located, and Glyndebourne remained a landlubber.

He is survived by his wife Diana, whom he married in 1944, and their three children.

The Guardian, 27th June 2003

Ian Hunter

Ian Hunter inherited from Rudolf Bing the direction of the Edinburgh Festival and for five years (1951-5) I was his assistant. At heart a canny Scot, he was fun to work for – and with. He taught me a great deal, most of all about negotiation with opera and theatre companies.

* * * * *

To describe Ian Hunter as the most successful impresario of his generation is to undervalue a large part of his achievement. He was surely unique in migrating from the promotional world of the performing arts, whether commercial or subsidized, to the sphere of disinterested charitable activity.

A highly imaginative festival director and initiator, an astute and considerate artist's agent, he was in due course to become chairman of the Council of the Royal Society of Arts, founder of the Young Concert Artists Trust (a non-commercial agency for young soloists) and chairman of the Musicians Benevolent Fund, whose work benefited substantially from his sound business sense. His father was a Scot, and Hunter strikingly displayed many of the talents of that gifted race. He was very shrewd: he never neglected a useful contact, he had a nose for future fashion, he went about his business with discretion and charm. He was unrivalled in the unobtrusive skill with which he coaxed large sums of money out of tough and apparently philistine city fathers, whether in London or Hong Kong. But he was more than merely a smart operator. As Isaac Stern observed at the amazing seventieth birthday concert in the Royal Albert Hall, Hunter went on enjoying music and the company of musicians. The galaxy of eminent artists who associated themselves with that concert was itself testimony to the affection and respect in which he was held.

Born in 1919, Ian Bruce Hope Hunter was the youngest of the five children of a Scottish stockbroker and his English wife. He was educated at a prep school in Dorset and at Fettes, where he learned the horn and resolved to become a musician, if possible a conductor. Unsuccessful in the Oxford entrance exam, he was already studying with Donald Tovey, then professor of music at Edinburgh University. Tovey was a fine musician and his lessons qualified Hunter for a post as assistant to Fritz Busch, then music director at Glyndebourne. For two years (1938-9) he was a jack-of-all-trades: he made notes for Busch, copied orchestral parts and even appeared on stage – in the silent role of Fleance in *Macbeth*. Barely twenty, he was highly susceptible and was known in the company as 'Cherubino'. At one point he accompanied Busch on a Scandinavian tour and encountered Rachmaninoff and Nathan Milstein, whom he was to represent many years later.

When war was declared in September 1939, Ian Hunter enlisted. He served in North Africa and Italy, reaching the rank of lieutenant-colonel. Before demobilization he found time to establish a symphony orchestra, the Philharmonica Romagna, which entertained the troops in and around Ravenna, and to re-open the opera house in Klagenfurt. He was given permission to fraternize with the Austrians and, in assembling a complete company, he tasted for the first time the pleasure and satisfaction of working with professional musicians towards the thrilling goal of public performance. The impresario was born.

Meanwhile John Christie, Audrey Mildmay and Rudolf Bing had visited Edinburgh and proposed a great international arts festival there. Leaving the army, Hunter approached Bing, then general manager at Glyndebourne and shortly to become the Edinburgh Festival's artistic director, and Bing engaged him as his assistant in planning the first festival, in 1947. Three years later, when Bing moved to the Metropolitan Opera, Hunter succeeded him.

He was in his element and the six festivals he directed (1950-5) demonstrated not only his flair and showmanship but also the wide range of his interests. He was particularly proud of having brought the visual arts into the festival. A Rembrandt exhibition in 1950 was followed by Spanish Painting and then a fine series of French Impressionists: Degas, Renoir, Cézanne, Gauguin. Most memorable, because most exotic and extravagant (Richard Buckle, the organizer, seemed daily to demand a bigger budget) was the Diaghilev Exhibition of 1954, the precursor, as yet unsurpassed, of all those exhibitions at which presentation has assumed the importance it deserves.

In music Hunter was equally innovative. In 1951 he brought over – they came by sea – the New York Philharmonic, who gave no less than fourteen programmes under Bruno Walter and Dimitri Mitropoulos.

He was not afraid, next year, to ruffle Glyndebourne's feathers by engaging the Hamburg State Opera to present six productions, never, of course, seen in Britain before, with Georg Solti among the conductors. He invited Beecham to preside over the *Royal Fireworks Music* on the Castle Esplanade. He brought dance companies from Communist Eastern Europe and from Japan. He persuaded great soloists to play chamber music together and in 1953, in celebration of four centuries of the violin, he commissioned the *Corelli Fantasy* from Michael Tippett, by no means then a fashionable composer.

He was already seeking to spread his wings and it was characteristic of his foresight that he took an interest in the firm of Harold Holt, whose board he joined in 1953. When Holt died not long afterwards, Hunter succeeded him as managing director, necessarily declaring an interest in any Holt artist he wished to engage at the Edinburgh Festival.

Harold Holt Ltd was to be the central platform of Hunter's professional life for many years. He resigned its chairmanship and became its president in 1988 but this was not simply a matter of being kicked upstairs: he was in the office four days a week until well into his seventies.

During his association with it, the firm expanded and diversified extensively but it never lost its original character as an agency devoted to the development of the careers of artists of importance – or potential importance: Daniel Barenboim was signed up when he was fourteen. And Hunter, who enjoyed creating and running arts festivals, was not slow to see that Harold Holt artists could advantageously be featured in festivals organized by Harold Holt.

This is not to suggest that the many festivals that he created so successfully – the City of London (1962), Brighton (1967), Windsor (1969), Hong Kong (1973) and Malvern (1977), among them – did not have their own character and integrity. The Bath Festival, where began a long association with Yehudi Menuhin, he had in any case launched in 1948.

Characteristic of Ian Hunter's capacity for thinking big was the Commonwealth Arts Festival of 1965. In preparing it he visited twenty-three countries, and it was held simultaneously, over two weeks, in London, Glasgow, Cardiff and Liverpool. Dance was strongly featured: Caribbean, African and Indian groups rubbed friendly shoulders with classical companies from Australia and Canada. Jazz jostled with the classics. Menuhin shared a platform with Ravi Shankar. Balloons were released and fireworks rocketed. Hunter believed festivals should be festive, and it was a nice touch that all the participants were rewarded with a handsome medal.

Meanwhile, Harold Holt flourished. Hunter's appointments to its senior staff were of a calibre to leave him more time to diversify his activities. In the late 1960s and early 1970s he sat on a number of Arts Council committees, and as president of the British Arts Festivals Association from 1978 to 1981 he established himself as the doyen of festival animateurs.

In 1981 he was elected chairman of the council of the Royal Society of Arts. His inaugural address, delivered in November 1981, was devoted to 'Aspects of the Arts in Postwar Britain'. He was not a natural speaker, but the imaginative range of his lecture was impressive: 'I do implore the authorities,' he said, 'not to consider education in the arts as a "recreational" subject and peripheral to the main concerns of education.' At much the same time he was associated with the Royal College of Music's ambitious and successful appeal.

Ian Hunter was knighted in 1983 and having moved, whether by accident or design, in the direction of the Establishment, he now indubitably ranked as one of the great and the good. He was always careful to maintain useful contacts in the diplomatic corps, and these enabled him to mastermind two very large festivals, those of America (1985) and of the German Arts (1987). In 1991 he was vice-chairman of the grandiose Japan Festival.

His family life was certainly happy, but without doubt tempestuous. He married Susan Russell in 1949 and with her had four daughters. During her long illness and until her eventual death in 1977 from cancer, his concern for her took firm precedence over his professional commitments. His undisguised grief at her memorial service was touching. Seven years later he married Marie, the widow of Sir Keith Showering. ('I don't have to make a lady of her,' he remarked.) A common interest in parrots, they claimed, was what brought them together.

Hunter developed other hobbies. He had a modest but attractive talent as a painter and he enjoyed gardening. He also took up hunting, and had a serious fall in 1979. The circulation to one leg was interrupted and he was lucky that it was saved. This accident noticeably slowed him down, both physically and mentally, but he was courageous and robust, and within a year or two he was on form again. His marriage to Marie Showering, perhaps because of her relative lack of interest in the arts, did not last into his old age.

The programme for his seventieth birthday concert contained two portraits: on the cover, a water-colour by Hugh Casson; inside, a sketch by Gerard Hoffnung. (The latter is inscribed 'For my little 10 per cent, with love from Gerard'.) The two pictures neatly encapsulate two facets of Hunter's character. Casson's shows an unsmiling tycoon, the mouth a thin, hard line. It is not flattering, but the subject was a tough negotiator and sometimes seemed hard-bitten. Indeed there was some initial opposition to his appointment to the Musicians Benevolent Fund on these very grounds.

But those who knew him well must surely prefer Hoffnung's sketch. It too depicts a tycoon, but one exuding cheerfulness and warmth, the mouth an up-turned grin, the eyes screwed up in laughter. Ian Hunter was great fun to be with: he had a large repertoire of anecdotes, mostly comic, some touching; he was happy to deflate himself; at times he giggled, irrepressibly, like a naughty schoolboy.

Behind both façades was a fine character, devoted to his artists, among whom were musicians of the calibre of Kubelík, Milstein, Stern, Haendel, Haitink and Barenboim, and to the integrity of his profession, of which he was a most distinguished and enterprising practitioner. He was, above all, an ideas man. He was exceptional in having the flair, expertise and tenacity to realize them.

The Times, 10th September 2003

John Drummond

Though I did not emerge unscathed from John Drummond's memoirs, *Tainted by Experience*, I found it impossible not to warmly admire a man with such passionate concern for the highest possible standards in music and the arts. And I sometimes envied his voluble articulacy.

* * * * *

In 1958 John Drummond applied for the job of assistant to the director of the Edinburgh Festival, Robert Ponsonby [this was an anonymous obituary]. He made a good impression and was offered the job on the spot. But there was a snag: the annual salary was a non-incremental £600. So, sensibly, as it turned out, he soon afterwards joined the BBC, as a trainee, at £625 with increments. He was to return to the festival, as its director, twenty years later, having meanwhile made his mark not only as a gifted director of TV arts programmes, but as a man obsessed by the arts in general and dance in particular.

To everything he did he brought a highly personal stamp, which derived as much from his conviction that none of the arts should be self-contained as from his passionate concern with quality. In a book that made him laugh, Caryl Brahms and S.J. Simon's A *Bullet in the Ballet*, an elderly dancer, once himself a noted Petrushka, shoots dead three younger interpreters of the role on the sole ground that they dance it badly. *Mutatis mutandis*, Drummond would cheerfully have slaughtered a considerable number of his colleagues – and not only the younger ones – who fell short of his own high standards or who failed to understand the transcendent importance of the arts.

Born in London in 1934 to a Scottish sea captain and an Australian singer (mainly of lieder), John Richard Gray Drummond grew up with parents of contradictory temperaments. His father was tone-deaf and often away at sea. Drummond, an only child, was much closer to his mother, who made him a happy home in Bournemouth, where the family moved in 1939, and where in due course the young Drummond haunted the local music library and the concerts of the municipal symphony orchestra.

After schooling, latterly at Canford, where he distinguished himself as an all-rounder, he embarked upon National Service with a major scholarship to Trinity College, Cambridge, already in his pocket. Poor eyesight kept him from active service and he took a course in Russian, qualifying as an interpreter. This skill turned out to be a valuable asset.

At Cambridge he at first thought he might become a history don but, like those of his contemporaries who became actors, musicians and impresarios, he was seduced by theatre and found himself involved in undergraduate productions, in cabaret and revue. He discovered that he had a talent for performance, he could make people laugh and had a sponge-like memory. Though never a Cambridge 'star' like Derek Jacobi or Jonathan Miller, he had glimpsed his métier, which seemed to lie in the communication of his passion for the serious arts.

The eighteen years that Drummond spent in the BBC heralded an unprecedented, and, alas, unrepeated, burgeoning of arts programmes on BBC Television. But he had first to go through some radio hoops, among them an unwelcome assignment to religious broadcasting. Within a year, though, he had a foothold in television and within two he was directing his first programmes, albeit for schools.

Not for the last time, however, he got up the noses of his bosses by speaking his mind with blistering candour, and his future at the BBC was in serious doubt until he was called on to act as an interpreter for Richard Dimbleby and David Attenborough in Moscow. Later, in the Paris office, he met, among others, Marlene Dietrich and Maurice

Chevalier, and he heard Pierre Boulez. He was happy in Paris, but his annual report noted that 'he does not suffer fools gladly.' He claimed to have taken this as a compliment and it has to be said that there were some fools he did not suffer at all.

He returned to London on the eve of the launch, early in 1964, of BBC2. Encouraged by Humphrey Burton, but not by the more senior Huw Wheldon, he made programmes around master-classes with Tortelier, the Leeds Piano Competition and, most memorably, about Diaghilev. For these he interviewed such legendary figures as Karsavina and Stravinsky, interviews which were printed, among others, in his absorbing *Speaking of Diaghilev*, published in 1997. His assistant on this project was Bob Lockyer, to whom the book was in effect dedicated and to whom he referred in his autobiography as having been 'central to my life for over thirty years'.

Irked by what he saw as harassment from Wheldon, who told him he lacked 'the common touch', and feeling that he may have shot his bolt at the BBC, Drummond cast around and was successful in his application for the directorship of the Edinburgh Festival. His predecessor, Peter Diamand, had tended to concentrate on the musical side of the programme and upon a somewhat repetitive roster of very eminent artists. Drummond saw his chance both to vary this formula and to bring into play his interest in the inter-relation of the arts.

This interest manifested itself most clearly in his first (1979) and last (1983) festivals, the linking themes being 'Diaghilev' and 'Vienna 1900', respectively. In 1979 Diaghilev's influence was apparent in opera, ballet, concerts, lectures and an exhibition. 'Vienna 1900' proved even more pervasive, performances of music by Schoenberg, Berg, Webern and Zemlinsky being complemented by manifestations of Kokoschka and Charles Rennie Mackintosh, of Rilke, Hofmannsthal and Werfel. This festival was Drummond's most successful demonstration of cross-fertilization in the arts and he was rightly proud of it.

In other respects his record at Edinburgh was uneven: there were superb discoveries such as the Rustaveli Company and the Opera Theatre of St Louis, but there were also some serious disappointments. Nobody could say, though, that things were dull. The lowering of four near-naked Japanese actors, upside-down, from the roof of the Lothian Regional Council's offices was the apogee of various street activities; there was a rapprochement with the Fringe, fireworks from the Castle battlements to accompany Handel's music in Prince's Street Gardens, and the Big Tent (for dance) in the Meadows. All these demonstrated

Drummond's concern to involve the man in the street and to placate that element among the city fathers who, ignoring that the festival brought millions of pounds into the city, begrudged the niggardly contribution they made to its finances.

It was upon this rock, and the lamentable neglect of the King's and Lyceum theatres, the Usher Hall and its organ, that his relationship with his employers foundered. Invited to extend his contract he decided, at a very late stage, not to do so; his departure was in effect a resignation.

Between 1983 and 1985 Drummond recharged his batteries, worked on his Diaghilev book, travelled restlessly, stayed with Hans Werner Henze in Italy and Elizabeth Frink in Dorset, founded and chaired the National Dance Co-ordinating Committee and flirted with the Adelaide Festival, whose 1988 season he was invited to direct. But in 1984, he had a call from Alasdair Milne, director-general of the BBC, which led, first, to his appointment as Controller, Music, and then to the controllership of Radio 3, the former post being sensibly subsumed in the latter. Both brought with them the bonus of planning the Proms, which Drummond addressed with relish.

His annual press conference generally produced some quotably controversial comment, among them, apropos the artists appearing that year, 'You can see I am using a prepared script. If I have left anyone out, it was deliberate.' But during his Proms reign few important musicians were left out, the programmes were imaginative and audiences steadily increased. Indeed, the Proms had never had so high a profile. This was helped by the happy coincidence of the series' hundredth birthday, which Drummond ingeniously exploited in 1994 ('the first hundred years') and 1995 ('the centenary season').

In the latter year, his last, he commissioned from Harrison Birtwistle – for of all nights the Last Night – a piece called *Panic*, for saxophone and orchestra. Predictably, he got into trouble with the Hooray Henrys, and BBC Television; the antithesis of his first season, when his announcement of 'Dance' as the linking theme got him into trouble with the purists.

The BBC's symphony orchestras, notoriously described by John Birt in answer to a question from Drummond as 'a variable resource centre whose viability depends upon the business plan of the Controller of Radio 3', were another of his responsibilities and with them, despite such admirable appointments as Andrew Davis to the BBCSO, he was not so happy: he thought the musicians truculent, while they reckoned he addressed them *de haut en bas*. The orchestras' usefulness was nevertheless central and Drummond pioneered the negotiation of a new contract which was advantageous both to the musicians and to the BBC.

As to the network and its tone of voice, Drummond believed in providing more stimulating information and, above all, a sense of spontaneity. As he put it: 'I did not like being read at all the time.' But some of his announcers were not confident enough to improvise and some of his producers were not good broadcasters; so there were casualties.

Radio 3 nevertheless changed perceptibly, and for the better, while there were exciting experiments such as the 1990 weekend from Berlin, which offered not only opera and concerts, but features and talks. A similar weekend was broadcast the following year from Minneapolis and St Paul, and Drummond regarded these two events as peaks in his achievement for Radio 3.

Rather gangling in youth, John Drummond grew into a bulky and imposing middle age. His eye was beady, his voice orotund (he could snort, even harrumph), his delivery so torrential that there were those who believed that, like some oboists, he had mastered circular breathing. A frequent public speaker, generally extempore and often in some charitable cause, he had an apparently inexhaustible fund of anecdotes, some funny, all telling.

He could be scathing: he described Brian Kay, a popular presenter, as 'someone who never uses one cliché when two will do and has all the unctuousness of a stage curate.' And his contempt was caustic. He reserved it for people such as Birt, and, famously, Nigel Kennedy, whose distracting sartorial self-indulgence and artificial estuary accent outraged him.

Kennedy, who had got under his skin by telling him he had 'an attitude problem', asserted that Drummond exemplified 'the typical arrogance of a self-appointed guardian of the arts world'. And it is true that Drummond could be arrogant and vain and intolerant, and that he could drop names like confetti at a society wedding, that he did, indeed, enjoy moving among the glitterati, that he claimed as friends some who were surprised by that description and that he was capable of taking credit for the achievement of others.

But these failings stemmed from the personality of someone formidably intelligent and well informed, who cared passionately about the arts and about artists (even the censorious Wheldon reported: 'I have never met an artist who did not respect and admire him'), and who was as a result inordinately impatient: impatient to reach his artistic goals, impatient with those who irrationally resisted change, impatient with intellectual nonentities and petty bureaucrats.

No wonder he offended people. But his autobiography, *Tainted by Experience* (the title quoted from the sneer of a desk-bound BBC suit) is testimony to a man who had panache, the guts to take risks, and who didn't mind – who indeed enjoyed – putting supercilious noses out of joint. How grey and narrow the arts world will seem without his gadfly brilliance.

John Drummond was appointed CBE in 1990 and knighted in 1995. Bob Lockyer survives him.

The Times, 8th September 2006

Chris Samuelson

Chris Samuelson was an unsung hero whose friendship, and whose professional support between 1972 and 1982, were wholly indispensable.

* * * * *

In May 1972, William Glock, whom I was shortly to succeed at the BBC, invited me to join him on the BBC Symphony Orchestra's Swiss tour so that I could familiarize myself with the orchestra, with BBC procedures and, particularly, those relating to public concerts. Describing the unit known as 'Concerts Management' he said, 'The key figure is Chris Samuelson. He is first class. You can rely upon him absolutely.'

Accordingly, I asked Chris to come to talk to me within a day or two of taking over as Controller, Music, in early December. I took to him immediately and for nearly ten years he was in and out of my office every day; he was always welcome. He was slight, grey-haired (he was already fifty), quick and energetic. Nothing was too much trouble, no problem insoluble. Once, in William's time, he had located and retrieved, from his office in London, a 'lost' conductor by arranging a public address announcement in Grand Central Station, New York. If I was on tour with the Symphony Orchestra, whether in Russia or Japan, he would phone me at precisely the time agreed, which often meant, for him, some altogether unearthly hour. By the end of the Proms quite yellow with fatigue, he was nevertheless invariably good-tempered and when I asked him how he managed this he explained that during the Normandy landings his tank had been hit, the man beside him killed and himself very badly burned. 'You see,' he said, 'I am so glad to be alive.'

Chris's face did indeed show the scars of plastic surgery, and he once said something to me which suggested that the burns had affected his generative capacity, perhaps had actually mutilated him. In any case, he did not marry and had no steady girlfriend. But he was a devoted and much loved godfather.

Outside his work, he had a single hobby, photography, and in the studio, at rehearsals, back-stage, in green-rooms, he took hundreds of photographs of innumerable important musicians, among them Adrian Boult, Pierre Boulez, Rudolf Kempe and Gennadi Rozhdestvensky. In his late seventies he offered this documentary archive to the BBC, who declined it. I thought this a mean response, but one not uncharacteristic of the Birtist regime which had at its heart a mechanistic philistinism.

Chris died in the spring of 2001. At his cremation there was music by Bach and Mozart. The BBC was not represented (unless, informally, by myself), but amends were made at a Prom on 12th August 2001 when I ended a short printed tribute to him with these words:

> Loyal, modest and kindly, there was not a grain of malice in Chris; he was a lovely colleague and a mainstay of the Proms.

William Glock

William Glock was of course 'a hard act to follow'. A natural insurgent, with immense authority and energy, I found him helpful and supportive; and I was happy to invite him to play – the Mozart E Flat Piano Quartet with members of the Lindsay Quartet – at my first Proms season in 1974.

* * * * *

'Your charm may be important, but your obstinacy is infinitely more so.' Pierre Boulez's remark astutely captured two of William Glock's most characteristic qualities. For Glock was a man with a mission. In his autobiography, *Notes in Advance* (1991), he spoke of music as 'a cause' to which he had devoted himself. It particularly embodied the necessity 'to campaign for ideas that seemed forward-looking'. From time to time it amounted to 'a campaign of insurrection'.

In one sense, Glock's passionate commitment to contemporary music was surprising, for his early years were musically conventional.

Born, in 1908, to a mother not specially musical and a schoolmaster father who was a choral conductor and a modest composer, he learned the piano as a child and, at the age of nine, was playing Mozart, Beethoven and Chopin to the boys at his father's school.

Two years later he won a scholarship to Christ's Hospital, where he took up the viola and the organ; his piano repertoire grew to encompass Debussy and Rachmaninoff. As an organist he became an associate of the Royal College of Organists at the age of sixteen, and in 1926 he won an organ scholarship to Caius College, Cambridge, where he read history, devoting his fourth year to a music degree, which he failed, despite many successes as a keyboard player.

Early in 1930, Glock heard Artur Schnabel playing Beethoven and Schubert in Oxford. He was bowled over and immediately determined, at whatever cost, to study with that great musician. Helped by Edward Dent, an influential mentor, he travelled to Berlin and was accepted as a pupil, though not without some hesitation on Schnabel's part.

The three years which followed – two in Berlin, the third in Italy, where Schnabel moved when Hitler came to power – profoundly influenced Glock, as a musician of course, but more particularly as one with a European, rather than an insular, viewpoint. (Vaughan Williams and Howells, interviewing him for a bursary, had told him that it was quite unnecessary to study abroad and turned down his application.)

It was not until after returning to England in 1933 and beginning to review for, first, *The Daily Telegraph*, then, as a regular critic, *The Observer*, that Glock began to interest himself in contemporary music. Stravinsky, Bartók and Hindemith came first. Berg followed in 1936, when he heard the first performance in Britain of the Violin Concerto. Very early in the Second World War Tippett, who once told him that he 'suffered the pains of an artist, but enjoyed few of the rewards', became an object of his enthusiasm.

In 1941, Glock joined the RAF, somehow managing to combine his military duties with a fortnightly column for *The Observer*. There was not much free time: such as there was he occupied with learning Köchel numbers and Shakespeare sonnets, occasionally playing cricket with Cliff Michelmore. His reviews attracted much favourable attention, but they were not to the liking of Ivor Brown, the theatre critic who had taken over from J.L. Garvin, as general editor, and Glock was sacked in October 1945. He was soon to write for *Time and Tide* and, later, for the *New Statesman*.

Meanwhile, he left the RAF in 1946 and began to lecture, fortifying his apparently frail self-confidence with a Benzedrine tablet. Despite his nervousness, he had an obvious aptitude and, when the Third Programme was launched on 29th September 1946, he was regularly engaged for music talks. In the spring of 1947 the BBC despatched him upon a *tour d'horizon* to find out what had been going on in Europe since 1939. Germany, Austria and Prague did not yield much of exceptional interest but at the International Society for Contemporary Music (ISCM) Festival in Copenhagen he met Roberto Gerhard, whose principal champion he was to become, as well as Luigi Dallapiccola and Frank Martin.

Glock now had three powerful strings to his bow: he was a gifted, 'classical' pianist; he wrote with expert acuity about a wide range of music; and, as a lecturer, he was an able communicator. He was consequently the ideal candidate for the directorship of a new summer school which opened at Bryanston in 1948.

He was in his element. He enticed two great teachers, Nadia Boulanger and Hindemith, to give lectures. He planned, he played, he lectured. Later visitors included Enescu, Elisabeth Schumann and the inimitable Imogen Holst. For five years all went well, despite financial crises, one of which caused Glock to take on the responsibility himself. But in 1951 he visited Dartington and was captivated by its atmosphere – and its facilities. The summer school moved there in 1953 and Glock was to remain its director for twenty-six years, a span of time during which composition classes were given by, among others, Berio, Maderna, Nono, Lutosławski and Maxwell Davies. The pianists included Ashkenazy, Barenboim, Brendel, Postnikova and Perlemuter. Stravinsky, visiting in 1957, 'greatly enjoyed himself.'

Glock's energy was formidable: he had founded *The Score* in 1949 and continued to edit it until 1961, when the BBC, whose Controller, Music, he had become in 1959, insisted that he give it up. (To give up the alternative, Dartington, was unthinkable.) From 1954 to 1956 he was chairman of the music committee of the ICA, a position which kept him in touch with the ISCM. For a year or two, in the mid-1950s, he ran the International Music Association, an elegant club for musicians – 'your café', as Isaiah Berlin called it – which had been founded by Corinne Hubbard, his patron of *The Score*.

Early in 1959 he was, as it turned out, the favoured candidate for the post of principal of the Guildhall School of Music and it was 'with half an hour to spare' that he extricated himself from this commitment in order to accept the BBC's belated offer, strongly endorsed by Michael

Tippett, to become Controller, Music. Such was the BBC's current reputation for dull conventionality that Walter Legge, writing to congratulate him remarked that it was 'as though…Luther had just been elected Pope.'

Glock now had a uniquely advantageous platform to advance his campaign: through the orchestras and the Proms, through commissioning, through Third Programme and Music Programme, he could exercise a pervasive, hands-on influence both on studio recording and, particularly, on public concerts. He plunged in, and within a few months had embarked upon the Invitation Concerts, at the very first of which Boulez's *Le Marteau sans Maître* was sandwiched between two Mozart string quintets, a programme which also established his firm belief in the principle of mixed programming. At the 1960 Proms he determined 'to venture a few yards further out to sea where contemporary music was concerned'. Audiences declined, but the corner was turned in 1962.

Glock had first encountered Pierre Boulez in 1952, when the young composer had contributed to *The Score* a highly controversial essay, 'Schoenberg is Dead'. The two first met in 1955, but Glock did not hear Boulez conduct until 1963; the work was Berg's *Wozzeck*. He immediately engaged Boulez as a guest with the BBC Symphony Orchestra and there began a fruitful relationship of two like minds and, in due course, a radical campaign to transform the London scene and, through broadcasting, the taste of Third Programme listeners.

To the BBC Symphony Orchestra Glock had appointed Antal Dorati (in 1963) and Colin Davis (in 1967). When Davis moved to the Royal Opera House in 1971, Boulez succeeded him, staying on for four extraordinarily stimulating years and for a further two as a special guest. It was a percipient appointment for he had, initially, only a tiny repertoire and, as an interpreter, tended to be inflexible. With Boulez as *animateur* the Proms, and some winter season concerts, invaded the Round House for small-scale contemporary works, which were introduced and discussed.

When Glock, who had been knighted in 1970, retired from the BBC in 1972, he occupied a position of unique standing and his sheer authority was redoubtable. Under full sail, he could be awe-inspiring, though some junior colleagues, left bobbing, breathless, in his wake, had complained that they were not much consulted, while others wished that he had been more willing to share, outside a small charmed circle, some of the encounters with eminent musicians which naturally came his way. But, if not a loner, he was certainly self-sufficient. 'Do it first. Tell *them* afterwards,' he advised me when I succeeded him at the BBC. (By 'them' he meant the bureaucrats, including, particularly, his superiors.)

Already on the Covent Garden board, he now joined the Arts Council. But this was committee work and he needed more practical activity. This materialized in two invitations: to lecture at the Royal Northern College of Music and to edit a new series, Eulenburg Books, under the aegis of the publishers Schott. Even more welcome was his appointment to run the Bath Festival, as Michael Tippett's successor, a post he held for nine years until 1984.

Over the same period he took on the chairmanship of the London Orchestral Concerts Board, a body set up to bring some rational order to London's often chaotic, and always under-funded, orchestral life. To all of these activities, but most of all to those which involved him in programme building, he brought expertise, energy – and obstinacy.

There is a photograph of him, with John Amis in about 1950, in which he appears positively pugnacious: shoulders squared, jaw set, lower lip thrust out. That was one aspect of him. Another was his undoubted charm. A third was his vulnerability to emotion. The prospect of playing domestic piano duets was so beguiling that even in middle age he would admit to over-excitement. At a deeper level, he said of the early death of his daughter by his first wife, Clement Davenport: 'From such a loss one seems never to recover.' His second wife, Anne Geoffroy-Dechaume, was a wonderfully supportive woman, charmingly serene, whose long illness and death (in 1995) darkened his last years.

To the end, Glock remained, in his own words, 'possessed by music'. In 1996, at Radio 3's invitation, he planned a small-scale programme (as did each of his successors at the BBC) to celebrate the fiftieth birthday of the 'Third'. It was wholly characteristic, comprising, as it did, works by Pierre Boulez (*Dérive*, written for him); Roberto Gerhard, whom he had championed; Elliott Carter, a dear friend; and the ever-essential Mozart.

Glock was fond of quoting Edward Dent's remark, apropos resigning, 'There is no strength in absence.' Sadly, William Glock's own dauntless strength is now absent from the musical community.

The Independent, 1st July 2000

1 Dinner at the Mitre Hotel, Oxford, 2nd February 1912, including Adrian Boult (*left*) and Noel Ponsonby, the author's father (*right*)

2A Adrian Boult in old age at the Royal Albert Hall, *c.*1977

2B Sena Jurinac coaching Amanda Roocroft at Canterbury Festival master-classes in 1988

3 Sena Jurinac, *c.*1950

4A
Thomas Beecham at Edinburgh, 1956

4B
Isaac Stern and Myra Hess at Edinburgh, 1960

5 Clara Haskil at the keyboard, Lausanne, 1957

6A
Clara Haskil, Besançon Festival, 1956

6B
Sam Bor, Jacqueline du Pré and Daniel Barenboim playing chamber music in the author's Glasgow flat, 14th January 1967

7 Günter Wand rehearsing the BBC Symphony Orchestra, *c.*1983

8 Pierre Boulez rehearsing the BBC Symphony Orchestra, *c.*1975

Ernest Warburton

Very soon after my arrival at the BBC in 1972, Ernest Warburton, then head of music at the BBC in Manchester, sensibly made it his business to suss me out. He was the complete professional, knowledgeable, energetic and thorough, if not always easy. But the range of his interests – J.C. Bach, Wagner, Britten – was amazing and I was grateful to him for very sympathetically producing some programmes I made for the World Service about 'The Mysterious Art of the Conductor' (see Pierre Boulez, page 152).

* * * * *

Ernest Warburton, who has died aged sixty-four, was an expert on the work of Johann Christian Bach (the son of Johann Sebastian who settled in London), and a long-time producer with the BBC, first with the BBC Northern Symphony Orchestra and then with Radio 3 and the World Service.

His voracious appetite for work ensured that he was almost perpetually under the stress of several projects simultaneously. His achievements, whether scholarly or practical, were remarkable, the more so because, as an albino, he suffered from eyesight so bad as to verge upon blindness.

Born a Lancastrian, in Irlam, Warburton had the toughness and shrewdness of that breed. His musicality emerged early: he achieved his Associate Royal College of Organists (ARCO), while in the sixth form of the Royal Masonic School, Bushey, and went to Oxford as organist and choirmaster at Wadham College. His DPhil, on the operas of J.C. Bach, was interrupted for lack of funds, but his completed thesis became the basis of his life's work – publication of the collected edition, in forty-eight volumes, of J.C. Bach's music, and the recording, on twenty-two CDs, of the orchestral works.

Between 1960, when he married Jenny Carding, and 1967, when he joined the BBC, Warburton taught music to support his family, but teaching was not his true métier. This emerged at the BBC in Manchester where, within three years, he became head of music, and immediately made his presence felt. With Edward Downes, conductor of the BBC Northern Symphony (now Philharmonic) Orchestra, he launched a series of public, free master concerts at the Free Trade Hall, much to the outrage of the Hallé. Warburton believed that a studio-bound orchestra could not have the vitality or responsiveness of a 'public' orchestra, and the immediate improvement of the BBCNSO proved his point.

He produced his first broadcast opera, Puccini's *Le Villi*, in 1967, and this was followed over the years by nearly fifty other productions, ranging from J.C. Bach and Stephen Storace to Lennox Berkeley, Alan Bush and Elizabeth Maconchy. Most ambitious of all was the recording of Wagner's first three operas, *Die Feen*, *Das Liebesverbot* and *Rienzi*. The last was a gargantuan undertaking: well over an hour of music was thought to exist only in vocal score, and Edward Downes (whose eyesight was also very bad) had orchestrated this section.

Then Warburton unearthed some of the original full score in the British Museum. Those who saw them working together, both peering myopically at Wagner's profusion of notes, found the spectacle both touching and comical. But all six hours of the score was completed, and Warburton, who always thought big, involved both the Hallé and the Royal Liverpool Philharmonic in the recording.

Before moving to London as Head of Music Programmes, Radio, in 1977, he recorded Britten's opera, *Paul Bunyan*, and in January 1976, he and I went to Aldeburgh to play the tapes to the composer, who, though unwell, was clearly pleased by them. Two years earlier, Warburton invited me to chair the jury of the first Lancaster University national piano competition, which he had established.

Arriving in London, he was both a breath of fresh air and a vigorous new broom. Some junior colleagues found his working methods uncomfortable, but he was admirably supportive of his staff. Relations with Ian McIntyre, Controller of Radio 3 – and no musician – were strained, to say the least, but Warburton's producers knew they could rely on his backing.

In 1986, he escaped from McIntyre's antipathetic tyranny and transferred to the external services, where he was appointed Music Organizer for the World Service, then Managing Editor, and later Editor, BBC World Service, English, a role into which music was subsumed. He retired in 1995.

Warburton sometimes spoiled his case by assuming that frailer colleagues were capable of his fastidiously high standards, and by simply driving them too hard. As a producer, though, he was sensitive and encouraging, provided always that one was as well prepared as he was. He deserved many more years of creative musical productivity.

When he relaxed, he enjoyed the shop talk of his profession and was humorous and companionable. He is survived by his wife Jenny and two sons.

The Guardian, 28th September 2001

Norman Platt

In 1987, Norman Platt brought Kent Opera to the Canterbury Festival, which I was then directing. A brilliant production of Judith Weir's *A Night at the Chinese Opera* was complemented by an admirable *Die Zauberflöte*. My negotiations with Platt were strenuous, not to say stormy, but absolutely worthwhile.

* * * * *

The Arts Council of Great Britain did a good many deplorable things during its more recent history, but none was more deplorable than its decision, in December 1989, to axe its grant to Kent Opera.

Norman Platt, who has died aged eighty-three, had founded the company in 1969, and it had presented more than sixty productions of a standard at least as consistent as that of any of the other companies vying for the Council's patronage. Platt was outraged by the decision, and he had the public support of many luminaries, among them Sir Michael Tippett, whose *King Priam* would shortly have been presented by Kent Opera at Covent Garden. In the event, the long-publicized visit was cancelled.

Though Kent Opera was Platt's crowning achievement, he came to it gradually; he was nearly fifty when Monteverdi's *The Coronation of Poppea* set the company afloat. But his early years had equipped him admirably for its creation and management.

His father sang Handel arias rather well, albeit about the house; piano lessons began at the age of six; at nine he became a 'pro', joining the parish church choir of his native Bury – and being paid for it; at eleven, while a pupil at Bury Grammar School, he sang Pamina (*The Magic Flute*), and was capable, he said, of singing the Queen of the Night as well. At fifteen, he was knocked for six by Wagner, having been taken to Munich and Bayreuth, where he heard his first *Tristan*, 'the most shattering and dangerous experience of my life'.

Then a committed Christian, Platt went up to Cambridge in 1939 to read theology, later admitting, though, that it was as much the King's College choir (which he joined) as the liturgy of the Church of England that motivated him. He embraced pacifism, but not ordination, and reverted to music, since he knew he could make a singer, but probably not a priest. Lessons with the great Elena Gerhardt led to a job in the chorus of *The Tales of Hoffmann* at the Strand Theatre, which he combined with his duties as an air-raid warden.

Gerhardt recommended Platt to Gerald Moore, who accompanied

him at a Wigmore Hall recital in 1947, by which time he had become a principal with Sadler's Wells Opera, his first role being Ned Keene in *Peter Grimes*. Other parts followed, but Platt was restless, and, in 1947, he accepted an offer to play Feste in *Twelfth Night*, in Regent's Park.

That autumn he joined the choir of St Paul's Cathedral, met Alfred Deller and later became a founder-member of the Deller Consort. During the 1950s he was constantly busy, singing, acting and teaching. Particularly important was a spell with Britten's English Opera Group, whose policies were a partial model for those of Kent Opera.

For several years Platt had brooded over the possibility of forming a regional company, with repertoire extending from Monteverdi to the present day. His second wife, Johanna Bishop, and Deller now spurred him into action and eventually enough money was raised; in December 1969, *Poppea* opened in Canterbury and Tunbridge Wells. Roger Norrington was the conductor, as he was for more than forty subsequent productions.

Platt's nose for producers was evident in a list which, over twenty years, included Jonathan Miller, Elijah Moshinsky, Nicholas Hytner and Adrian Noble. Among the singers – not all of them yet famous – were Rosalind Plowright, Jill Gomez, Sarah Walker, Patricia Rozario, Felicity Palmer, John Tomlinson, Andrew Shore, Paul Esswood, Thomas Hemsley and, of course, Alfred Deller.

Self-evidently, there was nothing wrong with the artistic direction of Kent Opera but, from 1985, as the result of serious under-funding by a philistine Tory government, the Arts Council had to make cuts. In the field of opera, though, it had recently approved the appointment of the outstanding Iván Fischer as music director (and Platt's eventual successor), and although Kent Opera made do with less subsidy than any other company, it did not fit in with the council's bureaucratically conceived master plan.

Kent Opera, the Arts Council said, was 'middle scale'. It should not have put on *Peter Grimes* and rumours that Platt was considering *Tristan* just went to show what a cussed fellow he was. There was a temporary reprieve in 1987, but the axe fell two years later.

It is true that Platt was a difficult customer, as I myself found when, in 1987, I invited Kent Opera to the Canterbury Festival, which Platt had founded in 1983.

In retrospect it is clear to me that Platt's single-mindedness, sometimes sheer bloody-mindedness, was at the heart of his achievement;

he was a dogged fighter, often committing his own financial resources to keep the show on the road.

Kent Opera was fitfully revived between 1994 and 1998, Platt retiring in 1996. In 2001 he published his memoirs, which reminded me of his own productions and libretto translations. He did not pull his punches where the Arts Council was concerned; his attitude had already been encapsulated in two articles for *Opera* magazine: 'Justifying the Dunghill' and 'Art Made Tongue-tied By Authority'.

In old age, Platt was virtually blind; the recreations listed in his *Who's Who* entry included, 'being read to by my wife'. I hope that, in his mind's eye, he was able to bask in the warm lustre of Kent Opera's finest achievements – its appearances at the Vienna and Edinburgh festivals, in Lisbon, Venice and Singapore; its commissions, notably from Judith Weir, whose *The Black Spider*, like Alan Ridout's *Angelo* and Adrian Cruft's *Dr Syn*, was written for children; and its, and his, relentless pursuit of the highest standards.

Platt received the OBE (1985), and honorary doctorates from the universities of Kent (1981) and Greenwich (1996). By his first wife, Diana, he had two children, Tristan and Mariana; that marriage ended in divorce. By his second wife, Johanna, he had a son, Benjamin, and two daughters, Rebecca and Lucinda. Johanna and his children survive him.

The Guardian, 6th January 2004

FRIENDS

Andrew Pavlovsky

Andrew Pavlovsky was a very special man and a very special friend.

* * * * *

Andrew's face was of a particularly Russian type: rounded, blunt. Prokofiev had such a face, Rozhdestvensky has just such a one. His parents were immigrants; he himself, his face apart, had left his Russianness behind.

On 10th March 1949 I observed, but did not meet, Andrew, who was playing the piano in a performance of a Victorian oratorio notorious, to connoisseurs of the genre, for the hilarious ineptitude of its text and the banal sub-Sullivan nature of its music. The performance was in Oxford; the piece was *Ruth*, by George Tolhurst. The piano part was not taxing, so it was well within Andrew's capacity for he had had lessons with Solomon, who later told me that, though he had the talent, he was too much of a polymath to apply himself single-mindedly to the instrument. Had he done so his friends would have been deprived of the regular company of an enchanting companion.

Within a few weeks of the *Ruth* performance Andrew recruited me for *Così fan Tutte* in the Holywell Music Room; I was the Guglielmo and the rehearsals gave me intense pleasure, the *Così* ensembles being, surely, flawless. And the concert was successful, the room packed, the audience involved. Andrew's tempi and overall control were exemplary and when we repeated *Così* the following year I was touched – and flattered – by a letter from him:

> I particularly want to thank you for singing so well, especially in the second half and for your acting, which was appropriate in the fullest sense and really extremely funny.

I was flattered by this because Andrew could be very candid. 'I don't know what you're doing in this *galère*,' he told me during rehearsals of *The Trojans* (in which I was Narbal and he played timps). Similarly, when I had arrogantly claimed that I had no problems with intonation, he was quick to observe, 'You sing out of tune sometimes, you know.'

But he was not always severe. Indeed, Andrew's fits of giggles were infectious. Once, walking with him in the woods on Boars Hill, I all but trod on a partridge which rose to its wings with a startling clatter from under my feet. Andrew was convulsed, as he was when, staying in a fairly grand house, he contrived to knock some jug or pot off the breakfast hot-plate which, in turn, brought crashing to the floor several dishes and plates. His hostess did not see the joke.

When we came down from Oxford in 1950 I was engaged by Glyndebourne to organize the Festival of Sussex (a county manifestation of the Festival of Britain) and Andrew wrote,

> Good luck in your Sussex ventures, but beware of homespun, Belloc and Cold Comfort.

He became a civil servant and our friendship continued over lunches and evening expeditions to riverside pubs in the East End of London, *The Grapes* at Limehouse being a particular favourite. But it must have been at around this time, over two separate meetings with his friend Lucy Faithfull, that he asked her to describe to him the symptoms and nature of leukaemia; then told her he did not expect to live long.

In the autumn of 1953 I returned from a holiday in Sicily to learn that Andrew was ill, with leukaemia, but was said not to be aware of his condition. In view of his premonitory talks with Lucy Faithfull I found this hard to believe, but I – and other friends – played along with this protective fiction and I visited him at his home, having first promised him, hand on heart, that I was free of any infection whatever, particularly the common cold.

He surely knew the score.

After his death, on 22nd April 1954 at the age of thirty, Frank Howes, chief music critic of *The Times*, wrote, in a longish obituary, that Andrew's

> intellectual energy was inexhaustible. He taught himself Hebrew and Old Slavonic and was fluent in Russian, German, French and Italian ...His musical knowledge and maturity of judgement were extraordinary in so young a man...His many friends will miss the bubbling laughter and untiring conversation in which he so eagerly shared with them his own intense delight in life...the springing vitality (reflected in his walk) of a richly imaginative and capacious mind...

And an anonymous obituary appeared in a musical journal (which I can't now identify):

Andrew Pavlovsky's sudden and tragic death leaves a gap no one will ever quite fill. Indeed a series of gaps: for one of the astonishing things about Andrew was the range of his activities, the versatility of his talents, the enormous number and variety of his friends.

He was an amateur musician, but no one talking to him or listening to him play would have guessed it. One sometimes hears, as an unkind criticism, that 'he always knows better than anyone else', but Andrew really did: his knowledge of the piano repertoire was encyclopaedic, his taste impeccable, his memory prodigious; and his own playing could certainly have risen to the highest professional standard. This made him a brilliant critic; it was also an element in the delight one took in his company.

But only an element. His quirkish, inventive humour, his breadth of knowledge, his unforgettable comments on people and things, his vivid enjoyment of everything, his generosity and friendliness: what fun he was. How one will miss him.

How one still does.

Anthony Besch

Going up to Oxford in 1948, I soon learned that Anthony Besch was a 'swell'. President of OUDS, he regularly appeared in OUDS productions, among them Ben Jonson's *Epicene*. (Also in the cast were Robert Hardy and John Schlesinger.) Later we were colleagues at Glyndebourne and became good friends.

* * * * *

Anthony Besch, who has died aged seventy-eight, was one of the most intelligent and musical opera directors of his generation. Though he maintained public silence about the conceptual extravagances of younger colleagues, his career demonstrated his belief in traditional methods. This is not to say that his productions were uninventive: far from it. But they were certainly never anti-musical; and they were always precise and illuminating.

Born in London, Besch was educated at Rossall School, Fleetwood, Lancashire (as was Thomas Beecham, with whom he was to collaborate), and at Worcester College, Oxford, where his rooms overlooked Nevill Coghill's garden staging of *Twelfth Night*. Besch produced *The Beggar's Opera* for the University Opera Club in 1943. After National Service he returned, in 1947, and threw himself into musical theatre with as much abandon as was compatible with gaining first-class honours in English.

He was game for anything, including Gilbert and Sullivan, which I discovered to my cost when accompanying him in a headlong patter song: 'Faster, Robert, faster!' rings in my ears to this day. Much more important was his production for the Opera Club of Mozart's *Idomeneo*, then a very rare piece. Its success probably gave him an entrée to Glyndebourne where, between 1950 and 1953, he was assistant to the general manager, Moran Caplat, and so was on hand, with direct experience of the opera, when Glyndebourne produced it in 1951.

Besch's first professional production was of Verdi's *The Sicilian Vespers* for Welsh National Opera in 1953. Two years later, he worked with Beecham at the Bath Festival on Grétry's *Zémire et Azor*, and in 1957 he had his own Glyndebourne production: Mozart's *Der Schauspieldirektor*, which featured the young Joan Sutherland.

At much the same time he became a leading light in the New Opera Company which, between 1957 and 1983, presented over forty new or neglected operas at a high standard. Besch himself directed fifteen, among them Dallapiccola's *The Prisoner*, Ravel's *L'Heure Espagnole*, Shostakovich's *The Nose* (at the end of which he contrived, for those who had not got the message, a neat stage picture which made it crystal clear that the protuberance of the title was not nasal but genital), Szymanowski's *King Roger*, Martinů's *Julietta* (which became an ENO production) and a number of British operas, including two works by Elisabeth Lutyens, which he seemed to understand better than the composer herself.

During his long career, Besch was a guest all over the world: at the Teatro Colón (Buenos Aires), La Monnaie (Brussels), Australian Opera, New York City and San Francisco operas, the Deutsche Oper (Berlin), the Canadian Opera Company and others. At home, his best work was for the Royal Opera House – including *La Clemenza di Tito* (1974), with Janet Baker, which Colin Davis conducted – and for Scottish Opera where, again with Janet Baker and with Alexander Gibson conducting, he directed *Così fan Tutte* (1967) and *Der Rosenkavalier* (1970).

The former, which many people thought his finest achievement, was exquisite, as were Baker and Elizabeth Harwood; it opened, unusually but aptly, in a Turkish bath. The subtlest imaginative touch emerged in the sets and costumes which, initially, were white, but which, as passions changed and developed, became imperceptibly more vivid, reverting, as the charade (if charade it be) played itself out, to the original pallor.

They were the work of the Australian designer, John Stoddart, who for many happy years shared Besch's private life. Of numerous professional collaborations their best, after *Così*, was probably a wonderfully atmospheric *The Turn of the Screw* at the 1979 Edinburgh Festival.

In 1993, Besch directed Haydn's *L'Infedeltà Delusa* at Garsington, *Tosca* (for the second time) for Scottish Opera, and in 1996 *Un Ballo in Maschera* for Holland Park Opera.

Between 1986 and 1989, he headed opera studies at the Guildhall School of Music and Drama, and in 1988 he brought a group of young singers to the Canterbury Festival, where I had invited Sena Jurinac to give master-classes. It was characteristic of Besch that he came with a good deal of stage furniture, although Jurinac had specifically requested that there be none.

But his singers were exceptionally well prepared, as he himself invariably was. And his introductory talks to his casts were inspiring: no one was left unenthused about the nature of the production ahead. At rehearsal, his concentration was intense, and he could be impatient, sometimes fierce, if he was not getting precisely what he wanted. An actor colleague remembers a production of *A Midsummer Night's Dream* in New College garden, with Besch saying to him during rehearsal: 'No, don't stand there! Over there! No, there! By that daisy!'

That was quintessential Besch, but it sprang from the clarity of his visual imagination (he was particularly fond of Edward Lear's luminous water-colour landscapes) and his natural sense of how the music paced the action. His range was extraordinary, but he was at his very best in operas in which detailed characterization grew out of the music, Mozart and Rossini in particular.

In 1999, Besch suffered a minor stroke which slowed him down, and much frustrated him. His sharp mind, his musicality, his grasp of style and his meticulous attention to detail are not, these days, too often found in practitioners of his art.

The Guardian, 2nd January 2003

Thomas Armstrong

Thomas Armstrong had gravitas and a self-evident wisdom. He seemed to know by instinct when I was in trouble and his letter of 17th June 1980 was characteristically perceptive and comforting.

* * * * *

> I hope you're well and can bear to live in London. And do you yourself still enjoy music? I still enjoy some music very intensely, but not all music; and I find now that I often get tired during long pretentious masterpieces, and inclined to put on a record of [Poulenc's] *Les Biches*. How I should love to see that ballet again, but I suppose I never shall.

This letter from Tom Armstrong was written when he was ninety-two and was the last I was to get from him. Over the years he had kept an eye on me, probably because my father, Noel, had been godfather to his son, Robert.

Tom's letters, of which I kept a considerable number between 1975 and 1990, were unlike anyone else's. Written in a kind of cursive Roman which tended to drift upwards from the horizontal, they were elegant, courteous and old-fashioned. They often contained sentiment, but were never sentimental; their writer wore his heart on his sleeve, but he could be formidably direct. After a career during which he was organist of two cathedrals, Exeter and Oxford, conductor of the Oxford Bach Choir, principal of the Royal Academy of Music and chairman of the Musicians Benevolent Fund, he had accumulated a large store of sheer wisdom from which – when I needed it – he generously dispensed wise thoughts and sound advice. And his compliments, when they came, were treasurable.

Though he came to our Oxford home in the 1920s I did not encounter him regularly till I joined the Oxford Bach Choir in 1948. Under him I sang in performances of the B Minor Mass, *The Dream of Gerontius* and the Brahms Requiem. He must have thought me better than average because the following year he accompanied me in a group of Schubert songs at a Balliol College concert, a well-regarded series devoted to chamber music and song.

Between 1950, when I left Oxford, and 1972, when I returned to London (from Scotland) to join the BBC, my contacts with him were irregular, but we met, socially, from time to time. Once, at a pleasant party which had loosened all our tongues, he told me of an occasion when, as young men, he and Constant Lambert had gone to the Proms, in the Queen's Hall, of course, and found that the programme included Ethel Smyth's *Two Interlinked French Melodies*. Lambert detested Smyth's music and at the end booed loudly. 'Connie,' protested Armstrong, 'you can't do that.' 'Boo! Boo!' went Lambert. 'Stop it, Connie,' said Armstrong. 'Boo! Boo! Boo!' went Lambert.

'We fell to blows,' Tom told me, 'and were thrown out.' The idea of

Lambert and Armstrong exchanging punches in the arena of the Queen's Hall, and then being frog-marched into Regent Street, is nicely comic, not so much because of Lambert's characteristic role, but because Armstrong, then organist of Exeter Cathedral, was usually a most decorous man.

And he had style: an eightieth birthday speech on the theme, 'Old Men Remember', was memorably evocative. But his apple-red cheeks overlay a formidable jaw, which his son, Robert, inherited, and he could be stubborn, occasionally sharp. I heard him describe Ursula Vaughan Williams, the composer's widow, as 'a most un-wise woman', because her entourage tended to include a number of sycophantic young composers. Of Robert Simpson he wrote (in 1981):

> He is a humourless chap who takes himself far too seriously and has persuaded a number of other people to support him – people who in some cases also have a chip on their shoulders.

But let his letters speak for him. Here are some dated extracts:

> 27th July 1978
> I can't say it's a lot of fun being eighty years old; too many diminuendos and rallentandos: but the love of friends makes it tolerable.
>
> I'm glad of the opportunity to say how much I admire what you're doing in that extremely difficult job, and the spirit in which you do it. So apparently unworried, and stepping so confidently among all the traps.

This was a treasurable compliment indeed.

> 9th April 1979
> That was a wonderful occasion[1] last night, and I can't tell you how grateful we are to you for associating the [Musicians Benevolent] Fund so closely with the celebration.

> 17th June 1980 (in the middle of the musicians' strike, an agonizing period for me)
> I was sorry to learn that the troubles the Corporation is suffering were a cause of personal unhappiness to yourself. Naturally, they must be a matter of regret, especially when you're a musician yourself, the son of a musician, and a man with many good friends in the profession. But you can have no feeling of individual responsibility, and this is so widely

1 Boult's ninetieth birthday concert.

and fully recognized that any sense you might have of being criticized, still less blamed, would be seriously over-sensitive...I can assure you, Robert, that your work for music and musicians in the BBC is *very highly valued* by the profession, and I hope your knowledge of this will help you to hold on...God bless you, Robert, and please forgive me for intruding in this way, which my affection for your father perhaps entitles me to do.

These, too, were words to treasure and they lifted my spirits.

24th August 1983
It would be splendid if there could be a real revival of *Hugh the Drover*, with a little tidying-up of the second Act: it has, that Act, such beautiful music in it, but as a whole it never quite came off. I think the first fifteen minutes of Act 2 is some of the most beautiful music VW ever wrote. And he thought so too.

It gave me a lot of pleasure that my mention of Alan Bush interested you. I think he is a '*great man*' – in the sense that VW was. I am of course biased, and devoted to him; and I don't like *all* his music; and I understand the various factors that have stood in the way of popular acclaim. But there's a certain nobility about the man and his music.

29th September 1983
The real object of this letter is to ask you to consider the possibility of a programme about F.S. Kelly, a very wonderful man who was killed on the Somme in 1916. Jelly d'Arányi never got over his death; and there were many who believed that he would be what VW and Holst were, after the war...Would you be good enough to look into this, and also into the possibility of having another programme about Ernest Walker.

I know how very busy you are, and how many *important matters* are waiting on your decision. But there's something in these ideas...

Was there a note of irony in that last paragraph? I think perhaps!

4th December 1983
I can't remember the first time I met Adrian [Boult] – it's so long ago, but I remember Dean Strong [of Christ Church, Oxford] telling me of his astonishment when Adrian, at his first interview as a freshman, when asked what career he meant to follow saying quite cheerfully, 'I am going to be a conductor.'

21st July 1984
I'm hoping to go to Ely tomorrow to see my poor sister who is, like me,

in an advanced state of decrepitude. When I go there I always think of your father, and your mother in that glorious house[1] which is now no more than a noble white elephant, which you could buy, with a basketful of troubles and expense, for a song. I hope the Proms will be a resounding success, and bring you satisfaction and appreciation. N(icholas) Maw is the best of the younger composers – now well advanced into middle age and conservative values. Alan Bush is a *great* man, but gullible.

19th September 1984
I thought that article in *The Times* was a good one on the whole...but one or two of the suggestions about your possible successor at the BBC made my blood run cold.

Tom died on 26th June 1994 at the age of ninety-six. A memorial service was held at Christ Church Cathedral, Oxford, on 15th October. The music was by Handel, Vaughan Williams, S.S. Wesley, Parry, Byrd, Gibbons, Schubert, Debussy and Tom himself – a setting of Thomas Campion. He had also written the poem which Jan Morris read: 'Lines written in Budapest in August 1960 during a summer school "when it was very hot and my lodgings were in a noisy street".' It was quite long, imaginative and, like Alan Bush, it had 'a certain nobility'. Tom's son, Robert, read from *Ecclesiasticus*, Ch.44: that great passage which reminds us that great men may also be good men and that men 'which have no memorial', their names, too, will live 'for ever more'.

Tom partook of both characteristics.

Robert Mayer

Robert Mayer was ninety-four when I first met him, but his love of music and his passion for musical education were undimmed. And I was tickled to know someone who had been hugged by Brahms.

* * * * *

I first met Robert Mayer on 6th February 1973. Ian Trethowan, then the BBC's Managing Director, Radio, had told me that he wanted the Corporation to take over the Robert Mayer Concerts which, with his wife Dorothy, he had founded in 1923. He had been alone since Dorothy's death. He was a legendary figure said to have been dandled on Brahms's knee as a child, but when I referred to this story in an

1 The Bishop's Palace, my grandfather then the Bishop.

article about Robert, I received an authoritative note from Gerald Abraham (whose notes were invariably authoritative: he was general editor of the New Oxford History of Music):

> No, the young Mayer was neither dandled by Brahms nor patted on the head. As a boy of fourteen he was taken by his father to Brahms, who gave him advice or a warning – I've forgotten which – about music as a profession. He then put his arm around him, which Mayer demonstrated to me – by doing the same (so that I felt I'd been embraced by Brahms at one remove).

The BBC had taken over the Proms in 1927. Would the Robert Mayer Concerts thrive as well under BBC management? The problem of finding a way of presenting them simultaneously to a live audience of children and to an unidentifiable audience of radio listeners was a tricky one. (Eventually, Christopher Seaman found a happy mean; Edward Heath, on a single occasion, was less successful.) However, when I called on Robert to discuss this proposal I soon realized I had not the smallest chance of declining it. Outlining the scenario of the takeover, he referred constantly – with twinkling irony – to 'the great BBC'. He persuaded me, easily, that we would enhance his concerts. He assured me that no safer hands than the BBC's could be found.

We took them over.

And it is shameful that the BBC later abandoned them, for it was understood that Robert sought the perpetuation of the concerts, and of his name, which now has no public platform. Another small disgrace surfaced in 2001 when, in the BBC's staff magazine, a photograph of Hans Feibusch's excellent bronze bust of Robert was printed with an appeal to any reader who could identify the sitter. I was able to do this for the bust had adorned my office for a while, was then appropriated by Aubrey Singer, Managing Director, Radio, at the time, and subsequently lost sight of, though it was said to have been displayed in the Governors' dining-room at some stage. But Birt's BBC had no room for the honouring of benefactors, let alone for works of art.

Robert was ninety-five when, in 1974, we promoted our first Robert Mayer Concert. The programme was:

Mozart: Overture, *The Marriage of Figaro*
Dukas: *The Sorcerer's Apprentice*
Sibelius: *Valse Triste*
Copland: Suite, *Billy the Kid*
Dvořák: *Slavonic Dances*

In 1980 I called on him to ask for his blessing on a small change in the description of the concerts: from 'for children' to 'for young people'. He gave it gladly and even wrote to me a day or two later (on 22nd July):

> I cannot thank you enough for your idea which will draw attention to the activities of Youth and Music [which he had founded in 1954] and secure also practical support.

I was in the middle of the musicians' strike at the time and I was touched by a tactful reference to my 'present anxieties'.

Over ten years or so I had grown to value his approbation and it pleased me when, as he sometimes did, he muttered, 'Good man!'

Ursula Vaughan Williams

To meet Ursula Vaughan Williams, which I suppose I first did in about 1986, was to encounter a warm and lively woman, not quite eccentric, but distinctly original. She was also most hospitable: visits to her Gloucester Terrace home were always a pleasure.

* * * * *

Ursula Vaughan Williams was a complicated person. Her father and her first husband were soldiers, so her early years were conventional and there was apparently a Betjemanesque touch of 'jolly hockey sticks' about her. Yet her own psyche was creative, poetic; and she was to marry the great English composer Ralph Vaughan Williams, to write verses for him and single-mindedly to cherish him.

Born in Malta in 1911, she was the daughter of Major-General Sir Robert Lock. At the age of twenty-two she married J.M.J. Forrester Wood who, with the rank of Lieutenant-Colonel, was killed in 1942. Until that time her life was therefore a nomadic affair and it was a surprising preparation for the years of fulfilment which began when she met Ralph Vaughan Williams early in 1938.

She had been 'bowled over' by his ballet, *Job*, while a student at the Old Vic, and had sent him a scenario of her own. 'VW' was not much impressed, but he forwarded it to Douglas Kennedy, of the English Folk Dance and Song Society. An unsatisfactory tripartite correspondence followed and it was characteristic of Ursula that she asked Kennedy to suggest that VW should take her out to lunch. This he did and things must have gone well, for they went on to see a Walt Disney *Silly Symphony* and 'ended up sitting by the Serpentine'.

At the time VW had been married to Adeline Fisher since 1897. She was now sixty-five and already much handicapped by arthritis. She was to die in 1951 and Ursula, who married Ralph in 1953, later recorded her 'early beauty, her lively mind, her austere discipline, her tenderness and edged wit'. The relationship of the two women who, in whatever sense, shared Ralph for thirteen years, was civilized, apparently affectionate: when Ursula was widowed in 1942, Ralph took her to his home in Dorking, where Adeline made her welcome.

Ursula's own interests were not really musical; they were literary. An avid reader, as was Ralph, she was also a poet and in 1953 he set her 'Silence and Music' for four-part chorus. Her ballet scenario, which in 1938 had been the occasion of their first meeting, was adapted and Spenser's *Epithalamion* newly chosen as its subject. With the title *The Bridal Day* it was later recorded for television, but the recording embarrassed both writer and composer. More successful were *The Sons of Light* (1950), 'our joint cantata', and *Song for a Spring Festival*, a unison piece written for the use of Leith Hill Choirs. There are also interpolations by Ursula in Ralph's *The Pilgrim's Progress* (1921-49, revised 1951-2), whose performance at the Royal Northern College of Music in 1992 gave her special pleasure.

R.V.W., Ursula's biography of Ralph, published in 1964, is a document of great value, but it tells us almost nothing about her feelings for him, or his for her. Those who knew her best are clear, though, that she adored him and that when he died in 1958 the book became an imperative obligation and an act of piety.

But it would be for her own creative writing that she would no doubt have liked best to be remembered. Her novels, among them *Set to Partners* (1968) and *The Yellow Dress* (1984), are surprisingly conventional, coming, as they do, from a woman who at lunch one day responded to the proposition that 'All women are either mothers or tarts', with, 'Well, I'm a tart.' Some, but not all, of this sharpness found its way into her libretti, of which *The Sofa* (1957), with Elizabeth Maconchy, was perhaps the most effective. Other collaborations were with Malcolm Williamson, David Barlow and Charles Camilleri. None, sadly, made much of a mark.

She was at her best in verse, of which she published at least six volumes, the latest being *Aspects* (1984). Often personal, they employ a rich vocabulary that reflects her love of nature and her extensive reading. One poem, 'No Hand in the Night', suggests that she never really got over Ralph's death. But she filled her life with useful activity – and with expeditions. 'I love gadding about,' she said, and no year passed without a journey overseas. Even after a fairly severe stroke in 1995 she holidayed in Rhodes. In 2002, astonishingly, she attended a Vaughan Williams festival in Brisbane. There were those who wondered if she would survive the journey, but they were utterly confounded.

Her memory will probably be perpetuated not in her writing but in her work for others. She served for thirty-three years on the executive committee of the Musicians Benevolent Fund – 'the Musben' – and for fifteen years on its Homes and Cases Committee, to which she brought compassion and a refreshing candour. From 1956 until her death she concerned herself devotedly with the RVW Trust. This had been established to promote the music of living British composers and when, in 1983, Ralph's performing rights reverted to her personally, she re-assigned them to the trust, thus making available very large sums of money. These funds. sometimes rather idiosyncratically, even partially, distributed to individuals, nevertheless handsomely subsidized an impressive range of corporate musical enterprises. It is regrettable that her disinterested generosity was never publicly acknowledged.

Till the end of her days Ursula Vaughan Williams relished activity, friends young and old, new enthusiasms. These, if diverse – Stefan Zweig, a new larder in her welcoming Regent's Park home, the adoption of a Pyrenean wolf – were always wholehearted. But Ralph remained her lodestar.

The Independent, 25th October 2007

MISCELLANY

The seven pieces in this section are not about single individuals, except, in one sense, the last one. The first two recall visits to Italy, where I called on William Walton, and Austria in 1973; and to Budapest in 1976. The third records some random thoughts which occurred to me on the eve of my departure from the BBC in 1985. Then come two pieces about the Proms – a major preoccupation between 1972 and 1985. 'A Mysterious Business' is about the conductor's art, and the final piece preserves a long interview with Pierre Boulez, much more seriously about the same subject. The words are almost all his, but I seem to have asked the right questions: what he has to say is altogether fascinating, and nicely humorous.

Moving South: Walton, Henze and Boulez

Naples is noisy and hot. Cars are driven *con malizia* and barely one is to be seen that has not a dented bumper, bonnet or wing. Fortunately the Bay is less crowded, navigators less angry. The hydrofoil heaves itself out of the water, gathers speed and pounds away to the north-west. In half an hour it subsides into Porto Ischia. The Waltons are on the quay and we fold ourselves into an Italian Mini, Sir William in the back. Their front gate slides aside, electronically activated by a dashboard switch. We extricate ourselves and climb up inside the cool house, built on a steep hillside with a view of mountain and sea. The terrace looks down on a lily-pond set in a rich garden of shrubs and trees, all planted by Lady Walton in the last twenty years. They seem to have been there for ever. When Gillian Widdicombe, who is writing a book about Walton, joins us, we are shown over (no less imposing words will do) the thermostatically-controlled greenhouse. A thermostat signals, and we are lightly drenched with warm water. I ask Sir William if Gillian carries a tape-recorder and he replies: 'Yes, she is discreetly bugged.'

Walton's talk is low and murmured, quite without the accented energy of his music, but with all its wit. After dinner he shows us his music room. It is extremely tidy: books and records are in their place on the shelves. There is hi-fi and an amazing upright piano, whose upper parts seem to have been carved out to furnish space for immense manuscript paper. 'I found it in Harrods,' says Sir William. 'It makes a horrid sound.' On the wall is the original feliform manuscript of a song about a cat written and presented to Walton on his seventieth birthday by Hans Werner Henze.

Returning to Rome next morning to join the BBC Symphony Orchestra for the European premiere of Pierre Boulez's tribute to Stravinsky, '*...explosante-fixe...*', I find an invitation from Henze to visit him at his home in the Apennine foothills. We have barely met since the Edinburgh Festival performances of his compellingly dramatic *Elegy for Young Lovers*, his Sixth Symphony and *Versuch über Schweine*. On that occasion he bought a bulldog and I had frankly feared for its health – indeed its life – in the transfer to Rome, but the animal bundles across the front meadow panting contentedly, and it has acquired a mate. The meadow is alive with creatures: whippets, goats, a turkey and various other birds. The garden at the back of the house is patrolled by a number of cats almost as idiosyncratic as T.S. Eliot's. One is in disgrace: she has been multifariously unfaithful while her mate was ill with flu. Henze hums:

Aprite un po' quegli occhi,
Uomini incauti e schiocchi,
Guardate queste femmine,
Guardate cosa son.[1]

Over a vegetarian lunch I ask, knowing the answer (it is a *num* question), whether he will come into Rome to hear the orchestra's second concert which, like the first, includes '*...explosante-fixe...*', but there is no question of it: Boulez's criticisms of Henze were, and remain, wounding. It is a pity, but there is a certain inevitability about the situation, given Boulez's tough intellect and uncompromising directness, and the florid lyricism of much of Henze's music. The two men, almost exactly contemporary, are at opposite poles of musical style: almost as remote as Hindemith and Strauss; and indeed Tovey's celebrated description of the 'lean, athletic' style of the former would fit the Boulez of the piano sonatas.

1 Mozart's Figaro inveighs against the wiles of women.

In any case, Henze does not join me at the concert, at which, for the second time, the deplorable Roman audience does its best to bring the performance to a halt. There are four elements: those who are prepared to listen in silence, a minority; those who simply and steadily talk; the Fascists, who abhor all 'modern' music; and those who abhor the Fascists. The Fascists express their abhorrence by pointed outbursts of clapping: their opponents shush loudly. The conflict is somewhat sharpened by the fortuitous resemblance of one of Boulez's cues to the Fascist salute. Nevertheless, '...*explosante-fixe*...' continues, and is concluded. A majority of the audience applaud it, though the electronic equipment has, in fact, worked imperfectly. In Vienna, a few days later, all goes well and the excellent performance is rewarded by a festival audience both open-minded and apolitical. The main concert starts at 7.30; Boulez introduces '...*explosante-fixe*...' at ten. He is still answering questions at midnight, when several hundred concertgoers remain. His replies are succinct and humorous. He makes clear that the work is 'about' communication – one of the mainsprings of his life – and insists that each generation must exploit the newest means at its disposal to thrust outward the boundaries of musical language: hence his use, in this work, of highly sophisticated synthesizers. 'Fascists' would probably say that the synthetic modification of the instrumental sounds produced by the eight soloists is mere gimmickry and that the sequence of the twenty sections is apparently inconsequential. (They might be surprised to learn that the eight parts are scrupulously notated.) They might well say that the work does not communicate. If they meant that it evoked no response, in any degree or at any depth, from mind, heart or sexuality, then they would surely only confirm one well-established fact: that new ideas cannot make headway against the inertia of the closed mind.

It is this inertia which Boulez has consistently made the principal target of his professional energy. Today he conducts his campaign in London (at the Round House), in New York (at his 'rug' concerts) and in Paris (at his developing acoustic research centre). One of his favourite words is 'contact', contact with new audiences. Ironically, his personal warmth and generosity are somewhat belied by an austere, not to say brusque, platform manner. There are signs, though, both audible and visible in his conducting, that, as Walton and Henze have moved south to make their homes in Italy, so he too is 'moving south'. Perhaps his new work for the BBC Symphony Orchestra's 1973-4 season will confirm this tendency. Whether it does or not, I would be sorry if the Michelin guide to posterity did not award all three composers a rosette.

The Listener, 5th July 1973

Hungary Diary: Music for a Lime-green Cat

Because of the deaths of Rudolf Kempe and David Munrow, and of their involvement in the Proms, I had phoned Budapest to tell my hosts, Editio Musica, that I must reluctantly curtail my visit. When I arrived, it was clear that my programme had simply been compressed. 'Tonight,' they said, 'the Puppet Theatre. Tomorrow morning – before you record your piece for the radio – a gentleman will come to tell you of Hungarian soloists. Then there is the quiz, and lunch with representatives of the radio. Perhaps you would like to visit the music shop in the afternoon? The concert is early, and there is a small reception afterwards. On Wednesday, there will be time to visit the Kodály Institute before your flight leaves for London. It is a pity you cannot stay longer.' It was indeed: Editio Musica proved most considerate hosts,

Their invitation to Budapest had come as a consequence of the Hungarian programme given by the BBC Symphony Orchestra under Pierre Boulez in February. Bartók's *Duke Bluebeard's Castle* had been preceded by Ligeti's *San Francisco Polyphony* and Sándor Balassa's *Iris*; Balassa had come to London for the performance. Now he was involved in the radio production of a concert of contemporary British music which coincided with my visit. The eight composers represented were Bedford, Birtwistle, Cardew, Dalby, Maxwell Davies, Musgrave, Skempton and Smalley. Hungarian Radio's orchestral studio was used, and there was a capacity audience, mainly of young people, who listened attentively to a programme which, by chance, gave the impression that the younger generation of British composers is passing through a phase of gentle lyricism.

At the State Puppet Theatre, the programme comprised Stravinsky's *The Soldier's Tale*, Ravel's *La Valse*, Ligeti's *Aventures* and Prokofiev's *Classical Symphony*. The techniques used cover an immensely wide range. In the Stravinsky, two puppeteers are actually on stage. They speak the dialogue and manipulate suspended puppets, scenery and backdrops: others beneath the stage operate puppets, supported on sprung wires, and sliding scenery. The confusion of scale is distracting only initially. Ligeti's *Aventures* is a tour-de-force involving an empty, male suit and two headless, female wigs: the three enact a surrealist tragi-comedy of jealousy, love and lust, hysteria infecting every sound and movement. *Classical Symphony* is a tour-de-force of a different kind. We are sitting behind an eighteenth-century prince in his private marionette theatre. He is alone – except for his pet dachshund. Immediately in front of him, the orchestra-pit is occupied by a conductor and small orchestra, the bowing of whose strings is of unimaginable unanimity. Beyond is the puppet stage, on which a *commedia dell'arte* is being played out. All goes well until an enchanting lime-green cat strays on to the stage. The consequence is foreseeable. As the French translation of the scenario puts it, 'Le chien du seigneur met fin au spectacle, en se jetant sur le chat qui joue sur la scène et, déchaîné, il dénude, démasque tous les personages.'

The following morning, I recorded a half-hour talk about the BBC and serious music. Preparing this, I had been glad to discover a number of links with Hungarian composers. Bartók had recorded a recital of his own music in 1928, and had appeared with the Symphony Orchestra during the 1933-4 season. I recalled Dohnányi's visit to the Edinburgh Festival in 1956, when he played his *Nursery Variations* with the BBC Scottish Symphony Orchestra. I remember him describing how he had played his Op.1, the Piano Quintet in C minor, to Brahms. This must have been between 1895, when it was completed, and 1897, when Brahms died. The work may, I suppose, have been heard by telephonograph subscribers at the same period, for though broadcasting in Hungary began in December 1925 (with a gala concert of music by Liszt, Bartók and others), the telephonograph had been available since 1893. After a year, the telephonograph had 700 subscribers – not absolutely a large number, but astonishing if you consider that, at this date, Brahms was still alive and Hindemith had not been born,

Today, Hungarian Radio has three networks, Kossuth, Petöfi and the Third. They are not organized generically, and there is serious music on all three, a preponderance on Kossuth and the Third. Among many more substantial programmes, Kossuth transmits, five days a week, a ten-minute programme, *Ki nyer ma?* (Who will win today?) which has achieved such phenomenal popularity that the shores of Lake Balaton are said to empty of holiday-makers between 12.20 and 12.30. On 25th May, the programme came from the lounge of the Astoria Hotel in Budapest and I was invited to take part, as inquisitor rather than victim. People gathered informally round the presenter, an unassuming figure who introduced the two contestants, selected a moment before by ballot, and then myself. The producer had found the perfect question for someone in music from the BBC: 'On this day (25th May) in 1934, a work was given its first performance by BBC forces in London. What was the work?' Part of the music was then heard. The first contestant, a medical student, identified it immediately: 'Bartók's *Cantata Profana*.' (And it was so. Trefor Jones, Frank Phillips, the Wireless Chorus and BBC Symphony Orchestra were conducted by Aylmer Buesst.) The medical student then succeeded in identifying music by Weber and Liszt, so qualifying for a cash prize. The second contestant, an older man, faced only one question. He recognized the music, but could not identify it. The question was passed to bystanders anxious to catch the presenter's eye. A ninety-four-year-old man was successful: 'Delibes – *Coppélia*'. He received a gramophone record. We all dispersed, as did the largish crowd outside on the pavement who had been peering in, many – for I could see only one transistor among them – without being able to hear a word or a note of the proceedings.

On the morning of my departure, my host from Editio Musica drove Sándor Balassa and myself to Kecskemét, fifty miles or so south-east of Budapest. There was a good deal of traffic, and the road, a minor highway, was in good order. The flat plain is heavily cultivated. Acacia trees and wild blue irises were in full bloom. Balassa, for whom 'iris' means not only the flower, but the eye and the rainbow, told us the plot of his first opera, due to be finished in the spring of next year. He is a man with deep feelings for nature who complimented me on my membership of the World Wildlife Fund. He grew up in the country and, as a boy, adored fishing. But he 'got sorry for the fish', and gave it up. An admirable man, more of whose music should be known in Britain, he is an almost exact contemporary of Zsolt Durkó, from whom the BBC have commissioned a work for the Leeds Festival this October.

The Kodály Institute, now established in a monastery beautifully converted for the purpose, was opened last September in the same town as the now celebrated General School of Music and Singing, the first primary school of its kind to have been founded, in 1950, by Kodály himself. The school is linked by closed-circuit TV to the institute, so that the teachers who come from all over the world to the latter can observe Kodály's methods in use without disturbing the children in class. It is by no means fanciful to attribute, in part, to Kodály's influence the richness of musical life in Hungary at the present time. Apparently, though, Kodály was himself a harsh teacher. A surprising contradiction.

At the airport, I recorded a final interview and said a word about the Proms: music by Liszt, Bartók and Ligeti would be included. The warmth of our farewells proved, if proof were needed, that music is in more than one sense absolutely the best means of communication.

The Listener, 17th June 1976

Langham Diary

I have owned a tiny cottage in the Cumbrian hills for sixteen years and though I enjoy passing the time of day with the retired shepherds who live opposite and the farmer and his family who live down the road, I still feel an 'off-comer'. So I was pleased when I heard recently that I was referred to in the village as 'that lang boogger' or 'old Pons'. I felt I had begun to belong.

I have similar feelings about the BBC. I am not an old hand. I have a mere thirteen years of service and having, it seems, only just recovered from the trauma of joining the Corporation I am now faced with the trauma of leaving it. How insidiously it invades the system. It can probably damage your health. It is certainly habit-forming. I shall miss the routines and the disciplines – the fixes of institutional life. I shall miss the daily encounters with congenial, like-minded musical colleagues; I sometimes think I shall even miss those shameful, necessary duels which are mostly the consequence of fierce professional commitment, but sometimes, alas, a symptom of shameless personal ambition. I read in *The Times* the other day that I lacked 'the killer instinct'. It hadn't occurred to me it was a good thing to have.

It is held that conductors need some such instinct if they are to get to the top, but it wasn't true of those I have most admired – Mitropoulos, Walter, Kleiber, Boult, Kempe. It certainly isn't true of Boulez or Haitink. It was sometimes true of Toscanini, who once explained some failure of generosity with the words 'Sono una bestia'. Toscanini was indeed a volcanic character and the story of his fierce altercation during rehearsal with a wayward brass player has passed into orchestral legend. The offending musician eventually left the platform, turning as he reached the door to fling a final, conclusive shaft. Misunderstanding him, Toscanini yelled back: 'Too late to apologize.'

Always apologize, sometimes explain. I wish I had adopted that motto unequivocally years ago. To explain may or may not be a kindness. To apologize never demeans, almost always enhances the apologist. I recall that dear and good man, Henry Ley, who tried to teach me the organ, telling a story about Brahms, who while performing his own Piano Quintet for some friends, lost his temper, hurled insults at random and stormed from the room, only to return a moment later to shout: 'And if there is anyone I haven't insulted, I apologize.' Brahms was not enhanced – but to have been insulted by him: that would have been something!

I suppose the nearest I have come to Brahms [as I have said elsewhere] was with Robert Mayer, who – legend has it – was either dandled on the knee of, or alternatively patted on the head by, the great man. Robert, whose life the BBC Symphony Orchestra celebrated at the Barbican recently, was someone we could all emulate to advantage. Very small (in that respect I am disqualified), very astute and very dogged, he loved music and young people with passion, and the two kept him young for a hundred years. At that age he was asked (by some idiot interviewer) what it felt like. Robert was equal to that: 'There isn't much future in it,' he replied. In fact, there were five years and a second marriage ahead of him. When his adored first wife, Dorothy, died he lost, he said, his moral courage for a while. But he found it again. And by then he had asked the BBC to guarantee the future of his (and Dorothy's) concerts for young people.

An even weightier responsibility was entrusted to us by Henry Wood. The Proms were in financial difficulties in the mid-1920s and Wood reached agreement with the BBC that it should have the exclusive right to use the title 'The Henry Wood Promenade Concerts' and should promote the concerts 'as at present'. The year 1987 will mark sixty years of our association with the Proms. It will be John Drummond's first year as a planner of them and I wish him every possible success. If he is like me, he will enjoy the programme-building as much as anything in his professional life. I reckon that, over twelve seasons, I have attended getting on for 700 Proms. I would willingly plan, and attend, many more, but I would not so willingly write about them. There is a limit to the number of ways in which to explain, and sometimes defend, the policy you believe in; and I have reached it. That book I drown.

The Proms are, I suppose, the single most prominent musical event broadcast on Radio 3 and they are, I would say, more secure than Radio 3 itself. In times of crisis – and now is one such time – the BBC establishment tends to transmit two conflicting signals. One proclaims, *con tutta forza*, 'Radio 3 is the jewel in the crown.' The second emerges *sotto voce*, 'It is *very* expensive.' There follows talk of Radio 3's inaccessibility and Sir Michael Tippett is quoted as finding it 'unlistenable'. Even if true, I don't find that surprising: Michael is no ordinary mortal and I prefer to cite the Durham miner who wrote not long ago to say that Radio 3 made his whole life tolerable, and the retired Cumbrian hoteliers who, I know, each week ring with a felt pen all the Radio 3 programmes listed in *Radio Times* which, the garden permitting, they want to listen to. Radio 3 is no less accessible than other channels (though, sadly, it is less audible) and its audience will never compare, in numbers, with other audiences. Why should it? Sales of, say, E.M. Forster will never compare with those of, say, Barbara Cartland. But it is worth remarking that, by that analogy, sales of Forster have recently been going up, sales of Cartland going down. And it is necessary to affirm that a work of literature is absolutely more important than any quantity of treadmill pulp.

Forster the essayist is one of my heroes and his broadcast talk, 'What I Believe' should be compulsory reading for the powerful and the rich. I met him only once, in the Nag's Head, Covent Garden, before a performance of Strauss's *Salome*. He was perched on a barstool and I introduced myself. He was kindly and talkative, remarking at one point that 'the trouble with *Salome* is that Oscar Wilde was such a goose.' That went straight into my commonplace book.

As a broadcaster Forster was unusually listenable and he had interesting views about music, just as musicians tend to have interesting views about other disciplines, including literature. This fact was a discovery which surprised the late John Vaizey. He was chairing a Gulbenkian Foundation inquiry into the training of musicians and he had already chaired similar inquiries into the training of actors and dancers. He was so bowled over, he said, by the intelligence and articulacy of the musicians that he reckoned that music ought to be regarded as a discipline equipping its practitioner just as effectively as any other professional qualification.

He was right, of course, and it was good to read the other day that Her Majesty's Inspector of Schools had declared that 'music should be part of every child's daily experience'. Amen to that. Music should never again be an 'extra'. If it were central, its civilizing influence would surprise the philistines, just as its healing influence has surprised the doctors. The BBC could set a good example here by appointing a musician as Controller, Radio 3, and by occasionally admitting a musician to the counsels of its board of management. They would benefit.

I shall await the good news of these developments in my Cumbrian eyrie, the only conceivable disadvantage to which is that Radio 3 is less than perfectly audible.

The Listener, 28th November 1985

Prom-bashing

After ninety years the Proms are alive, and their critics, thank heavens, are kicking. If they did not inspire controversy, they would certainly be dead.

My Welsh correspondent ('Ponsonby, poisoner of the Proms') has given up in disgust, but Tunbridge Wells still writes to complain that *every* programme is ruined by a modern work, and Robert Simpson continues to rumble like a 32-foot organ pedal. Specific complaints have come this year from two mutually compatible, but surely unconnected, sources: anti-Americanism and – if I may call it that – the British music lobby. The inclusion of an enjoyable march by Sousa in the second half of the Last Night programme has brought letters of fierce accusation that there has been a political sell-out to the USA. President Reagan and Mrs Thatcher have both been invoked, unflatteringly. My argument that the Proms are about music, not politics, falls on stone- and, I dare say, tone-deaf ears. Where is your patriotism? my correspondents yell. Down with the Stars and Stripes! Up with the Union Jack! Their arguments are incomprehensible to me: the Last Night is conceived solely as a musical celebration of the end of a great international concert series. The touts, not the BBC, sell the flags. Elgar and Parry and Arne wrote superb tunes.

The British music lobby deserves a more considered response. It was alerted, this year, by Simon Heffer writing in *The Times*. Some doctors weighed in. It was argued that there was a strong case 'for including a staple of English classics as the backbone to every Proms season'. The *backbone*? To pursue a medical metaphor, are Bach and Handel, Haydn and Mozart, Beethoven and Schubert and Brahms to become ribs on a British spine? Thirty years ago, the doctors said, British music had a proper place in the Proms. So, taking them at their word, I studied the 1955 prospectus. It was illuminating. There were certainly more British works. But, as a consequence, some great international names were conspicuously absent: there was not a note of Mahler, Bruckner, Bartók or Schoenberg and only one work by Stravinsky. Oddly, of the 'neglected' British composers cited in *The Times*, these were also absent: Brian,

Berners, Finzi, Moeran, Warlock, Foulds, Bridge, Howells and Butterworth. What was present was even odder: forty-four overtures (eight by British composers) and about thirty snippets from about twenty-five operas. Concerts were very long and, by today's standards, surely underrehearsed: the BBC Symphony Orchestra, in four concerts over five nights (all under Sargent), gave twenty-one works including, in one programme alone, Prokofiev's *Classical Symphony*, the *Emperor Concerto*, Britten's *Young Person's Guide*, and Ravel's *La Valse*, with none-too-lightweight trifles by Smetana, Sibelius and Delius thrown in. Programme-building was eccentric. One Beethoven Night ended with Seiber and Bizet, another with Bush, Alwyn and Bizet; a Tchaikovsky Night with Panufnik, a Bach-Handel Night with Vaughan Williams. A Brahms-Mendelssohn Night had two works by Brahms, one by Mendelssohn and others by Rossini, Respighi and Sibelius. The concert which included Beethoven's *Choral Symphony* ended with Ireland's *These Things Shall Be*.

To my way of thinking, the programmes were indigestible; they contained too many unimportant works; they conspicuously lacked music by recent and contemporary international figures. And that, of course, is where Henry Wood excelled. His flair for what was going to prove important was surely unrivalled. Promenade concert audiences were introduced by him to Strauss in 1895, Rachmaninoff in 1900, Sibelius in 1901, Mahler in 1903, Debussy in 1904, Ravel in 1907, Schoenberg in 1912, Stravinsky in 1913, Bartók in 1914, Prokofiev and Scriabin in 1916, Hindemith in 1924, Kodály in 1928, Janáček in 1930, Webern in 1931. Shostakovich was first heard in 1935. Moreover, once introduced, these composers' works recurred; as of course did the works by the really important British figures.

But times have changed, Shostakovich's first appearance was fifty years ago and in 1985 we have to take account of all the music that has been composed meanwhile. Where British composers are concerned, that includes the whole output of, among many others. Bainbridge, Benjamin, Bennett, Birtwistle, Blake, Buller, Cowie, Crosse, Maxwell Davies, Goehr, Hamilton, Harvey, Holloway, Knussen, McCabe, Mathias, Maw, Musgrave, Patterson, Swayne, Williamson and Wood. Is it important to promote the music of these living composers or to revive the music of the English late-romantics, of what has been affectionately called the 'green and pleasant' school? (A recent Great British Music Festival held in London attempted such a revival. Against all hope and expectation it was not well supported. Equally disappointing was a 1984 Prom comprising works by Delius and Maw and Bax's Fifth Symphony.) Of course, no objective answer is possible. Subjective value-judgements (influenced in some degree by public taste) have to be made and programmes built accordingly. But one fact must surely remain unarguably true: that nothing could be more unflattering to any British music than that it be included in the Proms *because* it is British.

I have often argued that our programme policy for the Proms has not changed fundamentally since Henry Wood's time. That means that the totality of works performed in any one season must be balanced between the masterpieces of the central repertoire and what is most vital and interesting about unfamiliar music, whether new or old. The trouble is that the central repertoire is vastly greater than it was: it stretches – let us say – from Monteverdi to Stravinsky. Similarly, the 'early' music field can now take us back to the twelfth century, while in the late twentieth a considerable number of obviously very gifted composers, both at home and abroad, are writing in a rich variety of idioms: in itself an entirely healthy phenomenon. The task of selection therefore gets harder every year, since the Proms can get no longer. Without a firm editorial policy they would become shapeless, all things to all lobbies. They would contain more early music, more 'ethnic' music, more brass-band music, more wind-band music, some jazz, a Hoffnung concert, more funny music, more bleeding chunks of Wagner and much more music by those composers on whose behalf supporters' societies are formed.

If one way to destroy the Proms would be to plan sixty popular and uncontroversial programmes, another would be to listen too attentively to any of the lobbies.

Happily, it seems clear that, having a recognizable editorial profile, the Proms are going uphill rather than down. Since 1980, when the musicians' strike lost us some concerts, a fact which in turn affected attendances in 1981, the number of concertgoers has increased steadily. It looks like increasing again this year. And that is happening, I am convinced, *because* of the risks we take, not despite them. Without inherent risks our programmes would be faceless and, considering the competition (there was virtually none thirty years ago) on the South Bank, at the Barbican and in London's parks, it is essential that our programmes are instantly recognizable. They surely are, and, as surely, we are attracting to them a very large audience which is genuinely curious about what is new and unfamiliar. Would that I could answer, on behalf of other promoters, that hoary question: where do Promenaders go in wintertime? (I shall never forget the expression on the face of a senior South Bank official when he saw the huge audience which turned out last year to enjoy Michael Tippett's *The Mask of Time*.) Obviously, they disperse. Obviously, some – there are about 180,000 of them – attend some winter concerts given in London by some promoters, including the BBC. But there is the world of difference in appeal between an amorphous mass of symphony concerts – about two a night from October to May – and a coherently planned, compact music festival, with longstanding charisma, given during the summer, if not, this year, in summery weather, in an extraordinarily congenial and paradoxically intimate auditorium.

The BBC, currently neither very fortunate nor very happy, is fortunate and should be very happy, and very proud, to be responsible for the Proms. They give pleasure, and offer enlargement, to concertgoers in Britain and listeners around the world. They will continue to do this for just as long as risks are run, experiments made, horizons extended, ears stretched, minds challenged – all within the tremendous international framework established by great musicians and great music.

The Listener, 12th September 1985

Planning the 1986 Proms

Isaac Stern's memorable dictum, 'If nobody wants to come, nothing will stop them', applies less acutely to the Proms than to any other concert series I know of. But it applies; and whoever plans the programmes can run only so many risks. Assessing the number and size of them puts a sharp edge on the job.

This year there are plenty of risks and, I believe, some good programmes. Not every detail has fallen into place as I would have liked; certain problems were even more recalcitrant than usual and stubbornly resisted solution until after I had left the BBC. By and large, though, the overall scheme represents what I wanted, even if some cherished ideas and one cherished composer have perforce fallen by the way.

I chose Italian music to flavour the series, at the same time beginning to regret my adoption, in 1982, of 'national' themes; the Proms should not really need any artificial characterization. Opera apart, British promoters neglect the Italians and I am glad that Maderna, Nono and Berio are represented, and overjoyed that Dallapiccola can be heard three times, most notably in his tremendous *Il Prigioniero*.

Verdi and Puccini are reasonably provided for, Rossini barely so (a projected *Petite Messe* collapsed). Respighi is revived. Alessandro Scarlatti, Carissimi, Monteverdi and the Florentine Intermedii lead back to the sixteenth century. And, among others, Wolf, Elgar, Stravinsky, Walton and Henze speak in Italian accents of varying authenticity.

But, of course, the Italian works are a tiny part of the whole – seventeen out of nearly a hundred and eighty – and in fact are fewer than the French. The German repertoire predominates and, for the first time, there is more Bruckner than Mahler. The Russian ingredient is strong and there are four Sibelius symphonies, but no Janáček, a fact I much regret. As to British music, twenty-two composers, fourteen of them living, are present in thirty-four works. Who is to say if that is 'fair'? There must be at least as many people who would prefer more Beethoven, this year's chief sufferer from other pressures, to more British music.

In the past I have made the point that the Proms could not play a big part in the celebration of anniversaries without distorting their own essential policy. This was certainly so in 1985 (Bach, Handel, Scarlatti and others) and in 1984 (Elgar, Delius and Holst) when other promoters were anyhow very active. Liszt seemed to me a different case and on the hundredth anniversary of his death there is what a mischievous colleague urged me to bill as a Lisztorama, while, later on, Peter Eötvös (countryman and champion of Liszt) offered his *Ce qu'on entend sur la montagne*. This was a case, all too rare, of a conductor proffering a substantial work well worth reviving and particularly apt.

Programmes are made in many different ways and consultation is essential if the needs of the planner are to be reconciled with the tastes of the conductor. But consultation sometimes veers towards disputation and no doubt there are conductors who carry the scars of flesh-wounds inflicted by me. I certainly carry some such scars myself. Sometimes – as with those wholly single-minded and very important musicians Günter Wand, Claudio Abbado and Simon Rattle – discretion has sooner or later seemed the better part of valour. Sometimes a particular annual struggle goes one way, sometimes the other: this year that endearing eccentric and brilliant trainer, Jerzy Maksymiuk, was the winner. Oliver Knussen did not need to win; he took some ill-digested ideas of mine and transformed them into a formal mosaic of dazzling ingenuity. Similarly, Pierre Boulez offered three works so 'right' for the Proms (and for him) that there was nothing more to be said.

Sometimes it happens the other way round. I have a scrap of paper on which, at a dull committee meeting when I was near Sir Charles Groves, I wrote: 'What about Wagner *Faust* Fauré *Pavane* Chausson *Poemè* with Jessye and Brahms 2?' He handed it back immediately with the reply 'I'll buy that!' Amelia Freedman and Michael Vyner will recall successions of meetings at which we would push ideas to and fro until – as one supposes Ben Nicholson organized his beautiful abstract shapes – a coherent and satisfying structure emerged.

The most severe difficulty tends to arise when a particular work, or a programme, seems to demand performance. It then has to be cast, and a conductor and soloists cajoled into undertaking it with sympathy. In my experience Boult and Boulez have been the two conductors who least betrayed whether their complete professional commitment concealed personal enthusiasm – or indifference. In this connection I am grateful to David Atherton for responding so warmly to the idea of *Il Prigioniero*. Similarly, Andrew Davis readily accepted works by Stravinsky, Dallapiccola, Tippett and Henze; and Richard Hickox – though we argued about the order – welcomed a British programme of Delius, Britten, Walton and Nigel Osborne. Would that the most eminent international figures were so responsive.

The making of programmes is one thing, the choice and engagement of soloists another. I have generally tried to put the programmes first (and to cast them afterwards) but there are great musicians who are specially popular at the Proms and whose current stock of works, not to mention their very limited availability, has often dictated part of a programme. Alfred Brendel is a case in point: his wish to play the Brahms D Minor was irresistible and fortunately his diary permitted him to perform it with Abbado. Again, that wonderful pianist Alicia de Larrocha particularly asked to be allowed to play Franck and Falla, and happily she was free on the August Bank Holiday. Sometimes the concerto arrives backwards, as it were. Imogen Cooper, whose Schubert seems to me unsurpassed today, wanted to play other than Mozart, but her alternatives were either bespoke or had too recently or too often been heard at the Proms. So we finally agreed the relatively rare K415.

The choice of soloist in new and unfamiliar works is particularly problematic. The great international figures are rarely willing to find time to learn such music. (A distinguished colleague recently said to me 'Why engage young X when you could engage the great Y?' To which the answer is that if 'the great Y would learn, say, the Muldowney Piano Concerto, I would gladly do so.') This year the prodigious Håkan

Hardenberger gladly took on the then uncomposed *Array* of Gordon Crosse, and Phyllis Bryn-Julson committed herself to Oliver Knussen's *Chiara*, a work not certainly complete. From earlier periods Debussy's *Fantasy* and Bartók's *Scherzo* were offered by Anne Queffélec and Zoltán Kocsis. These were offers to be jumped at.

At the end of the day there has to be a willing collaboration between planner, conductor, soloists and – bless them – the audience. Isaac Stern, admirably undertaking Maxwell Davies's Violin Concerto in Orkney this summer, would agree that if nobody does come the exercise is pointless. Happily, the Proms audience responds uniquely to the challenge of the unfamiliar. I leave the concerts in safe hands.

The Times, 14th May 1986

A Mysterious Business

The late, great Carlo Maria Giulini, who died in June aged ninety-one, was an honourable exception to the general rule that orchestral musicians do not often love conductors. He had started as an orchestral string-player, so, when he became a conductor, he had a sympathetic insight into the mind of the apparently subservient instrumentalist, and he knew that his authority had to be tempered with courtesy and consideration.

For it is the case that the nature of the symphony orchestra is such that ninety-odd experts must submit to the musical will of the conductor, who may not play any instrument expertly and whose gestures may not always be helpful. Moreover, the instrumentalists may not agree with the conductor's interpretative instructions, but *they cannot answer back*. Occasionally, of course, they do. The very young Andrew Davis, rehearsing a hard-bitten orchestra, stopped to clear up a difficulty, then looked down at the score and said, 'Now, where shall I go back to?' An orchestral voice suggested, 'King's College, Cambridge'.

But orchestras will not generally be so unkind, provided that the conductor knows the score (in every sense), is clear, and treats his musicians as colleagues, not as menials, which Malcolm Sargent did. Then he is likely to secure what Charles Mackerras describes as their 'willing collaboration'. If, in addition, he can bring some wit to the proceedings, so much the better. 'Kindly pull the chain,' Thomas Beecham said after his tuba player had muffed an exposed passage.

Beecham was unique: mercurially gifted, boundlessly energetic, irresistibly persuasive – who else could have cajoled Bruno Walter into conducting Ethel Smyth's *The Wreckers* at Covent Garden? From October 1946, when he launched the Philharmonia, I went to his concerts whenever I could, the finest of them being some given at the 1956 Edinburgh Festival, which he would have opened with Beethoven's *Missa Solemnis* had not the Free Church violently objected to a Latin Mass being heard on 'the Sabbath' in the presence of the Queen. His orchestras adored him, as I did, and, perhaps unknown to them, he had one of the conductor's special gifts: he enabled his orchestral soloists to play the music their way while preserving his own conception intact. No wonder Norman Del Mar's recurrent nightmare was of a concert he was conducting which was going very well except in one respect: he could not identify which piece they were playing.

No performance will be much good unless the conductor has a clear and mature conception of how he wants the music to go and, of course, how the composer intended it to go. The latter point shouldn't have to be made, but I find it hard to forgive Leonard Bernstein (a musician with an extraordinary mastery of orchestral control) for his recording, with the BBC Symphony Orchestra, of the *Enigma Variations* in which 'Nimrod' very nearly dies of a snail-paced tempo. Bernstein should have listened to Adrian Boult's reading, which was crisp and authoritatively Elgarian.

For Boult was not only a devout servant of dead composers but also an indefatigable champion of living ones. And his sense of professional duty was such that, though released from his contract, he flew to Amsterdam for a concert with the Concertgebouw Orchestra, which included the *Enigma Variations*, on 29th February 1940, a few days before the German invasion. He was at his very best in Elgar and Vaughan Williams, Schubert and Brahms, his passionate readings of whose symphonies entirely belied his apparently prim exterior.

Over the question of the baton, he was adamant that it was indispensable. So what he made of the precision which one of his successors at the BBC, Pierre Boulez, achieved without one I do not know. But the debate was surely rendered pointless by Otto Klemperer who sometimes did, and sometimes didn't, use a 'stick'. Klemperer attached great importance to the movements of the hands, and during his greatest years, before accident and illness afflicted him, he brought a fine technique to his immense authority. He was revered by his musicians, who also enjoyed his sometimes Beechamesque wit. 'Ein gutes Jahr,' he was heard to remark, having noted the recent death of several other conductors.

My own work with Boulez was specially enjoyable. Technically immaculate, though self-taught, and with a phenomenally sensitive ear, he is without side and is irritable only if the musicians are lazy or obstructive. I visited him in Bayreuth during rehearsals for the Boulez-Chéreau *Ring* Cycle and he was clearly exhausted by an orchestra, apparently xenophobic, which stubbornly resisted the changes he wanted to make. With the BBC Symphony Orchestra he achieved memorable results, particularly in Debussy and Stravinsky, and relations were good. Once, on his birthday, the orchestra conspired to produce during the rehearsal of one of his own works a massive chord of C major in place of what the score called for – a massive chord incorporating almost every note of the diatonic scale. Boulez's features flashed from stunned puzzlement to hilarity. As a very severe young man, he has found that laughter comes more easily to him as the years pass. And he has evolved his own wit: asked what he thought of Rachmaninoff, he replied 'With Rachmaninoff no *need* to theenk.'

Conducting is a mysterious business. Telepathy probably comes into it and nobody can convincingly explain how it is that two conductors will elicit from one orchestra a perceptibly different sound. However that may be, when everything is right – conception, technique, collaboration, acoustic and audience concentration – a great work of symphonic music under an inspiring conductor must be one of the highest peaks of corporate human achievement. I think with intense pleasure of Beecham in Haydn and Mozart, Furtwängler in Beethoven's *Eroica*, Klemperer in his Fifth, Günter Wand in Bruckner, Evgeny Mravinsky in Tchaikovsky's Sixth, Boult in Elgar, Dimitri Mitropoulos in Vaughan Williams's Fourth, and Boulez in Debussy's *Nocturnes*.

Not forgetting your instrumentalists, I thank you, Maestri!

The Oldie, August 2005

Pierre Boulez in Conversation

In 1981 I made six programmes about 'The Mysterious Art of the Conductor' for the BBC's World Service. These derived from interviews with nine conductors, among them Pierre Boulez, Colin Davis, Bernard Haitink and Charles Mackerras. Each programme lasted half an hour and included music examples. The interviews were much longer, but each was filleted and spliced so as to juxtapose, and sometimes contrast, the views of different conductors on particular aspects of their art. The interview with Pierre Boulez, reproduced here in full, was recorded in

Broadcasting House on 25th October 1986. It gave me special pleasure and is, I believe, of special interest.

* * * * *

RP: You recently wrote that 'There is almost nothing to teach or to learn about conducting,' and Klemperer is on record as saying that what one can teach is so minimal that 'I could explain it to you in a minute.' There must surely be more to it than that?

PB: Well, I spoke of technique. Certainly the way of conducting is not easy to learn and not easy to teach; it's not at all like an instrument. For instrumental technique you need many years, because it's a mechanical process. What you learn on an instrument is not only the music to be performed, but you learn how, mechanically, to achieve what you require from your instrument. In conducting you do not have any kind of specialized gestures; the gestures are very unsophisticated. The proof is that if you don't play the violin for five or six months, then you must train your muscles to play again; but if you have not conducted even for three years, you can be on the podium and immediately have the same contact with the orchestra as if you had conducted the day before. So it is the material proof that, technically, there is nothing very much to be learned. The gestures are very simple. It's like when you begin to drive a car: first rule, know how to stop; and second rule, know how to begin! And, if you know these two rules well, in between you can manage – more or less!

RP: You don't use a baton – a stick – but most conductors do and at least one, Sir Adrian Boult, attached the very greatest importance to the stick and to the point of the stick. Is there any loss in *not* using the stick? Is there actual gain?

PB: I think that's an individual matter. (If you ask singers, for instance, each singer thinks he has a better technique than another one.) And, stick or no stick, I think it depends on what you want or how you want to convey the things you have to convey. You can observe various conductors, and sometimes very good conductors have very awkward gestures, but they work; and some people have more elegant gestures, but it does not work; so it doesn't depend upon the elegance of the gestures, or whether you do it with a stick or without a stick. For me I can only give a personal answer: I always found it very awkward with a stick because for what I want to form – the rhythm, the dynamic – my five fingers are to me so much more expressive than a stick. Of course, it is economical, because

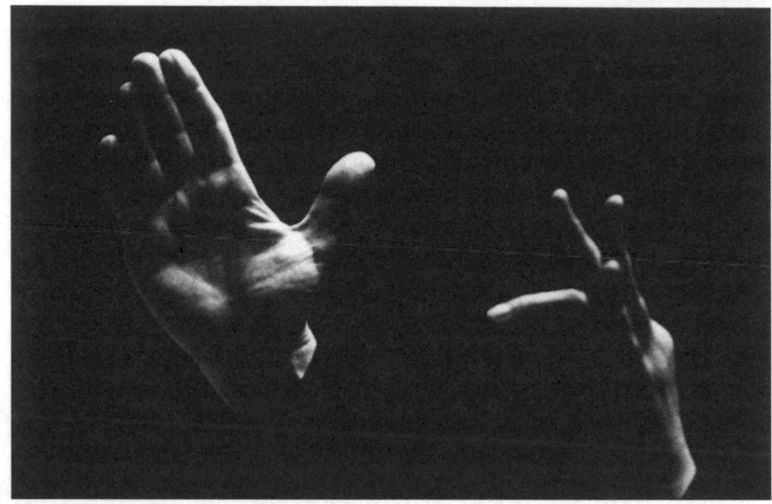

Boulez's hands

you can move the stick and the response is bigger to see, but I ask myself, 'Does the musician really look at the stick?' It is not terribly important, because I've conducted works which are difficult rhythmically and I have also conducted in the theatre at a great distance, and nobody ever complained about the lack of precision or difficulty to follow my beat. So, I conclude that, for myself, it is a good technique; I cannot say that it's a good technique for everybody.

RP: Did you ever use a stick?

PB: Never.

RP: Did you ever have any formal lesson of any kind from anybody?

PB: No, I am completely self-taught, because I did not mean at first to become a conductor at all. The first things I did were in the theatre with Jean-Louis Barrault. Just conducting incidental music for the stage, which is not terribly complicated; and you learn your métier with that, because you learn how to act with musicians and also how to react to a situation which is dramatic – a theatrical situation. But, confronted with a hundred musicians, it is quite different.

Then I founded the Concerts of the Domaine Musical, which were exclusively dedicated to contemporary music, and I was the least expensive conductor in my organization, so therefore I began to conduct the works, which were not the easiest to conduct; but I had the advantage that I had in front of me musicians who were as inexperienced as myself! So, we learned together and therefore my technique, my way of conducting, came out of this confrontation with contemporary music. Only afterwards did I enlarge my repertoire to everything that's in the history of music, but always with a preference for contemporary music, because it is more directly related to me. Not that I don't like the other music, but it is less significant to me, less directly significant, I have to say. Also, I find that for the audience it is better: there are so many people who do the standard repertoire and so few who do twentieth-century music, that I prefer to be involved in it because I have always thought that was my mission. And also I must say that I observed conductors like Rosbaud, like Désormière – people who were, in my opinion, very great conductors – and who were not specialized, but who were very involved in contemporary music. So I observed them much more than other conductors like Munch, like Karajan. I observed all these conductors, but the ones I related to most were the conductors who were conducting contemporary music.

RP: Whatever the music, most conductors have attached the greatest importance to the upbeat, the preparatory beat. How is it that so much can come out of such a small movement?

PB: That was my first difficulty and I remember the first advice I got. That was, 'Just breathe in the same time and you will give something to the musician and your gesture will correspond to the reaction of the musician preparing himself to give sound.' Of course, it is good for the wind instruments, but you cannot say it is the same for percussion or for piano. If you have four pianos, for instance, like in Stravinsky's *Les Noces*, or if you have a string orchestra, that's not at all 'breathing'. It is a kind of preparation to the action, which has to do with breathing for some instruments, but which is not expressly to do with breathing for other instruments. And also it depends very much on the education, the schooling of the musicians. For instance, in France and the Latin countries generally (although I have not much experience with Latin orchestras, only French) your upbeat gives the action immediately and the sound from the strings is immediately there. But in Germany you give the beat while everybody is preparing themselves, and then you give the downbeat, but the sound does not really come on the downbeat, it comes slightly later – which is in some cases extremely good because, if you play Wagner, you want this type of sound which comes out of the instrument without any brutality. It is rather difficult at first, especially when you are trained to conduct an orchestra which reacts immediately, to have this slight delay, and you must adjust yourself to this kind of delay. Therefore, it's not only the problem of the upbeat but the problem of how the sound comes out of the instrument, and how long it takes to come out of the instrument.

RP: It's interesting, isn't it, that certain orchestras play very late and this seems nothing to do with a particular conductor?

PB: No, certainly not. For instance, when you hear German orchestras, you find this kind of delay and you have to adjust to it because the sound quality is better. French orchestras, when they play romantic music, sometimes are too direct, especially the strings, and therefore you like a response which is less immediate, but with a small delay, and this response can also change from one work to another one. For instance, when you play Wagner, especially with the *sforzato*, you have first the beginning of the *sforzato*; then you push, like a spring, and you have the second *sforzato*, you have *sforzatos*. But if you play Stravinsky, this way of playing is absolutely obnoxious; you cannot get anything because when you play *The Rite of Spring* the rhythm should be there immediately, because otherwise you have a mess, it's not clear at all.

RP: Can we talk about the score now? You once said in my presence that, in order to get to know a particular piece of music, you simply had to read the score. This suggested to me that you read a score as a non-musician would read a book, and as easily. When you do that, can you hear in your head all the sounds that are there on the page, or does some of that come later?

PB: I think that's a question of training. When I was very young and I first looked at a score I had difficulties with the transposition of the instruments; you have this kind of material difficulty, especially when you look at the beginning of *The Rite of Spring*, for instance. To take just this example, you have a clarinet in E flat, you have a flute in G, you have other instruments in B flat, in A, some in bass clef and some in treble clef, the horns in F, the cor anglais in F, and so on and so forth. So not only do you have to transpose with the key system, which normally you are trained to do, but you also have to transpose with the accidentals. So it is a hard training physically to read a score really very well, because you have to know a lot of information, which is given in the score, especially when you have a page which is rather complex, and thick, and dense.

But that's not the point, that's just a kind of mechanical training. The most difficult training is to be able to imagine the sonority when you read a score and that, of course, cannot be dealt with just theoretically. You know, I had an experience which was to me very enlightening: I gave two classes of conducting in my life (although I don't believe in teaching, as you know, and especially in teaching conducting!), but I had two classes which were very hard. That was in Basel, where Paul Sacher invited me, and I had the orchestra at my disposal for three entire weeks, and I made for the students a repertoire, and there were three concerts at the end. So everyone, the orchestra as well as the students, had to study, because they could not blame themselves in front of an audience. So I chose a repertoire with *The Rite of Spring*, *Erwartung* by Schoenberg, the Berg Violin Concerto and so on and so forth, and then I discovered this difficulty of conductors. Some are very gifted from the point of view of gesture: they are physically gifted, but they are unable to analyse the score and really to make the texture clear, so they gave a kind of vitality but within this vitality it's very much *alfresco*. And you have the other kind (I take, of course, extreme cases). There is the other type of young people who can analyse very well and they know the score and they really are involved with it, but when they come in front of the orchestra, first, their gestures don't correspond to what they have seen in the score and, second, they are not able to give to the musicians the most simple and effective instructions to do this or that, do this note *forte* and that other one less.

Through instructions which are very simple, you can explain to a musician what you want. You read a score, you listen to it, you want to hear what you have listened to (I mean, just listening in your head), and then you correct some things you had not expected to hear exactly that way, especially if you do a score for the first time; and then you correct very rapidly. But for the scores you have already conducted and have heard, then you know very precisely what to do. And, in a very funny way, you can be sure that almost all orchestras, even the best, fall into exactly the same traps – difficulties of reading some passages which are very difficult, difficulties of balance, some rhythmical difficulties – and you can be sure that there is a kind of difficulty, which is difficult for everybody.

RP: I'm sure that the conversion of what the conductor imagines in his mind into a practical performance is one of the great problems. On the question of using the score, I think I am right in saying that you always do have the score there? This is, presumably, not because you can't remember it, but as an *aide memoire*.

PB: At the beginning I was conducting from memory. But later, when I was involved more and more in tactical things, I had not time to concentrate on memory, because you can learn a score very well, but memory is a second step and of course scores you have conducted a lot of times, you memorize automatically, you don't make an effort, it inscribes itself in the memory. So I have done that as a challenge. I remember the most challenging thing I have done was to conduct from memory the *Variations* by Webern which is very difficult to remember properly because you cannot rely on the response of the musicians, because they have very little to do – with a lot of rests in between – and they must be absolutely sure, if you give a cue, that it is for them and not for anybody else. So if you have a lack of confidence on the part of the musicians and if you are yourself fighting with your memory, it gives an uncertainty of performance which leads certainly to disaster.

I find for me that memory is a kind of gift which is totally independent from musicality. Like absolute pitch: you have conductors who have not absolute pitch but who listen carefully and it makes them work harder on this problem, because somebody with absolute pitch – I have it – will find that if you don't play a C sharp but a C you will immediately notice that the C and not the C sharp has been played, like you would say, 'That is blue, not red', for instance. You have a notion of pitch which is instantly there and which can help very much: you don't need to check the internal reference. I think that memory is exactly the same. For instance, you have conductors like Mitropoulos who have a photographic memory – I've never had that myself. What I remember is the whole structure of the piece and, in a funny way, when I come back to the printed score, I am very disturbed to find it on the page because I do not memorize photographically; on the contrary, I memorize by a kind of memory which does not take into consideration the printed page. I have the structure in myself, I have my own pages, not any more the printed pages. But other people have a photographic memory.

RP: Presumably the memorization of atonal music is in itself more difficult than traditional, tonal music?

PB: You have to absorb much more 'information', as one says today. For instance, I have conducted by memory very often the Berg pieces, Op.6, and now if I conduct them, after so many years, I don't look at the score every second. I know them. If you have absolute pitch it is not that difficult, because then you are aware of the pitch of each line and you know how it sounds. And if you have conducted a piece a lot of times, then you react like Pavlov's dog. If you have a wrong chord, at first you don't know why exactly, but you know this chord is wrong because you have heard it many times right, and suddenly it is wrong, and if you apply your listening capacity, then you find very quickly why it is wrong.

RP: On a different subject altogether, the question of the beating of a particularly difficult passage: I believe I am right in saying that a famous conductor, Sir Georg Solti, once phoned you to ask you how to beat a particular passage? Do even the most eminent of experienced conductors actually sit down in the privacy of their studies and practise the beating of very difficult music?

PB: I suppose yes. I would like to clarify this example with Solti: he asked me – not about Wagner for sure! – but he asked me about a piece by Ives, because in Ives there are two rhythms and he asked me how I beat it myself, which is very normal, because that was the first time he did this score. I can understand, if someone had conducted a piece many times, I would ask him in exactly the same way.

I find it very difficult in Wagner, for instance, to decide if I should beat in 4 or in 2, because you have a tempo which is possible to be beaten in 2 or in 4, and you can see that some conductors beat it this way, some the other way. The music is capable of being sub-divided, or not. I remember very well an instance – it disturbed the musicians very much, especially the first year, but I was stubborn and I was right, finally! In the second scene of the second act of *Siegfried* you have a dialogue between Mime and Wotan, and Wotan is very calm and very sure of himself, rather slow, and Mime is, of course, very agitated; but the tempo is unified. How do you do it? You can do it, of course the simple way, as it is done very often; you can beat all in 4, a little calmer in 4 for Wotan and a little more agitated for Mime, but you don't give this relationship, which is in Wagner very, very obvious, that Wotan is in 2 and Mime is in 4, and I decided to do it in 2 for the one and in 4 for the other. Of course, for the musicians to change the metre all the time was irritating and disturbing, but I stuck to my guns, and finally everybody, when accustomed to it, found the relationship was much more obvious. The calming 2 is a calming 2 – you don't need to make much movement – and the agitated 4 is of course agitated because of the doubling of the movement.

In some of my own music, there is no metre any more and you must really memorize where the people are on the platform, because you cannot at the last moment think, 'Oh my God, the harp is on the left, the extreme left, I must give this cue on the extreme left!' You must have an automatic reaction. For instance, you would not look at the keyboard and say, 'Where is the G sharp? Oh it is here', then hit the G sharp. You must have this automatic reaction to where the musicians are, and also when you have a series of difficult rhythms you have to practise that, and even more in *Gruppen* by Stockhausen, when you have three orchestras, and three conductors, who have to be synchronized in very specific ways. For instance, one conductor has 5 against 4 of the other one, the other one has 7 to 6 of the third, so you know there are points when you have to meet absolutely! Then of course the three conductors have to rehearse for themselves; after that they can go to each of the orchestras and finally to the three orchestras together. That's an example of where the conductor has to rehearse for himself.

RP: Rehearsal is obviously critically important in the preparation of any performance. Do you plan your own rehearsals down to the last minute?

PB: At the beginning I was more careful than I am now. Now you know more or less what you want to do, it's more instinctive, because I know the difficulties of the score, especially when I have conducted it a couple of times. I know where the difficulties are and I read the score with the orchestra. Even with all the disasters of the first reading, sight-reading, they have an idea of the continuity. I have done, for instance, *L'Heure Espagnole*, which is not very difficult music, but it constantly changes tempo, so you must here sub-divide, here not sub-divide, here you stop, here you conduct this way, here you conduct another way, and it's like that every two or three bars. With this piece no sight-reading is possible because everybody would be lost. So there are cases where you can really not do this sight-reading. But generally you can do the sight-reading and, afterwards, you take immediately the places which are difficult. I'm not the first one to do that: Stokowski was famous for choosing the places which were difficult and which would not improve without rehearsing. He also said there were places which do improve without rehearsing, partly because they are not that difficult and even if a musician has made a mistake, he will not do it the next time.

RP: When the musicians are trying very hard, I have noticed that you are very patient with them. Do you expect them to come to rehearsal knowing their parts, even in the most complicated contemporary scores?

PB: Utopically, I would like that they are completely prepared! But you cannot expect them to be prepared, especially for a score they don't know at all, because it's true (while it is sometimes laziness or lack of interest) that sometimes they don't know how to learn a part, how to work on a part, if they don't have any idea of the ensemble. I can understand that because, for instance, they don't know how I shall beat; they don't know the sonority; they don't know the exact tempo. There are lots of things they don't know if it is a score they are playing for the first time, especially if it is not a difficulty of an instrumental nature. Then they will not bother very much, but, if they have a challenge in the instrument itself, it's a personal challenge and they work for themselves and say, 'Well, that was difficult, but I did it.' But if there's a difficulty of style...

I remember very well a concert some thirty years ago when we had the Symphony Op.21 or the Concerto Op.24 by Webern. There is nothing difficult really for the instruments, but awkward, delicate. They have three notes and then eight bars rest, and then two notes and six bars rest. They cannot understand the music at first, so what to work on exactly? When they understand the music they can of course forge the sound in a better way; they can make a phrasing in a more smooth way. But only when they have a notion of what the work is about and how the ensemble will sound. Of course, if they have a solo part or a part which is very important, I find it very disconcerting when someone has not had the smallest look at the score, because you have to say, 'That's not a B natural, it's a B flat; no, that's not a crotchet, it's a quaver.' Then you give the impression of being a teacher in an elementary school, and that's not exactly the most pleasant task, you can imagine! There's immediately tension and everybody is irritated and waits, and you know the time is wasted, simply that.

RP: Rozhdestvensky used to say that rehearsal is not for practice.

PB: Yes, that's true, but at the same time you have to rehearse!

RP: On the question of tuning and intonation: it does seem that the public, including the critics, don't really notice bad intonation. Obviously it is of great importance, but what is the actual effect of bad tuning, apart from the pain which it causes to sensitive listeners?

PB: I think the sound of the orchestra is bad when the tuning is bad. In my opinion the two most absolute qualities of an orchestra, independent from any music, are, first, the tuning, and, second, the range of dynamic. You recognize immediately the orchestra that has bad intonation and dynamic, which has reduced everything to between *mezzoforte* and *mezzofortissimo*, and nothing else – and you have no range of dynamic possibilities. As to intonation, if you have a chord, they say, 'Of course this is in D major or in F major and you must have it perfectly tuned because it will be heard.' And they also say, 'If you have a more complicated chromatic chord as in twelve-tone music, it doesn't matter, because it will not be heard.' But it is heard! If you have an orchestra very well tuned, then the sound of the chord is quite different, because the sonority is much nicer to listen to. And then also it gives the impression of *truth*, you have something which is as striking as truth.

I remember with the BBC Symphony Orchestra (with which I worked a lot, as you know) I did sometimes find in some Webern pieces, when I wanted to draw attention to this intonation problem, I took some chords, very clear and very exposed, and I constructed the chords. For instance, I took out of the chords the fifth, or the fourth, or the third, and then I built the chord progressively and the musicians, without me saying anything, were aware how the chord could be properly adjusted to the tuning. Once you have done that with a couple of chords then everybody is alert and everybody is aware that the sonority will change completely.

It's the same for the strings. The intertwining of rhythmical accuracy and pitch is really the thing which is satisfying. Very often you hear the violin section: the notes are there, but the rhythm is not quite there. The G does not exactly come together, you have one G which comes too late and then, when you have a C-G sharp, for instance, the G sharp comes a little bit too late in some desks. That I taught the musicians very often and they believed me after a while! You can have perfect intonation, all of you, but if you are not absolutely together, it will give the impression of bad intonation, because this rhythmical inaccuracy spills over into the intonation and gives the impression that the tone is not really pure and not well tuned. So you have a mixture of rhythmical accuracy, tuning and also, especially for the wind instruments and for the brass, the *quality* of the sound, especially in contemporary music where we have the problem of mutes. If four trombones, for instance, don't care very much about the quality of the mutes, then you have four individuals who are playing a chord and you have not a chord! For me real quality is to achieve this unity not only in intonation, but in the time and in the rhythms.

RP: When you have got the intonation right and the notes right, you then have to get behind the notes to the meaning of the music. We all know that some apparently faultless performances are actually very dull, and we also know that some very inspiring performances have faults in them. What is the difference between a felt and moving performance, which may not be immaculate, and one which is just a play-through, though completely accurate?

PB: I think that's very difficult to define. Cocteau once said the musician can have talent but the public can also have talent, or not have it, according to different evenings. I think it's a conjunction of facts. First, there are different circumstances. For instance, when you have rehearsed, but only just as much as was necessary, not more, everybody is tense. This tension can bring disaster, or it can bring a marvellous performance. You never know exactly why. If everybody gives his best, the tension can add something which is absolutely unbelievable. But then sometimes, if there's too much tension, or if there's a small disaster in one area, everybody becomes nervous and the performance can fall apart, very rapidly. Of course, there are also performances in which you feel too secure and then you have no more interest, because the performance is just one more performance. That's very dangerous, particularly on tours. When you tour, you repeat the same piece four or five times and you begin to feel like a factory: you give *another* performance, not a *new* performance. It can bring on disaster. It happened to me that, suddenly, at the end of a piece everybody was apart because attention evaporated and there were pieces of the score which were practically chaotic. Everybody was surprised, because it was a routine performance and suddenly disaster happened – and that really makes the blood go into your toes! It is unpredictable, and happily so, because if you knew in advance that the performance would be very good, or awful, you would not have the courage to begin!

RP: In every other art, I think, technique is essential, but in music it does appear that you can give great performances without a faultless technique. Furtwängler would be a very good example of this. Toscanini had a naïf, rather primitive technique, and Stokowski also. How can this be?

PB: I observed Furtwängler, I saw many of his concerts. Toscanini I never saw because he refused to conduct in France after a kind of political feud between France and Italy, and therefore I never heard him, apart from his recordings. I would not say that the technique of Furtwängler was primitive, not at all, he was a very refined conductor. He had not the technique of nowadays, but that's quite a different matter. It's like listening to Casals's recording of the Bach Suites. You cannot say that Casals was a bad performer. He was a veteran of his time and the view we have is different. For instance, on string instruments (not to speak of conducting now) they did sliding, which to our ears is horrible, but their ears were not shocked by it. There is a style which has disappeared progressively – and the same in conducting.

I suppose that Furtwängler was a man who wanted flexibility and therefore, if a chord was not exactly together, for him it was less important than phrasing. He had some priorities, we now have other priorities, and I suppose that is due to the recording industry. I remember there is a recording of a performance by Furtwängler of *Die Zauberflöte* in Salzburg and, really, if you hear the first three chords of that opening, you cannot believe your ears. I suppose, maybe, that for once in his life he did not really convey very well and, as I say, accidents can happen very often, more often than you wish! But I have also heard *Walküre* with Furtwängler and the feeling of time in *Walküre* was absolutely wonderful; of course, I would not see *Walküre* with the same eyes as he, but I find that his way of saying it was really remarkable. I remember I had a lot of conversations with Strobel, who watched the conductors in Berlin in the 1920s, and Furtwängler was, for this new generation which Strobel was associated with, the conductor they could not stand, because of his romantic approach. For them Toscanini was the big man, because he was exact, he was just doing what the score said had to be done. But if you hear the recordings of Toscanini they are not that accurate either.

And that notion of accuracy also relates to the standards of our period: if now you hear a recording, even only twenty times, you cannot stand a chord which is not together twenty times – hence all the editing. We must not forget that editing came rather late in the recording industry – I mean tape – and now of course our listening habits have changed completely, and also the dynamics. I remember very well once I was on tour with the Cleveland Orchestra and we played *The Rite of Spring* rather loud, at least not especially timidly, but it was in a big hall, and after it a student came to me and said, 'Oh! your performance this evening was not very loud. I have the recording, and when I listen to it, it is much louder than you did it tonight.' I said, 'Yes, of course, but there you have just to push a button for that sound.'

RP: There is one very mysterious fact about conductors and orchestras, which I don't think anybody has been able to explain fully, and that is that a particular conductor can come to one orchestra and produce from it a particular characteristic sound of his own, and the next day a different conductor can come and produce his own, quite different characteristic sound. How can this be explained?

PB: I think that's because he chooses the sonority. For instance, he wants the strings louder compared to the woodwinds; he wants the woodwinds sharper for some accents; he wants the brass, on the contrary, to be very soft in the background; and so on and so forth. Mainly it's a combination of what he requires from a group of instruments, and the balance he establishes between the groups. There are so many ways of changing the music. I find, for instance, that if you hear Haydn or Mozart by one conductor or another, you can hear what they do only with the strings. There are many ways of doing a staccato: you can make a staccato very short; or you can make a staccato more flexible; you can make a staccato with an accent; or you can make a staccato very fluid. And the whole character of the music is changed with that.

RP: But, I suspect, you see, that it isn't necessary for the conductor to say any of these things, that there is something to be conveyed in the hands alone. Klemperer said it was very mysterious, but he thought it depended on the hands, the way in which the hands and the arms are actually moved, whether they move quickly and violently, or gently and elegantly – this is enough to make the sound of that orchestra particular.

PB: I would say 'no'. Of course the way of conducting is critical; the way that Karajan is conducting, and the way Solti is conducting –

visually it isn't the same so obviously the response can't be the same. But I think more important is the conscious relationship between what the conductor wants and the response of the musician – the type of bowing, the type of accent. You notice it when an orchestra has worked for a long time with one conductor. In America, for instance, the Philadelphia sound is very famous, because it was Stokowski and Ormandy who were in the same line, and the Philadelphia sound is a sound by itself, it cannot change easily because these musicians have played most of the time like that and they will not forget it very easily. But you have orchestras which are less under the influence of a personality, and then they are more flexible and they can change from one conductor to another. In Cleveland when they had a very strong disciplinarian in Szell, this orchestra played really the way Szell wanted them to play, and it was a sound which was recognizable. I don't think therefore that a kind of hypnotism affects an orchestra, but a very conscious relationship, and you see it especially when this relationship is on a long term.

RP: Another aspect of musical performance: Furtwängler used to talk a lot about spirituality in performance. Is it possible for a conductor who is spiritually a charlatan to be a success?

PB: Yes, of course! Well, you know, some charlatans are successful in life, so why not in music? Music is not an exception and certainly there is this kind of success. I would not say that it lasts for ever, because the musicians are very much aware of it and very quickly, and, if the musicians are aware of it, you can be sure that the audience is also very quickly aware of it. I think there is a chain in performance: first the composer, the work, and then the conductor and the orchestra, and the audience. Everything is a kind of chain, which is circular and which reflects the behaviour of everybody and this behaviour is the mirror of the behaviour of each part of the chain. There is a continuity between the various elements of this chain and if the chain is broken, well, everybody is aware of it very quickly.

RP: You are a composer as well as a conductor, like Weber and Mendelssohn, and Wagner, and Mahler and Strauss, all of whom were important if not great conductors. What has conducting done to your own idea of composition or, indeed, to your own work as a composer?

PB: A lot, I must say. I have learned a great deal through conducting orchestras. First, it's corrected my tendency to be sometimes very theatrical and stubborn. It has taught me how to deal with difficulties of performance and how to be more effective, more efficient in my writing. You know, if you are rehearsing a piece and you have really worked, say, thirty times on the same spot and even then you have a chance in a thousand that it goes right during performance, somehow that is wrong, because the relationship between, as we say in French, the quality and the price, is not really right! It's like writing for an instrument in such a way that, individually, all the chords are possible, but the relationship is not possible in the right tempo. So, if you want to be stubborn and say it is possible, okay, you can stick to your point of view but you will never be performed successfully, in the sense that the performance will never achieve what you have in mind. If you write a score to be performed at only fifty percent or forty percent, that's not really a great achievement, and you cannot say, 'That's forty percent, but in the future, in twenty to thirty years from now, it will be sixty or seventy percent.'

Of course you can rely on a certain progression in mastering the difficulties. I will give an example. *Le Marteau sans Maître*, my own work, was first performed thirty years ago with Rosbaud as conductor and I think he had something like fifty rehearsals because, especially with the percussion instruments, there was a lot of difficulty, and also for the viola, and for every instrument there were some technical difficulties. Now when I do it with my group in Paris, the Ensemble Intercontemporain, I need half a rehearsal. So that is proof that things which are possible can be mastered much quicker now than they were thirty years ago. I needn't have taken this example; I could have as well taken *Pierrot Lunaire*, when now you need two rehearsals and that's absolutely all right, if you have musicians who are well trained. But in the time of Schoenberg they needed thirty or forty rehearsals. So I believe in, not an improvement, but a better relationship between the musicians and the score, better knowledge.

I was amazed recently: I was asked, 'Why do you revise your scores all the time?' I have done a new version of my *cummings ist der dichter*. In the earlier version I did fifteen or sixteen years ago, I had to explain to the musicians, 'You do *that* if I do this gesture; you do *that*, if I do this', and so on. It was very tedious to rehearse and to repeat always the same instructions, which could be given in a much easier way. So I re-orchestrated this work for many reasons and also I made it richer in texture; I had a new look at the composition itself. Now when I do it, I have almost nothing to say – it comes by itself. And I have not simplified; on the contrary, this score is more complex than the previous one but, from the performer's point of view, the material is there, completely prepared for the musician. I am aware now, when I write a score, especially when I do the final score, of the problems of conducting, and I remember that I will need so much time to rehearse if I rehearse this score.

You find that very much in Mahler, for instance. He knows very well the dynamic balance of everything, the relationship of the instruments between one another; and also Stravinsky: with Stravinsky you have absolutely no problems rehearsing a piece, because he's very practical. But with Berg – and it's nothing to do with the quality of the music – with Op.6, for instance, you have to change the dynamic because, if you want to have the main voices and the secondary voices in the right proportion, then he was not as experienced as Mahler, and therefore you have to readjust it, and it is this re-adjustment of my own writing which I have learned during all these years of conducting. And also it gave me a lot of ideas for using the orchestra in a way I would never have considered before.

RP: When you conduct your own music, as an interpreter, do your own ideas of it sometimes change?

PB: Certainly, with distance it changes completely. I'm conducting *Le Marteau sans Maître* right now, but I'm no more involved with this work, because it's a work which is thirty years old, and I don't want to relate with it directly, as I did when I was composing it. My relationship with this work is in the memory and therefore one has more ability to conduct the piece because you take it as an object, not by yourself, but by somebody who was yourself. And, therefore, not only because I am a better conductor than I was thirty years ago, but because also of this distance, I can interpret this piece in a way that I could not dream of thirty years ago; for I was more stiff then, less at ease; I mean stiff in performing the piece, in the relationship I had with it. But now I can take pleasure in the piece because I have read it from the same distance as I have, for instance, a piece of Debussy. Yes, exactly the same way.

When I do *Jeux* I take a lot of freedom with the score, and with *Marteau* I have my own indications, which I respect of course *in toto*, but I am also more flexible. So I take pleasure with it practically and, when you conduct, you play with the score and you are just not respectful of it; you play with it and make it your own thing; and with my own scores it's exactly the same. And I notice, even for the most recent ones, for instance, *Répons*, I think of *some* revolution of tempo, some density, some texture, but it needs a couple of performances to become natural: the musical material asks you to do something else than what you conceived when writing it. So I mean, you thought of the material, of a musical object, and then this musical object, when you begin to manipulate it, asks for some freedom or for some changes: not very big ones, but some changes of what I call manipulation, taking it from this point to this other one. And that's the relationship between an object which is your life, but your life inside, and you bring it outside and it needs fresh air, a fresh approach, and breathing.

RP: How great a part does emotion, or how great a part should emotion, play in a conductor's work?

PB: Emotion should not be everything. You know, very often I think that emotion is an excuse for laziness; very often it is that, unfortunately! I will not go also to the paradox of Diderot, who wrote on the comedian, who says that only the actors who have no emotion at all can convey the maximum of emotion because they can master the emotion of the audience; but the actors who are too emotional convey only their own emotion, not the emotion of the work. There's something true in that, because if you just convey your personal emotions that's not enough to convince everybody, but if you convey the emotions that are in the work, and you convey them through a tool which is really perfect, then the emotions in the work will be there. Of course, if you bring *only* the tool, then that's not enough: the tool, as you said before, can be just dull and uninteresting. But when I hear some passion in the orchestra, but with wrong intonation, then I find the passion very difficult to enjoy!

RP: I think it was Strauss who said that the conductor should not perspire, only the audience should get warm.

PB: Exactly that.

RP: We've all of us been at performances which in some mysterious way have declared themselves as great performances, and everybody has recognized that, the orchestra, the conductor, the audience. I don't suppose such occasions can be analysed, but can you remember attending such performances and would you tell me about one, or more than one?

PB: I have a very bad memory for that. I cannot really remember such a performance. I remember very good performances, but I cannot say, 'That's a perfect performance which I will remember all my life,' because I never live in the past and for me performance is always in the future. A new performance destroys always for me the previous performance. So, for instance, in the years I had with the orchestra here in the BBC or with the New York Philharmonic, I remember very many occasions where everybody was absolutely together and the level of performance much higher than one expected. But that's a very individual judgement, because I remember some musicians telling me there was a beautiful performance of a Mahler symphony in Japan and I don't remember that performance as very exceptional myself. But I do remember very well a performance of the *Concerto for Orchestra* by Bartók in Vienna, for the opening of the Vienna Festival, which was to me quite exceptional, but we did other performances of this work which were as good. Maybe the circumstances were more exceptional in Vienna, but I cannot say that I remember really very exceptional performances. I can remember very exceptional circumstances of my life when a performance was important; that's another matter.

RP: Other people's performances, you mean?

PB: Other people's or my own performances. But I don't trust people who remember one performance especially; that's like people who tell me, 'Oh! I was in a restaurant twenty years ago and I had a meal I can never forget!' Maybe I have a bad memory, or a memory which is very selective, but, no, I cannot remember either a meal or a performance which I could consider really as exceptional. I can remember performances which were very important in my development, that's for sure, but were they exceptional performances? I don't know.

RP: Thank you very much, Pierre.

Tempo, January 2008

RETROSPECT
at January 2009

Looking back to 1951, I am astonished and elated by what has been achieved during my professional lifetime. In Britain we now have excellent opera companies, occasional blips notwithstanding, and excellent orchestras – also a quite extraordinary number of very gifted conductors, at least one of them unarguably a great artist. Our specialist ensembles are among the best in the world. Young string quartets of real quality are popping up with welcome frequency. Our singers and instrumental soloists are engaged world-wide; and we have very fine accompanists. British composers, after a grey patch in the 1970s, when Darmstadt was too influential, now exhibit an admirable range of idioms; there is originality, imagination, energy and colour in today's new music.

Music festivals have mushroomed since Edinburgh's opening in 1947. *Classical Music*'s 2008 festival supplement lists 225, a figure which excludes the numerous summer schools. There are youth orchestras, the superb National Youth Orchestra sometimes outshining the grandest of professional ensembles; Wales and Scotland, which hosts a festival of British Youth Orchestras, have similar fine bodies. Our choir-schools, specialist music schools, universities and conservatoires are producing technically impressive young musicians, though personality and interpretative insight seem rather too often to be missing. The National Opera Studio provides advanced training for the most gifted young singers, and there are a surprising number of small-scale touring opera companies. Scholarships and awards are available from about eighty organizations – some of them quite small – and there are, of course, competitions, the most eye-catching of which, BBC TV's Young Musician of the Year, has, I'm sorry to say, seriously lost its way.

Amateur activity, mostly in the choral field, is profuse and enthusiastic, semi-professional orchestras are plentiful, while, on the clinical/palliative front musicians, mostly young, play and sing in care-homes, hospitals and hospices, under the auspices of Yehudi Menuhin's Live

Music Now and the Council for Music in Hospitals, often with heart-warming results.

Architecturally, too, there have been striking developments. Birmingham, Manchester, Gateshead, Cardiff and Belfast have fine new halls, Wales its Millennium Centre. (London's monstrous Millennium Dome, actually a tent, should be, pretty nearly is, beyond the pale.) Glasgow, having lost by fire its superb St Andrew's Hall, rediscovered its City Hall, then built the Royal Concert Hall. Edinburgh – not before time – is refurbishing the Usher Hall and has brilliantly converted the dire Moss Empire (where, nevertheless, Margot Fonteyn and other great artists danced) into the Festival Theatre. In London, the wonderfully sited Royal Festival Hall has been retuned and refurbished; the Barbican Centre, not ideally accessible, has very valuable facilities; the Cadogan Hall, recently converted, is useful for middle-scale concerts; and the Royal Albert Hall, for which I have a self-evident soft spot, had its acoustics transformed by the 'flying saucers' and, more recently, has been updated for the comfort of artists and audience. The Wigmore Hall, refurbished (but not with increased leg-room)[1] attracts musicians of international status for chamber music and recitals. Of the new Kings Place complex it is impossible to speak too warmly. Handy to King's Cross, it is spacious, light and airy. In the larger hall, whose wooden cladding produces a responsive, bright acoustic, there is a raked floor (hence good visibility) and good leg-room. The smaller one will be useful for less formal events. And, upstairs, the London Sinfonietta and the Orchestra of the Age of Enlightenment have found convenient and practical offices. Praise and gratitude are due to Peter Millican, the enlightened developer of the building.

St John's, Smith Square, despite its innate beauty and its wonderful organ, has never, sad to say, quite found a niche for itself. But in smaller centres around the country, new halls have been built, old buildings and churches adapted.

At the apex of this multifarious activity stand two benign deities – well, Grand Oldish Men, and geniuses, surely – Peter Maxwell Davies, who has brought to the formal role of Master of the Queen's Music an active enthusiasm and who speaks eloquently on behalf of the musical community; and Harrison Birtwistle, who, unfettered by Royal formality, and coming to the matter from a different angle, has confessed – apropos pop music – that he 'didn't know so many clichés existed' and

1 I declare a prejudice: I am six foot six inches tall.

asked, 'why is your music so f***ing loud?' Bravo Sir Peter! Bravo, Sir Harry!

On the face of it, things are looking good for 'classical' music and musicians.

And yet, and yet…

The principle of state subsidy for the arts was firmly established in 1948 when the Arts Council of Great Britain was created as the natural successor to the Council for the Encouragement of Music and the Arts (CEMA.). In its first year the infant Council had £235,000 at its disposal. Over sixty years it has changed shape in various ways and has hived off to Scotland and Wales their independent responsibilities. But in 2008-9 Arts Council England alone has over £400,000,000 to disburse: a large sum indeed, but proportionately a good deal less than the state subsidies available in a number of other European countries.

That the Councils still exist at all is something to be thankful for. It is also surprising for, under the chairmanship of William Rees-Mogg and his successor, Peter Palumbo, the 'arms-length principle' (i.e. the exclusion of the state from grants policy and artistic decisions) was perceptibly compromised, and there remains a risk that arts funding could be handed over to the politicians in the shape of a dead-handed Ministry of the Arts. Already we have a Department for Culture, Media and Sport (chronically uncomfortable bed-fellows, I would have thought), and, in Scotland, the Government now directly funds certain major companies. It remains to be seen whether the arrangement will prove to be in the companies' best interests.

But the Arts Council (I now mean Arts Council England), as it has become more moneyed and, simply, bigger, has also become more aloof and more loftily patronizing. In 2000-1 Peter Hall and John Tusa headed a campaign whose aim was to proclaim the message that the Arts Council(s), once on the side of the artists, had deserted to the other side, to the committee-men and the penny-pinchers. The campaign never quite got off the ground, but its heart was absolutely in the right place. For in the early days, if you were applying for a grant, you met men and women who spoke your language because they had been active in the field, had managed festivals or orchestras, had themselves desperately struggled for financial backing. These days ACE seems to be staffed by office-bound bureaucrats who condescendingly disburse funds on a basis whose logic is hard to discern. Thus, in 1989, the Council destroyed Kent Opera by withdrawing its grant at impossibly short notice (the flyers for performances of Tippett's *King Priam* at Covent Garden were already distributed, as I have said) despite the fact that the company had met its conditions to the letter. More recently it did much the same to, among other ensembles, the London Mozart Players. And just the other day some ill-advised and impertinent pen-pusher introduced into the Council's application form a question[1] regarding the sexual orientation of the applicant's constituents.

ACE must surely re-humanize itself by employing staff with experience 'out there'. It must spell out unambiguously the criteria by which it makes its decisions. And it should certainly take better, professional advice. The musical community must hope that Dame Liz Forgan, recently appointed to the chairmanship of ACE, will attend to these matters for, though her cultural credentials are slightly cloudy, she is nobody's poodle.

As for the British Council, which is charged with propagating our language and our culture overseas, this august body in 2007 appointed as its arts director (*sic*) a lady who, on appointment, declared, 'I am here to do cultural relations. I am not here to do arts.' Not surprisingly, the musical community shivered, for it was reasonably assumed that the Council's music programme was in jeopardy. Recalling, with gratitude, the help I had had from the Council's overseas representatives when engaging, for the Edinburgh Festival, orchestras and opera companies from all over Europe, and the valuable reciprocal arrangements which often ensued, I shared the musicians' alarm. However, the lady in question left her post in April 2008 and it is to be hoped that, by the time this book is published, the Council will have emphatically repudiated her statement and will also have dissociated itself from the dismissive attitude which was implicit in what she said. If the arts are not 'cultural', what in heaven's name are they? And music, because it speaks an international language, is surely a vital ingredient in good cultural relations between states: witness only Daniel Barenboim's amazing West-Eastern Divan Orchestra.

The BBC, my bread and butter (and sometimes jam) for thirteen years, deserves unqualified praise for maintaining its orchestras, all at present very good, and the expert BBC Singers and for its commissioning of new works. And, of course, it has since 1927 promoted the Proms, a cultural flagship, now sailing into literary waters, which every year seems to get bigger, braver, more broadly based and more bizarre in its (rather condescending) efforts to reach out to the man on the

1 Quite soon, and ridiculously, declared 'voluntary'.

Clapham omnibus. Was it really necessary to invoke non-musical, populist TV programmes – *Blue Peter*, *Dr Who* – when seeking to interest new listeners in great music? But everything, including much great music, can be heard on Radio 3.

This channel, today's successor to the glorious Third Programme, remains a secure jewel in the Corporation's nowadays somewhat tarnished crown. But good as it is, I wish it were that much better. At its worst, Radio 3 appears to ape Classic FM, whose amateurish presentation and cavalier mutilation of important works, not to mention its commercial breaks, make it, to my mind, unlistenable. But some of Radio 3's presentation is also slapdash and it is obvious that no consistent guide-lines are observed; the word 'live', for example, is used in two contradictory senses: both 'simultaneous' and 'recorded at a public concert'. Chunks of important works are broadcast in isolation and there are often jarring juxtapositions; a Dowland song should not, surely, be followed by the *Warsaw Concerto*, as happened recently. Then again, there is altogether too much matey chat (with male chuckles ad lib) and too much reliance on young women with coy inflections who gratuitously, and presumptuously, offer us their opinion of this or that performance or work, while *not* giving us the information we really want to hear. As a result, Radio 3 too often resembles a guessing game. There are, of course, excellent programmes, but overnight and in the morning planning seems to operate on the bran-tub principle without regard to the mood or period of one piece when the next is selected. And there are odd obsessions. Time and again we hear arrangements, some quite inept, when the original would be preferable. Time and again we hear programmes from Baltic and Balkan regions and the orchestras of Bergen and Bratislava seem to be broadcast more often than those of Birmingham and Bournemouth.

Clearly there must be an obligation to contain rising costs and, if possible, to increase listening figures, but that either should be achieved at the cost of lower standards ought to be unthinkable. So I ask, why broadcast overnight? The audience is minimal and some sub-standard recordings are transmitted so as to fill up the time available. If, however, the channel were to close down from, say 1 a.m. to 6 a.m. there would be practical savings and a general improvement in quality.

Though the BBC's World Service is not essentially a music channel, its surrender to the pandemic of 'accompanying' music is deplorable. It is easy, for me at least, to remember the time when the World Service stood for a measured clarity of unaccompanied speech, delivered with intelligence, correctly pronounced and stressed. Nowadays speech, often not well delivered, is constantly underlaid by distracting jingles and bursts of what I can only call moron-music. Even the pips are now so underlaid. And, apart from the sheer offensiveness of this 'music', it undoubtedly compromises audibility, surely the World Service's very highest technical priority. *Lilliburlero*, too, has been sidelined. It is now only spasmodically heard, and then not in its original robust wind-band version, but in a bland arrangement for strings, so that the Service no longer has a readily recognizable non-verbal identification signal.

Below and beyond all of this, however, there is, I fear, a chronic malaise.

Writing in *The Listener* in November 1985 (see page 143), I noted that, 'it was good to read the other day that Her Majesty's Inspector of Schools had declared that "music should be part of every child's daily experience." Amen to that.' But did we not hear the very same declaration from an 'official' source just the other day? And the day before that ... But nothing much ever seemed to happen. Many schools continued to regard music as an 'extra', class singing or playing an inconvenience, one-to-one lessons an unaffordable luxury. In 2004, however, Government published its *Music Manifesto*, an ambitious document which proposed a radical review of music education and appreciation. The trouble was that it offered no financial commitment, let alone any guarantee; nor did it exclude non-classical music. As a result it had a mixed reception and was initially opposed by the Incorporated Society of Musicians, many of whose members are teachers. But gradually various plans were developed which had subsidy (albeit rather modest subsidy) attached. Singing came first and Howard Goodall, the composer and broadcaster, was appointed a kind of Singing Supremo. A national programme, *Sing Up*, was established with £10 million a year over three years. Then £40 million was allocated for the purchase of instruments and £3 million for a programme inspired by Venezuela's astounding El Sistema, the cream of which, the Simón Bolívar Orchestra, blew the minds of us all – and shamed us all – by its exuberant excellence. We were also shamed by the fact that while many Venezuelan children, a majority of them socially deprived, practise *after school* to fill the country's youth orchestras, it has emerged that in Britain it is not necessary to understand notation to achieve an 'A' grade in GCSE music.

But things are improving and slowly, very slowly, the benefits of music-making, whether singing or playing, are being understood –

and paid for. Moreover, 'Boys don't sing' is not as 'cool' as it was: the National Boys' Choir of Scotland and the Sage Gateshead's Male Voice Weekend are signs of the times; and other projects are afoot. I hope the politicians will take note.

For they set a wretched example. In my time Mrs Thatcher came only once to the Proms, and then only for the first item. I am not aware that Tony Blair ever did. (One wonders, if, misunderstanding the occasion, he would have brought his guitar with him.) And recently a silly minister, Margaret Hodge, declared the Proms 'elitist': a statement which revealed not just her ignorance but her prejudice as well. More seriously, Lottery funds, presumably including music grants, have been raided in favour of the highly controversial 2012 Olympics.

Nowadays I do voluntary work at the Handel House Museum, where Handel lived for thirty-six years, where he composed *Messiah* and where he died in 1759. The Museum opened, after a long period of crisis and uncertainty, in 2001, nearly 250 years after the composer was buried in Westminster Abbey. Though German-born, he was English from 1727 and was employed by the English monarchy. Yet nobody, till Stanley Sadie insisted, thought it desirable to preserve and restore his house.

The fact is, we are not good at honouring our musicians, and the reason is shameful: there is a thick seam of philistinism in our national psyche and it is by no means only to be found in what the Germans graphically call the *Lumpenproletariat*. Our millionaires (two a penny these days) and mega-millionaires, unlike their American counterparts, who admittedly enjoy more generous tax concessions, contribute, with a few very honourable exceptions, little or nothing to the performing arts. And new 'non-dom' regulations have already driven back to America a bountiful supporter of the Edinburgh Festival, Scottish Opera, the RSNO and the SCO.

It is a bitter irony that at a time when our musicians are performing – in every sense – at a standard never before surpassed, arguably never equalled, the recession is all too likely to mean the freezing, perhaps the reduction, of state grants, which have grown significantly in recent years. Commercial sponsorship, particularly by banks and building societies, already shows signs of collapse. Audiences, which have been increasing, may well shrink. (But perhaps, as in wartime, the hunger for great music will become sharper as the material world grows more harsh.) Whatever happens, musicians, whose *average* income, the Musicians Benevolent Fund has recently discovered, is £16,300, are unlikely to escape the effects of the credit crunch.

Nor will musicians in the rest of the world of 'western' music. But in one respect they are undoubtedly ahead of us: they value their musical heritage.

The Italians are demonstrably proud of their composers and their singers; the Germans and the Austrians idolize their composers; the Russians have their Tchaikovsky museums and their Tchaikovsky Competition; the Norwegians have built a Grieg Hall in Bergen, the Swedes a Berwald Hall in Stockholm; the Finns' monument to Sibelius is magnificent; the Poles, the Czechs and the Slovaks all have major public tributes to their own composers; in Budapest the Conservatoire is named after Liszt.

In London, near Victoria Station, there is a rather kitsch statue of Mozart, who, as a child prodigy, spent a year in England, once playing to George III. And by South Kensington station there is a handsome, but inconveniently sited, statue of Bartók, who stayed in a house nearby when he came to London in the 1920s. Not one English composer is similarly celebrated in our capital city. True, there is, in Embankment Gardens near the Savoy, a modest bust of Sullivan atop a monument whose lower, larger part, is dominated by a distraught, near-naked lady. (Can she be '*Patience* on a monument smiling at grief'?) There is the Purcell Room[1] on the South Bank, a mean, heartless place, and the Britten Theatre within the RCM. But there is no open-air statue of any native composer – and precious few outside London. The birthplaces of Elgar and Holst are preserved at Worcester and Cheltenham[2] and, in Hereford, there is now a charming sculpture of Elgar and his bike, propping each other up. On the beach at Aldeburgh there is an abstract sculpture honouring Britten and, in the vicinity, other Britten-Pears manifestations. But nowhere a great Elgar Hall; no Vaughan Williams Conservatoire. (Either composer, incidentally, could worthily occupy the vacant plinth in Trafalgar Square, on which we are threatened with stupefyingly unsuitable figures, down on which Horatio Nelson would look, aghast.)

Our concert-halls are more likely to be named after brewers than composers. Our conservatoires are all, monotonously, 'Royal'. As to our conductors and soloists, such memorials as exist are apologetically insignificant, and our greatest conductor, buried in a country cemetery next to Delius, has no public memorial at all. I wonder how Vernon

1 And the admirable Purcell School in Hertfordshire.

2 Where a statue of Holst has recently been erected.

Handley and Richard Hickox, both eloquent champions of English music, will be commemorated.

Music, and of course I mean 'classical' music, because it is both the most mysterious, the most moving and the most difficult of the arts, is without doubt the greatest of them, and musicians therefore have a specially honourable responsibility. They are, by and large, an extraordinarily nice lot, intelligent, interesting, companionable, and I am unshakeably on their side. They have my profound respect, my wholehearted good wishes – and my affection.

WHO'S WHO

Allen, Hugh, later Sir Hugh (1869-1946). English teacher and conductor, at one time both director of the RCM and Heather Professor of Music at Oxford. He conducted the London and Oxford Bach Choirs; Dorothy L. Sayers, a member of the latter, recorded in her vocal scores his most vivid comments.

Ansermet, Ernest (1883-1969). Swiss conductor, he premiered Britten's *The Rape of Lucretia* at Glyndebourne (1946) and brought his own Orchestre de la Suisse Romande to the Edinburgh Festival (1949), where he also conducted the Sadler's Wells Ballet (1954).

Armstrong, Robert, later Lord Armstrong of Ilminster (b.1927), son of Sir Thomas Armstrong. An eminent civil servant, latterly Cabinet Secretary, he is in private a good musician.

Bird, John (b.1936). English actor, best known for his comic duologues with John Fortune in *Bremner, Bird and Fortune*. A kindly neighbour of Sidonie Goossens, and an admirer of Boulez's music.

Birt, John, later Lord Birt (b.1944). Controversial director-general of the BBC, 1992-2000, whose innovations proved better in theory than in practice. Later, an adviser to Tony Blair.

Bor, Sam (1912-2008). English violinist, a founder member, in 1930, of the BBCSO, he was leader of the SNO for Alexander Gibson, 1958-73.

Busch, Adolf (1891-1952). German violinist and founder of the Busch Quartet, he was sonata-partner with his son-in-law, Rudolf Serkin.

Busch, Fritz (1890-1951). Brother of Adolf, he was music director of the Dresden Opera from 1922, but left Germany in 1933. He was Glyndebourne's first music director, 1934-9, returning in 1950 and 1951.

Bush, Alan (1900-95). English composer of leftish sympathies. His operas, among them *Wat Tyler*, were produced in Communist East Germany. His *Dialectic*, for string quartet, is greatly admired.

Campoli, Alfredo (1906-91). British, Italian-born violinist who graduated from the world of light music to become an important 'classical' artist. Bliss's Concerto is dedicated to him.

DeGaetani, Jan (1933-89). Accomplished American soprano, expert both in Bach and in contemporary music.

Dent, Edward (1876-1957). Musicologist, teacher, linguist and translator, he was professor of music at Cambridge from 1926 and a valuable influence in the affairs of the ISCM.

Elinson, Iso (1907-64). Russian virtuoso pianist who became a British subject and professor of piano at the RMCM from 1944 till his death. He taught John Ogdon.

Faithfull, Lucy, later Baroness Faithfull (1910-96). She was deeply concerned, professionally and personally, with juvenile delinquency and the welfare of young people.

Firkušný, Rudolf (1912-94). Czech pianist and composer, he was a pupil of Janáček, of whose music he became an authoritative interpreter.

Fournier, Pierre (1906-86). French cellist, he appeared at the first Edinburgh Festival with Szigeti, Primrose and Schnabel; and was noted for his aristocratic style.

Gerhard, Roberto (1896-1970). Spanish, naturalized British, composer who studied with Granados and Schoenberg, he settled in Cambridge. His opera, *The Duenna*, was very successfully revived in Spain and by Opera North in 1992.

Gerhardt, Elena (1883-1961). German, naturalized British, mezzo, she was expert in the lieder of Schubert, Brahms, Wolf and Strauss and, in London, became a sought-after teacher.

Goodman, Arnold, later Lord Goodman (1913-95). Influential lawyer, adviser to Harold Wilson's government, he was the peacemaker between the BBC and the MU at the end of the musicians' strike in 1980.

Goossens, Eugene (1893-1962). English conductor and composer, brother of Leon Goossens and Sidonie Goossens, his last major post was as conductor of the Sydney Symphony Orchestra.

Green, Gordon (1905-81). Pianist and admired teacher of, among others, John Ogdon, Philip Fowke and Stephen Hough.

Grumiaux, Arthur, later Baron Grumiaux (1921-86). Belgian violinist whose recordings, with Clara Haskil, of the Mozart and Beethoven sonatas are celebrated.

Günter, Horst (b.1913). German bass-baritone, he sang Papageno for the Hamburg State Opera at the 1952 and 1956 Edinburgh Festivals.

Hardy, Robert (b.1925). English actor in the theatre and on TV and radio. Winston Churchill was one of his many roles – and he has just the jaw for it.

Harewood, George, 7th Earl of (b.1923). Opera and festival administrator, founder of *Opera* magazine, he directed the Edinburgh Festival, 1961-5, and, from 1972, was successively managing director, chairman (from 1986) and president (from 1995) of ENO.

Hartog, Howard (1913-90). Expert in twentieth-century German music, he chaired the British branch of both the ISCM and the SPNM. Later, as managing director of the agency Ingpen and Williams, he represented, among others, Rudolf Kempe, Alfred Brendel and Pierre Boulez.

Hemmings, Peter (1934-2002). English opera administrator, he was Scottish Opera's first general administrator, 1962-77, then director of Australian Opera, finally of Los Angeles Opera, which was largely his creation.

Heyworth, Peter (1921-91). English critic, from 1955 *The Observer*'s chief contributor, he edited Ernest Newman's writings on Berlioz and, in the *New Yorker*, published a major profile of Pierre Boulez.

Hope-Wallace, Philip (1911-79). Knowledgeable critic and wit, whose writings, mainly for *The Guardian*, are anthologized in *Words and Music*.

Jacques, Reginald (1894-1969). English conductor and founder of the Jacques Orchestra, 1936. He was music director of CEMA, 1940-5.

Josephs, Wilfred (1927-97). English composer, best known for his film and TV scores, whose Requiem, winner, in 1963, of Milan's composition competition, was performed by Giulini.

Kell, Reginald (1906-81). English clarinettist who played for Beecham in the LPO and was professor of clarinet at the RAM, 1936-48.

Keller, Hans (1919-85). Austrian-born English writer, critic and BBC producer, 1949-79, he wrote authoritatively on the Haydn quartets. A controversial, gadfly personality.

Legge, Walter (1906-79). Dictatorial record producer for HMV and Columbia, he created the Philharmonia Orchestra in 1945. He married the German soprano, Elisabeth Schwarzkopf.

Ley, Henry (1887-1962). English organist, he was appointed to Christ Church Cathedral, Oxford when still an undergraduate. While precentor of Eton College, 1926-45, he taught the author the organ.

Lipatti, Dinu (1917-50). Superb Romanian pianist and friend of Clara Haskil, he died of leukaemia.

Mann, William (1924-89). English writer and critic, chief music critic of *The Times* from 1960, he translated *The Ring* into very singable English and, in a moment of likeable over-enthusiasm, declared the Beatles the best songwriters since Schubert.

Moiseiwitsch, Benno (1890-1963). British pianist of Russian origin.

His friend, Rachmaninoff, is said once to have complained that Moiseiwitsch played his music better than he himself.

Moore, Gerald (1899-1987). Doyen of English accompanists who wrote two entertaining books – *The Unashamed Accompanist* and *Am I Too Loud?* The singers at his farewell recital in 1967 were de los Angeles, Schwarzkopf and Fischer-Dieskau.

Mravinsky, Evgeny (1906-88). Eminent Russian conductor who led the Leningrad Philharmonic at the Edinburgh Festival in 1960.

Newman, Ernest (1868-1959). English writer and critic whose *Life of Richard Wagner* is a magisterial achievement.

Nikisch, Arthur (1855-1922). Austro-Hungarian conductor, celebrated in Leipzig, Boston, Budapest and Berlin, whose pupils included Boult and Horenstein.

Palumbo, Peter, later Lord Palumbo of Walbrook (b.1935). Adept in architectural matters, he was chairman of the ACGB, 1989-94.

Petri, Egon (1881-1962). Dutch pianist and teacher, he was professor at the RMCM, 1906-10.

Plaistow, Stephen (b.1937). BBC producer expert in contemporary music. In private a fine pianist, he played duets with William Glock.

Primrose, William (1903-82). Scottish violist, Toscanini's principal in the NBC Orchestra, 1937-42, he appeared at the 1947 Edinburgh Festival with Szigeti, Fournier and Schnabel. He commissioned Bartók's Viola Concerto.

Rees-Mogg, William, later Lord Rees-Mogg of Hinton Blewitt (b.1928). Journalist and bookseller, he was editor of *The Times*, 1967-81, vice-chairman of the BBC's Board of Governors, 1981-6, and chairman of the ACGB, 1982-9.

Riddle, Frederick (1912-95). English violist, played in the LSO and the LPO and led for Beecham in the RPO.

Rosebery, Eva, Countess of. Formidable chatelaine of Dalmeny and Mentmore, she was an influential member of early Edinburgh Festival committees.

Sadie, Stanley (1930-2005). English musicologist, he edited the sixth edition of *Grove* (1980) and published books on Mozart, Beethoven and Handel, the restoration of whose London home he championed.

Schlesinger, John (1926-2003). Internationally celebrated film director, whose *Billy Liar* first made his name and whose *An Englishman Abroad*, for TV, is a masterpiece.

Schnabel, Artur (1882-1951). Austrian pianist and Beethoven specialist. At the 1947 Edinburgh Festival, with Szigeti, Primrose and Fournier, he played Schubert and Brahms chamber-works. He gave lessons to Clifford Curzon and William Glock.

Simpson, Robert (1921-97). English composer and a BBC music producer until his resignation, in dramatic circumstances, in 1980; his idiom is essentially traditional. He published books on Bruckner and Nielsen and a polemic on the Proms.

Susskind, Walter (1913-80). Czech, later British, conductor and pianist, he was conductor of the (then) Scottish Orchestra, 1946-52, returning as a guest with the SNO.

Szigeti, Josef (1892-1973). Hungarian violinist who at the 1947 Edinburgh Festival led the quartet comprising Primrose, Fournier and Schnabel. He once asked the author to hold his left hand, to warm it, before an important concerto.

Teyte, Maggie, later Dame Maggie (1888-1976). She sang Mélisande for Debussy in 1908 and became a superb interpreter of the songs of Debussy and Fauré.

Thurston, Frederick (1901-53). English clarinettist for whom Bax, Bliss and Howells wrote works. He taught and married the clarinettist Thea King, later Dame Thea.

Tovey, Donald Francis (1875-1940). Scholar, pianist and composer, he was Reid Professor of Music at Edinburgh University, 1914-40, when he wrote his famous *Essays in Musical Analysis*. It is said that, cheered for an encore after performing Beethoven's *Diabelli Variations*, he played the work again.

Tusa, John, later Sir John (b.1936). English writer, broadcaster and administrator, of Czech origin. He directed the BBC's World Service 1988-92, and managed the Barbican Centre, 1995-2007.

Vaizey, John, later Lord Vaizey (1929-84). Academic economist with a strong interest in the arts, particularly music.

Webster, David, later Sir David (1903-71). English administrator who presided astutely over the post-war recovery of the Royal Opera House as its General Administrator, 1945-70.

Welitsch, Ljuba (1913-96). Bulgarian soprano who sang *Salome* in Vienna for Strauss's eightieth birthday in 1944 and at Covent Garden in 1947. For Glyndebourne, at the 1948 Edinburgh Festival, she sang Donna Anna (*Don Giovanni*). A sensational artist.

Westrup, Jack, later Sir Jack (1904-75). English scholar, teacher and conductor, he was active in the Oxford University Opera Club as an undergraduate, 1925-7, and returned as Heather Professor of Music in 1947. He conducted *Idomeneo* and *The Trojans* for the club.

Widdicombe, Gillian (b.1943). English writer, critic and possible biographer of William Walton, she married Jeremy Isaacs, general administrator of the Royal Opera House, Covent Garden, 1988-96.

ABBREVIATIONS

ACE	Arts Council England
ACGB	Arts Council of Great Britain
BBCPO	BBC Philharmonic Orchestra
BBCSO	BBC Symphony Orchestra
BBCSSO	BBC Scottish Symphony Orchestra
BBCWSO	BBC Welsh Symphony Orchestra
CEMA	Council for the Encouragement of Music and the Arts
DCMS	Department of Culture, Media and Sport
EBU	European Broadcasting Union
ENO	English National Opera
ICA	Institute for Contemporary Arts
IRCAM	Institut de Recherche et de Co-ordination Acoustique/Musique
ISCM	International Society for Contemporary Music
LPO	London Philharmonic Orchestra
LSO	London Symphony Orchestra
MU	Musicians' Union
NADFAS	National Association of Decorative and Fine Arts
NBC	National Broadcasting Company
OUDS	Oxford University Dramatic Society
RAI	Italian Radio
RAM	Royal Academy of Music
RCM	Royal College of Music
RLPO	Royal Liverpool Philharmonic Orchestra
RMCM	Royal Manchester College of Music
RNCM	Royal Northern College of Music
RPO	Royal Philharmonic Orchestra
RSNO	Royal Scottish National Orchestra
SCO	Scottish Chamber Orchestra
SMBF	Scottish Musicians Benevolent Fund
SNO	Scottish National Orchestra
SPNM	Society for the Promotion of New Music
UCLA	University of California, Los Angeles

PHOTO CREDITS

Acknowledgements and thanks are due to the estate of Paul Shillabeer (Thomas Beecham, Isaac Stern and Myra Hess); Alex von Koettlitz (Pierre Boulez and Günter Wand); Roger Hanert (Clara Haskil); *The Guardian* and Fayer, Vienna (Sena Jurinac); Lauri Tjurin (Adrian Boult); Malcolm Crowthers (Robert Ponsonby); and Edward Cornachio (Pierre Boulez's hands). The photograph of Sam Bor, Jacqueline du Pré and Daniel Barenboim was taken by the author.

On the cover: the author (Janet Baker); the Goossens family (Sidonie Goossens); *The Guardian* (Sena Jurinac); Roger Hanert (Clara Haskil); unknown (Jacqueline du Pré); the Scottish Tourist Board (Vittorio Gui, Ian Wallace, Lord Harewood, Alexander Gibson, Leonid Massine, Gennadi Rozhdestvensky, Mstislav Rostropovich and (obscured) Iain Cuthbertson).

ABOUT THE AUTHOR

Robert Ponsonby is the son of the cathedral organist and composer, Noel Ponsonby. Born at Oxford in 1926, he was educated at Eton, not then – as it is now – a musical school, and saw National Service in the Scots Guards. At Oxford he was organ-scholar of Trinity College (1948-50) and president of the University Opera Club in 1949. While involved in the Club's 1950 production of *The Trojans*, he taught music, part-time, at Abingdon Grammar School, where he quickly learned that music-teaching was not his métier.

Engaged by Glyndebourne in 1951, he organized the Festival of Sussex, a county-wide celebration under the umbrella of the Festival of Britain. At the same time he worked as assistant to the director of the Edinburgh Festival, Ian Hunter, whom he succeeded in 1956. Resigning from the directorship after the 1960 festival, he was 'hired' to create an arts festival on a small island, recently acquired by his American employer, close to Nassau, Bahamas. The project soon proved unrealistic, and he was lucky, back in London, to get a (very dull) job with the Independent Television Authority.

He returned to music in 1964, being appointed to administer the Scottish National Orchestra. His eight years in Glasgow were professionally happy and apparently successful, for he was head-hunted by the BBC, who, in 1972, appointed him Controller, Music, in succession to William Glock. This post he held – not without controversy – until 1985.

Robert Ponsonby directed the Canterbury Festival in 1987 and 1988 while working for the Musicians Benevolent Fund and the Esmée Fairbairn Charitable Trust. Since 1985 he has filled advisory roles with the Purcell School, the Young Concert Artists Trust, the Council for Music in Hospitals and Wingate Scholarships. He has regularly lectured on the Proms for NADFAS. Currently, he is on the committee of the Michael Tippett Musical Foundation, and is a guide at the Handel House Museum.

He holds the Janáček Medal of the Czech Government, is an Hon RAM and was made a CBE in 1983.

Thetis Blacker's caricature of the author and herself as Narbal and Anna in *The Trojans*, Oxford, 1950

INDEX

Because this book is primarily concerned with *people* involved in the world of music rather than with the music itself, this index deliberately concentrates on such references as relate to those people themselves. This general rule means that, for example, there are many more mentions of Strauss and Stravinsky in the book than are to be found listed here, because most (to adapt Stravinsky's own comment) refer to the composers simply as the vessels through which a specific work has passed, or as begetters of a complete *oeuvre*, and not to them as individuals.

Names and page references in **bold** indicate articles on those particular people. An asterisk indicates inclusion in the 'Who's Who' section (pages 180-5).

Abbado, Claudio 72, 148, 149
Abraham, Gerald 131
Aimard, Pierre-Laurent 71, 95
Albéniz, Isaac 77
Alcock, Walter 56
*Allen, Hugh 76
Alva, Luigi 20
Amis, John 116
*Ansermet, Ernest 12
Argerich, Martha 29
*Armstrong, Robert 127, 128, 130
Armstrong, Thomas 126ff
Arrau, Claudio 91
Ashkenazy, Vladimir 29, 91, 114
Atherton, David 6, 149
Attenborough, David 107
Auer, Leopold 68

Baker, Janet 4, 6, 8, 26, 29, 30, 50, 57, 89, 125
Balassa, Sándor 138, 140
Barbirolli, John 13, 26, 59, 78, 79, 82, 85ff
Barbirolli, Peter 85
Barchard, Hilary 38
Barenboim, Daniel 14, 26, 29, 87, 89, 104, 106, 114, 174
Barlow, David 133
Barlow, Stephen 71
Barrault, Jean-Louis 154
Bartók, Béla 16, 69, 82, 139
Beecham, Thomas 1, 2, **10ff**, 12, 22, 28, 32, 104, 124, 125, 150, 152
Benjamin, Arthur 56
Berberian, Cathy 62ff
Berg, Alban 31
Berio, Adolfo 62
Berio, Ernesto 62
Berio, Luciano 62ff, 68, 114
Berlin, Isaiah 114
Bernstein, Leonard 74, 151
Bertlova, Ludmila 24
Besch, Anthony 124ff
Bing, Rudolf 1, 2, 23, 100, 101, 102, 103
*Bird, John 94ff
*Birt, John 109, 110, 131
Birtwistle, Harrison 109, 172
Bishop, Johanna 120, 121
Blair, Tony 177
Bliss, Arthur 10
Blyth, Alan 30
*Bor, Sam 30, 90
Borkh, Inge 47
Boughton, Joy 85
Boulanger, Nadia 56, 114
Boulez, Pierre 4, 6, 16, 28, 39, 50, 62, 64, 65, 68, 93, 94, 95, 108, 112, 115, 116, **135ff**, 138, 141, 148, 149, 151, 152, **152ff**
Boult, Adrian 6ff, 8, 16, 22, 24, 26, 29, 33, 44, 59, 84, 93, 112, 128, 129, 141, 149, 151, 152, 153
Boult, Ann 6, 7

Brahms, Johannes 130, 139, 142
Brain, Dennis 32
Brendel, Alfred 26, 29, 39, 114, 149
Britten, Benjamin 3, 19, 52, 82, 88
Brown, Ivor 113
Bruscantini, Sesto 74
Bryn-Julson, Phyllis 150
Buckle, Richard 103
Buller, John 66ff
Burton, Humphrey 108
*Busch, Adolf 31, 81
*Busch, Fritz 1, 12, 22, 73, 75, 81, 100, 103
*Bush, Alan 129, 130
Busoni, Ferruccio 77, 78

Cairns, David 67
Callas, Maria 3, 23, 74
Camilleri, Charles 133
*Campoli, Alfredo 10
Caplat, Diana 102
Caplat, Moran 1, 75, **100ff**, 125
Cappuccilli, Piero 20
Carding, Jenny 117, 118
Carewe, John 6
Carter, Elliott 116
Casals, Pablo 77, 78, 164
Casella, Alfredo 56
Cassadó, Gaspar 83
Casson, Hugh 106
Cebotari, Maria 75
Checkland, Michael 92
Cherkassky, Shura 91
Chevalier, Maurice 107
Christie, John 2, 74, 100, 101, 103
Chung, Kyung-Wha 50
Civil, Alan 27
Claridge, Shirley 67
Clay, Diana 121
Cleobury, Nicholas 6, 71
Cocteau, Jean 163
Coghill, Nevill 124
Cohen, Raymond 27
Coogan, Jackie 81
Cooper, Imogen 149
Cortot, Alfred 78
Cotton, Bill 92
Cox, John 100
Craxton, Janet 27
Curzon, Clifford 12, 26, 29, 31, 47, 91
Cutner, Solomon *see* Solomon

Dalberg, Frederick 47
Dallapiccola, Luigi 62, 63, 114
d'Arányi, Jelly 129
Davenport, Clement 116
Davies, Peter Maxwell 63, 114, 172
Davis, Andrew 38, 52, 109, 149, 150
Davis, Colin 28, 46, 52, 54, 95, 115, 125, 152
*DeGaetani, Jan 4
Della Casa, Lisa 1
Deller, Alfred 120
Del Mar, Norman 7, **31ff**, 88, 151
de los Angeles, Victoria 3
*Dent, Edward 56, 113, 116
De Sabata, Victor 20, 23
Désormière, Roger 155
Diaghilev, Sergei 108
Diamand, Peter 108
Dickson, Joan 59
Diderot, Denis 169
Dietrich, Marlene 107
Dimbleby, Richard 107
Dohnányi, Ernö 139
Dorati, Antal 95 115
Downes, Edward 117, 118
Drummond, John 2, 55, 92, **106ff**, 142
Dunn, Vivian 51
du Pré, Jacqueline 4, 15, 26, 29, 33, **88ff**
Durkó, Zsolt 140

Ebert, Carl 100
Edinburgh, Prince Philip, Duke of 9, 11, 57
Elder, Mark 6, 38, 67
Elgar, Edward 81
*Elinson, Iso 90
Elizabeth II, HM The Queen 11
Enescu, George 77, 78, 80, 81, 82, 114
Enriquez, Franco 100
Eötvös, Peter 148
Esswood, Paul 120
Evans, Geraint 2, 9, 26

*Faithfull, Lucy 123
Farkas, Ferenc 69

Fauré, Gabriel 77, 78
Feibusch, Hans 131
Ferrier, Kathleen 47, 86
*Firkušný, Rudolf 21
Fischer, Iván 120
Fischer-Dieskau, Dietrich 3, 8 23, 29
Fisher, Adeline 133
Flagstad, Kirsten 1
Fonteyn, Margot 172
Forgan, Liz 174
Forrester Wood, J. M. J. 132
Forster, E. M. 143
Fortune, John 94
*Fournier, Pierre 49, 73
Freedman, Amelia 149
Frick, Gottlob 20
Fricker, Peter Racine 59
Fricsay, Ferenc 75
Frink, Elizabeth 109
Furtwängler, Wilhelm 1, 12, 20, 30, 31, 41, 44, 78, 83, 152, 164, 166

Gál, Hans 46ff, 58
Gardiner, John Eliot 38, 97
Gardner, John 97
Garvin, J. L. 113
Gentele, Göran 23
Geoffroy-Dechaume, Anne 116
*Gerhard, Roberto 114, 116
*Gerhardt, Elena 119
Ghedini, Giorgio 62
Gibson, Alexander 4, 6, 15, **24ff**, 29, 31, 56, 57, 58, 59, 60, 88, 89, 90, 125
Gibson, Veronica 25
Gielgud, John 2, 22
Giulini, Carlo Maria 21ff, 150
Giulini, Marcella 21
Glock, William 31, 59, 111, **112ff**
Glover, Jane 34, 35
Gomez, Jill 120
Goodall, Howard 176
*Goodman, Arnold, Lord 50
*Goossens, Eugene 44, 94
Goossens, Leon 86, 95
Goossens, Sidonie 93ff
Goren, Eli 27
Gould, Diana 83
Gray, Stephen 38
*Green, Gordon 90
Greenbaum, Hyam 94, 95
Greenbaum, Kyla 95
Groves, Charles 4, 27, **37ff**, 50, 54, 94, 149
*Grumiaux, Arthur 79
Gui, Vittorio 2, 12, 18, 75, 88, 100
*Günter, Horst 47

Haendel, Ida 84, 106
Haitink, Bernard 100, 106, 141, 152
Hall, Ernest 96
Hall, Peter 54, 101, 173
Haltrecht, Montague 75
Hamilton, Iain 58ff
Handley, Vernon 6, 7, 178
Hardenberger, Håkan 149
*Hardy, Robert 124
*Harewood, George, Earl of 17, 18, 23, 73, 74, 75, 76
Harper, Heather 54
*Hartog, Howard 28
Harwood, Elizabeth 26, 125
Haskil, Clara 1, **77ff**
Heath, Edward 131
Heffer, Simon 144
Heifetz, Jascha 84
*Hemmings, Peter 56
Hemsley, Thomas 120
Henze, Hans Werner 50, 51, 109, **135ff**
Hess, Myra 1, 3
*Heyworth, Peter 58
Hickox, Richard 149, 179
Hindemith, Paul 78, 114, 139
Hitler, Adolf 113
Hodge, Margaret 177
Hoffnung, Gerard 106
Holst, Imogen 114
Holt, Harold 104
*Hope-Wallace, Philip 18
Horenstein, Jascha 26, **29ff**
Horsfield, Basil 13
Hotter, Hans 1, 73
Howard, George 93
Howarth, Elgar 71, 97
Howells, Herbert 113
Howes, Frank 11, 123
Hubbard, Corinne 114
Humby, Betty (Lady Beecham) 11

Hunter, Ian 1, 46, 47, 52, 53, 100, **102ff**
Hytner, Nicholas 120

*Jacques, Reginald 76
Jakšić, Djura 34ff
Jakšić, Dušan 34
Jakšić, Seka 34, 36
Jakšić, Tichon 34
Jochum, Eugen 78
Jones, Gwyneth 94
Jones, Philip 96ff
*Josephs, Wilfred 19
Jurinac, Sena 73ff, 126

Karajan, Herbert von 72, 74, 155, 165
Karsavina, Tamara 108
Kay, Brian 110
Kaye, Danny 86
Kaye, Nina 91
*Kell, Reginald 8
*Keller, Hans 77
Kelly, F. S. 129
Kempe, Rudolf 27ff, 95, 112, 138, 141
Kennedy, Douglas 132
Kennedy, Nigel 110
Kentish, John 76ff
Kentner, Louis 83
Kenyon, Nicholas 71
King, Thea 94
Kleiber, Erich 84, 97, 141
Klemperer, Otto 3, 23, 40, 41, 75, 151, 152, 153, 165
Kletzki, Paul 26
Knussen, Oliver 148
Kocsis, Zoltán 150
Kodály, Zoltán 140
Krips, Josef 73
Kubelík, Jan 21
Kubelík, Rafael 21ff, 44, 76, 106
Kubrick, Stanley 70
Kurtág, György 69

Lambert, Constant 127
Langdon, Michael 76
Larrocha, Alicia de 149
Lederle, Josef 76
*Legge, Walter 17, 18, 20, 23, 24, 75, 115
Leppard, Raymond 101
Lewis, Richard 53
*Ley, Henry 49, 141
Ligeti, György 68ff
Ligeti, Lukas 72
*Lipatti, Dinu 78, 79
Lock, Robert 132
Lockyer, Bob 108, 111
Loughran, James 6, 7
Löw, Brigitte 72
Lucas, Brenda 90ff
Lutosławski, Witold 114
Lutyens, Elisabeth 125

McCallum, David 9
McDonall, Lois 61
McIntyre, Ian 118
Mackerras, Charles 6, 22, 150, 152
MacLiammoir, Michael 30
Mace, Margaret 57
Maconchy, Elizabeth 133
Maderna, Bruno 62, 63, 65, 114
Maksymiuk, Jerzy 61, 90, 148
Malleson, Miles 8
*Mann, William 60, 66, 70
Marshall, Margaret 41
Martin, Frank 114
Massine, Leonid 88
Matthews, Denis 91
Maw, Nicholas 130
Maximovna, Ita 48
Mayer, Dorothy 130, 142
Mayer, Robert 130ff, 142
Mehta, Zubin 35, 90
Mengelberg, Willem 26
Menuhin, Hephzibah 82
Menuhin, Yehudi 3, 29, **79ff**, 104
Meyer, Doris 57
Michelmore, Cliff 113
Mildmay, Audrey 2, 100, 101, 103
Milhaud, Darius 63
Millar, Norman 95
Miller, Jonathan 120
Millican, Peter 172
Milne, Alasdair 109
Milner, Anthony 66
Milstein, Nathan 103, 106
Mitropoulos, Dimitri 103, 141, 152, 158

*Moiseiwitsch, Benno 1
Monteux, Pierre 82
*Moore, Gerald 3, 53, 83, 119
Morison, Elsie 24
Morris, Jan 130
Moshinsky, Elijah 71, 120
Moule, Henry 56
*Mravinsky, Evgeny 3, 87, 152
Munch, Charles 155
Munrow, David 138
Murphy, Maurice 31
Musgrave, Thea 58

*Newman, Ernest 9
Newton, Ivor 81
Nicholson, Ben 149
*Nikisch, Arthur 7, 29, 30
Noble, Adrian 120
Nono, Luigi 114
Norrington, Roger 97, 120
Nott, Jonathan 71

Ogdon, John 26, 29, 54, **90ff**
Ormandy, Eugene 166
Orr, Robin 56ff
Oyama, Susan 65

Packer, Talia 65
Paderewski, Ignacy Jan 77, 87
Palmer, Felicity 120
*Palumbo, Peter 173
Parry, Marjorie 85
Patzak, Julius 1, 47, 77
Pavlovsky, Andrew 122ff
Pears, Peter 3, 88
Penn, Prue 50
Perlemuter, Vlado 114
Perlman, Itzhak 21
Persinger, Louis 80, 81
*Petri, Egon 90
Piatigorsky, Gregor 48
*Plaistow, Stephen 60, 66
Platt, Norman 119ff
Plowright, Rosalind 120
Poole, John 6
Ponsonby, Lesley 66
Ponsonby, Noel 49, 127
Postnikova, Victoria 114
*Primrose, William 73
Pritchard, John 2, 8, **15ff**, 35, 42, 49, 52, 59, 75, 95, 100
Prokofiev, Sergei 122

Queffélec, Anne 150

Rachmaninoff, Sergei 1, 31, 103
Rattle, Simon 39, 148
Raybould, Clarence 58
Redgrave, Michael 2
*Rees-Mogg, William 173
Rennert, Günther 100
*Riddle, Frederick 27, 48
Robert, Richard 78
Ronald, Landon 81
Roocroft, Amanda 75
Roosevelt, Eleanor 86
Rootham, Cyril 56
Rosbaud, Hans 155, 167
*Rosebery, Eva, Lady 46
Rosenthal, Harold 77
Rostropovich, Mstislav 15, **87ff**
Rothwell, Evelyn 84ff
Rozario, Patricia 120
Rozhdestvensky, Gennadi 29, 33, 42, 87, 88, 95, 112, 122, 161
Russell, Susan 105

Sacher, Maja 16
Sacher, Paul 19ff, 87, 88, 157
*Sadie, Stanley 177
Salonen, Esa-Pekka 71
Samuelson, Chris 111ff
Sargent, Malcolm 32, 49, 53, 95, 145, 150
*Schlesinger, John 124
*Schnabel, Artur 1, 73, 113
Schoenberg, Arnold 30
Schöffler, Paul 73
Schönzeler, Hans-Hubert 43ff
Schönzeler, Wilhelmina 44
Schumann, Elisabeth 114
Schwarz, Rudolf 95
Schwarzkopf, Elisabeth 20, 73, 74, 75, 76, 77
Sciutti, Graziella 20
Seaman, Christopher 131
Seefried, Irmgard 3, 47, 73, 75, 76
Serkin, Rudolf 78

Shankar, Ravi 104
Shaw, George Bernard 101
Shore, Andrew 120
Showering, Marie 105
*Simpson, Robert 128, 144
Singer, Aubrey 55, 131
Sitwell, Edith 48
Smith, Cecil 11
Solomon 122
Solti, Georg 19, 28, 74, 104, 159, 165
Spitz, Vera 72
Stadlen, Peter 66
Stead, Reginald 35
Steinberg, William 35
Steinitz, Paul 97
Stern, Isaac 3, 102, 106, 147, 150
Stockhausen, Karlheinz 62, 65, 68, 69
Stoddart, John 126
Stokowski, Leopold 160, 164, 166
Strauss, Richard 26, 28, 30, 32, 34, 169
Stravinsky, Igor 108, 114
Strebi, Ursula 97, 99
Strobel, Heinrich 164
Strong, Thomas B. (Dean) 129
*Susskind, Walter 6
Sutherland, Joan 2, 20, 77, 125
Szell, George 46, 78, 166
*Szigeti, Josef 9, 73

Taddei, Giuseppe 20
Talich, Václav 21
Tauber, Richard 40
*Teyte, Maggie 5
Thatcher, Margaret 93, 177
Thomas, Jeremy 8
Thompson, Michael 71
*Thurston, Frederick 5, 58
Tippett, Michael 52ff, 56, 104, 113, 114, 116, 119, 143
Tomlinson, John 120
Tortelier, Paul 29, 108
Toscanini, Arturo 18, 20, 26, 37, 84, 85, 141, 164
*Tovey, Donald 46, 103
Trethowan, Ian 93, 130
*Tusa, John 173

*Vaizey, John 143
Van Kampen, Christopher 27
Vaughan Williams, Ralph 61, 113, 132ff
Vaughan Williams, Ursula 128, **132ff**
Verity, James 9
Visconti, Luchino 23
Vyner, Michael 149

Wächter, Eberhard 20
Walker, Ernest 129
Walker, Sarah 67, 120
Walter, Bruno 81, 103, 141, 150
Walton, Susana 49, 51, 135
Walton, William 48ff, 52, **135ff**
Wand, Günter 30, **40ff**, 44, 148, 152
Warburton, Ernest 117ff
Ward, David 26
*Webster, David 23
Weingartner, Felix 15
*Welitsch, Ljuba 22, 73
Westhoff, Anita 41
*Westrup, Jack 77
Wheldon, Huw 108, 110
*Widdicombe, Gillian 49, 50, 51, 135
Wilbraham, John 27
Wilde, Oscar 143
Williamson, Malcolm 133
Willcocks, David 97
Wilson, Conrad 60
Wood, Henry 21, 85, 142, 145

Ysaÿe, Eugène 77, 78, 80

Zeffirelli, Franco 23
Zukerman, Pinchas 90